TOWARD A BETTER LIFE

America's New Immigrants in Their Own Words
FROM ELLIS ISLAND TO THE PRESENT

by Peter Morton Coan

Foreword by Barry Moreno
Preface by Stephen A. Briganti

Prometheus Books
59 John Glenn Drive
Amherst, New York 14228-2119

Published 2011 by Prometheus Books

Cover images: "Statue of Liberty, 1934" courtesy of the Milstein Division of
United States History, Local History & Genealogy, the New York Public Library,
Astor, Lenox and Tilden Foundations.
"Ellis Island, New York City, Postcard" courtesy of Picture Library,
the New York Public Library, Astor, Lenox and Tilden Foundations.
"Immigrants Waiting on Ellis Island" courtesy of Corbis Images.

Cover design by Nicole Summer-Lecht.

Inquiries should be addressed to
Prometheus Books
59 John Glenn Drive
Amherst, New York 14228–2119
VOICE: 716–691–0133
FAX: 716–691–0137
WWW.PROMETHEUSBOOKS.COM

15 14 13 12 11   5 4 3 2 1

Library of Congress Cataloging-in-Publication Data

Coan, Peter M.
    Toward a better life : America's new immigrants in their own words : from Ellis Island to
the present / by Peter Morton Coan.
        p. cm.
    Includes index.
    ISBN 978-1-61614-394-7 (cloth : alk. paper)
    ISBN 978-1-61614-395-4 (ebook)
    1. Immigrants—United States—Interviews. 2. Immigrants—United States—Biography.
3. United States—Emigration and immigration—History. I. Title.

JV6450.C63   2011
304.8'73—dc22

                                                                    2011014990

Printed in the United States of America on acid-free paper

For my wife, Nur, and my daughters,
Sara and Melissa

"*If you can share history through the individuals who lived it, and tell their stories through their eyes, from their lips, then you've really done something because you've personalized history in a way that gives it new meaning and new resonance. The history comes alive!*"
—Studs Terkel, author and oral historian

"*For sixty-two years, millions of immigrants passed through the corridors of Ellis Island on their way to becoming Americans. Their journeys, however, are only part of the story. What of those immigrants who continue to come long after?*"
—*USA Today*, September 24, 2008

CONTENTS

PART 2: AMERICA'S NEW IMMIGRANTS
1954–2010

FOREWORD

IMMIGRATION IN THE GOLDEN ERA

For more centuries than one can count, humans have traversed the world in search of a better life, one in which freedom, food, riches, jobs, or simply the thrill of adventure has loomed large. In the late fifteenth century, Columbus's discovery of the "New World" and the subsequent spread of colonialism throughout it made that hemisphere a natural magnet for more immigrants. Since 1800, the United States has attracted more immigrants than any other nation on earth. The country's political and economic liberalism, its vastness, the extraordinary wealth and resources of land, and the general prosperity of its inhabitants have drawn countless "greenhorns" to its shores.

Beginning in the 1830s, the waves of immigrants boosted the country's growth: they gave it the strength to achieve its aims, not the least of which was the opening of the West to white settlement. Not long after the Civil War, there was a marked decline in immigration due to a number of factors, including the effects of a severe economic slump in 1873. But the next decade, the 1880s, saw a massive upsurge of newcomers, mostly pouring in through New York's Castle Garden Emigrant Landing Depot. One reason for this development was that a great many people were coming from an unexpected quarter: the far distant kingdoms of eastern and southern Europe, lands that had previously sent few immigrants. Known as the "New Immigrants," these sorts of Europeans differed markedly from the "Old Immigrants," who hailed from such countries as Germany, Ireland, Great Britain, Scandinavia, Austria, the Netherlands, Belgium, France, and northern Italy. To English America, the earlier group was welcome in spite of their differences, while the New Immigrants, from lands far, far away, seemed much too foreign to be successfully assimilated into American society.

Fig. 1. Castle Garden was the immigrant processing station in New York's Battery Park before Ellis Island came into existence in 1892. Photograph used by permission of the Statue of Liberty National Monument (National Park Service).

Even worse, Protestant critics bewailed the fact that the New Immigrants were almost all Roman Catholic, Jewish, or Eastern Orthodox Christians, faiths that easily aroused Protestant suspicion and, at times, even open hostility. For this and other reasons, a good many Americans began to doubt the value of mass immigration, and some even proposed that it was time to close the "golden door" altogether.

In 1882, the federal government began enacting laws to bar undesirable immigrants, but in order to win the compliance of the states, the imposed Immigration Act charged each arriving alien a "head tax" of fifty cents, and the funds were then reimbursed to those states that actively enforced federal regulations. New York naturally received the bulk of this relief money, helping it to continue operating Castle Garden Emigrant Landing Depot as well as the state immigrant hospital and refugee buildings on Wards Island. The same legislation barred the entry of "convicts, lunatics, idiots, and persons likely to become a public charge." A separate law adopted in the same year was the racist Chinese Exclusion Act, which barred the entry of certain laborers based on their ethnicity. In 1885, another law was passed, this time barring all foreign workers brought in under contract. The federal government passed this law to silence the boisterous complaints by the union leaders in the Knights of Labor, who had alleged that a vast number of American workers were losing jobs through the deliberate importation of foreign laborers. This law was aimed partly at Italians, thousands of whom were being brought into the country on a regular basis by men called *padrones*. These small-time businessmen earned lucrative commissions from manufacturers and other American firms needing reliable workers whom they could pay the lowest of wages without much complaint. In addition, padrones' immigrant wards paid them a commission out of their meager earnings.

The padrones had long been importing southern Italians and Greeks to work in their own small-scale enterprises, such as blacking boots, playing music in the streets and cafés, peddling fruits and vegetables, and making candy. Other nationalities brought in by padrones of their own included Croatians, Mexicans, and Japanese.

Not surprisingly, the state that had the greatest difficulty in satisfying the federal government in this matter of turning away undesirables was also the nation's leading port. Each year, the port of New York received as much as 75 percent of all immigration. In consequence, when the question of immigrants arose, the eyes of the nation naturally turned to New York State's Board of Emigration Commissioners and its Castle Garden Emigrant Landing Depot at the tip of lower Manhattan.

The US government considered the New York immigrant landing system seriously flawed. What dissatisfied lawmakers most was the lack of any real scrutiny: What went on at Castle Garden amounted to no more than a mere recording and tabulation of personal details about each immigrant in large ledgers—there was practically no screening. In addition, unsavory conditions such as dirt, dishonesty, and corruption were commonplace. Some people also complained about the work of Mormon missionaries, who were assisting thousands of northern and western Europeans to emigrate. Because of the church's traditional advocacy of polygamy, many felt it should not be permitted this role.

Debates about these and related questions compelled the federal government to assume full control of immigrant reception in 1890, and the United States Department of the Treasury was put in charge. In terms of bureaucracy, this was a sensible decision, since the Treasury Department was already running the Customs Service and the Marine Hospital Service, both of which carried out their duties at domestic seaports. With the consent of President Benjamin Harrison and Congress, the Secretary of the Treasury approved plans to construct the nation's first federal inspection station over on Ellis Island in New York Harbor. Meanwhile, immigrant reception was temporarily transferred from Castle Garden to a nearby federal building called the Barge Office. In 1891, Congress created a new Treasury Department agency to regulate immigration: the United States Bureau of Immigration. At the time, a new set of immigration policies introduced entirely new procedures such as "immigrant inspection," as well as instructions for what steamship pursers should write on the ships' passenger lists and precise regulations governing the exclusion and the deportation of undesirable or inadmissible aliens.

The same decade saw an even heavier immigration of the newer ethnic groups: southern Italians, Orthodox Jews, Poles, Slovaks, Lithuanians, Finns, and Bulgarians, as well as Greeks, Portuguese, Spaniards, Armenians, Syrian Arabs, Turks, Hindus and Sikhs, West Indian blacks, and Gypsies. All arrived, ship after ship, much to the consternation of a growing circle of Americans demanding far stricter immigration laws.

From 1892 to 1910, a nationwide immigration control system was brought into operation: a chain of immigrant inspection stations was set up at all ports and border crossings. In addition to New York's Ellis Island, federal immigrant stations were opened at Boston, Philadelphia, Baltimore, Detroit, Chicago, Seattle, Portland, San Francisco, Los Angeles, Honolulu, El Paso, Galveston, New Orleans, Mobile, Jacksonville, Savannah, Norfolk, San Juan, and the foreign cities of Montreal, Toronto, and Vancouver, which required the consent of the Dominion of Canada.

At the turn of the century, immigration began to rise, and it continued to surge at an astounding rate. Ellis Island was tremendously overcrowded: as many as fifty thousand aliens had to be examined at the little island in the bay each week. In response to this situation, the government hastily began enlarging the isle through land filling; this was followed by the construction of desperately needed medical and other support buildings. Additionally, newer and stricter regulations came into force. Inspectors were more than ever on the lookout for undesirable aliens, such as foreign prostitutes and their procurers ("the white slave traffic"), unwed mothers, those certified as having "poor physiques," those considered "feebleminded," and those suffering from the dreaded eye ailment known as trachoma. In 1903, suspect political beliefs were added to the list when anarchists were barred under the Immigration Act of that year. This law also raised the head tax to two dollars and barred the entry of epileptics and beggars.

Meanwhile, the flow of eastern European Jews increased dramatically due to the outbreak of hundreds and hundreds of vicious pogroms against them (1903–1906). The Bureau of Immigration sent a number of immigrant inspectors to investigate the causes of the massive exodus. Yet it was also apparent that in spite of the ugly outrage of the pogroms, the vast majority of Jewish emigration was mostly impelled by a burning desire to escape the age-old poverty that had been their lot for generations. For them, coming to America was a dream come true.

Balkan and Levantine (the Levant region includes Lebanon, Syria, Jordan, and Iraq) immigration also rose in this decade. Greeks, Romanians, Serbs, Croats, Bulgarians, Albanians, Bosnians, and others made the long trek to America. The stream of ships on which they sailed usually came from Marseilles, Naples, Patras, Piraeus, Constantinople, and Alexandria; the same vessels were also crowded with hopefuls from Syria, Armenia, Turkey, and Malta, while more emigrants were setting out from Spanish and Portuguese ports. Although the basic reasons for migrating were pretty much the same for all these people—namely, to escape dire poverty and help their families better themselves—there were other causes, such as avoiding discrimination, bigotry, prejudice, war, violence, forced military service, Old World customs and traditions, or forced marriages.

As one might expect, the steamship lines made quite a bundle from the lucrative business of transporting emigrants. After the United States, they found that Canada, Argentina, Brazil, Australia, New Zealand, and South Africa were popular destinations for migrants.

In 1907, the federal government, reacting to rising opposition to Japanese immigrants, entered into a diplomatic understanding with the Empire of Japan to curtail immigration from that country. Called the "Gentlemen's Agreement," it consisted of promises by the United States government not to pass a Japanese exclusion law and by the Imperial Japanese government to halt further Japanese immigration to the United States.

In 1910, refugees from south of the border began fleeing into Texas, Arizona, and California to escape turmoil and save their lives. Called the Mexican Revolution, this civil war went on for ten years, during which the United States received 890,000 Mexican refugees. This eventually led to the 1924 founding of a new federal agency: the United States Border Patrol. That agency's task was to block illegal entry along the Mexican and Canadian borders.

During this same period, the immigration restriction movement gained momentum. World War I contributed to this in a big way by creating a lull in mass emigration, indicating that America's mills, mines, manufacturers, builders, farming estates, and other large concerns could manage sufficiently well without the massive numbers of newcomers to bolster the workforce. The restrictionists marched to victory on the political front, inspired on one hand by the swift growth of the fiercely anti-immigrant, anti-Catholic Ku Klux Klan, and, on the other hand, by the nationwide Americanization movement; the movement, represented by respected organizations like the YMCA and the Protestant Episcopal Church, took place primarily between 1895 and 1924 and aimed to help immigrants assimilate into American culture. In 1917, Congress enacted the Literacy Act, which barred the immigration of illiterate people. Its sponsors knew quite well that the new law would block the entry of groups known to have low rates of literacy, such as Orthodox Jewish women and Christian peasants from southern Italy, Portugal, and eastern

Europe. Although this was an important law, it did not satisfy the restrictionists, who had far higher ambitions: They wanted Congress to pass legislation to end European mass migration for good. Their goal was finally achieved with the passage of the immigration quota acts of 1921 and 1924. Of the two, the 1924 law was the more severe, as it cut immigration to a trickle by the end of the decade.

However, before the May 1924 law was adopted, the United States had already received an overflow of fresh immigrants and refugees following quickly on the heels of postwar peace. From 1919 to 1924, thousands poured into Ellis Island and other stations: Germans, Austrians, Russians, Hungarians, Romanians, Irish, Armenians, Greeks, Jews, Italians, and people of just about every other Old World nationality were trying to get in before any new restriction laws could come into force.

As mass migration came to an end, the Bureau of Immigration changed many of its operations. With far fewer "immigrant inspections" needed at Ellis Island and elsewhere, bureau officials decided to step up domestic enforcement on illegal aliens residing in the United States. Designating Ellis Island as the national headquarters for deportation and other warrant cases, they perfected a system of investigating, arresting, and transporting great numbers of aliens who had transgressed the laws of the land. These "deportation parties" involved the use of trains traveling across the country and halting in rural areas and urban communities to pick up deportees from the local law enforcement officials. The trains operated every four to six weeks, beginning their eastward journeys from two points: San Francisco and Seattle. The duty staff consisted of men called "immigrant inspectors," as well as armed guards, matrons, and physicians. The end of the line was Jersey City, New Jersey, from which the detainees were transferred to Ellis Island by steamboats. These deportation trains remained a significant part of US policy from 1920 through the 1940s.

During the Great Depression of the 1930s, immigration virtually ended; even the limited quotas often went unfilled. In fact, for the first time in American history, statistics showed more people leaving the United States than entering it. Of course, the gradual improvement in the economy began reversing this trend, especially as war clouds gathered over Asia, Europe, and east Africa just before the outbreak of World War II.

While nationalism and war fever convinced many loyal German and Italian immigrants to return to their beloved homelands in support of fascism, thousands of people over in Europe, abhorring the change of events there, began fleeing to the United States, Canada, England, Palestine, Latin America, and elsewhere. Hitler's victorious conquests of Poland, Czechoslovakia, Denmark, Norway, Belgium, the Netherlands, Luxembourg, France, Yugoslavia, and Greece meant the hundreds of thousands of refugees from those places would now have to be labeled as "stateless" aliens. Ellis Island became a way station for those seeking refuge in the United States.

The war also exacted a severe toll on German, Italian, and Japanese nationals living in the United States. In December 1941, President Roosevelt signed an executive order proclaiming them "alien enemies." This affected more than nine hundred thousand people. Thousands of them found themselves under FBI surveillance, and at least ten thousand were actually arrested and taken to immigrant stations such as Ellis Island for investigation. In fact, even respectable American citizens were not exempt; in a decision clearly motivated by racism and xenophobia, President Roosevelt stripped US citizens of Japanese descent of their civil rights by signing an executive order that forced them out of their homes and into internment camps throughout the western states.

With the end of the war, Congress passed the War Brides Act of 1945, which permitted spouses and adopted children of American military personnel to enter the United States without waiting for a quota number. Meanwhile, President Roosevelt had already set up a War Refugee Board and subsequent legislation for helping European refugees and displaced persons enter the United States more easily.

By 1950, the Cold War was in full swing and Communism had become distinctly unpopular. The Internal Security Act blocked the immigration of subversives, such as communists and fascists. Ellis Island once more came into play as a leading detention facility for arriving foreigners suspected or known to be involved in subversive activities. Perhaps the most notable of these cases were those of Ignatz Mezei, "the man without a country," who was held for forty-three months, and Ellen Knauff, a war bride who was held for twenty-two months; after long struggles, both eventually won their appeals and were released. By 1954, Ellis Island was determined to be too large and too expensive to operate, and it was closed permanently on November 12, 1954, ending the first great era of US federal immigration control.

It also marked the beginning of the next great era and America's "new immigrants." In *Toward a Better Life*, you will hear the first-person stories of immigrants from both eras and experience what they endured as you take the journey across one hundred twenty years of immigration to America.

Barry Moreno
Historian, Ellis Island Immigration Museum, and
Author of *The Illustrated Encyclopedia of Ellis Island*

PREFACE

*T*oward a Better Life is a celebration of all immigrants who have come to America seeking freedom and a better way of life. In it, you will read the firsthand accounts of America's "new immigrants" who have come to America since Ellis Island closed in 1954. They tell their stories in their own words. The book also includes the stories of immigrants from the Ellis Island era to illustrate how America's diverse multicultural landscape has changed over the decades and generations.

To reflect this transformation, the Ellis Island Immigration Museum is making changes of its own. More than two million people visit Ellis Island annually, and some have said that they did not see a reflection of their own family's experience as immigrants to America.

That is about to change.

In 2012, the Statue of Liberty–Ellis Island Foundation and the National Park Service will unveil the new Peopling of America Center on Ellis Island. This exciting new center, being built at a cost of $20 million, is a significant expansion of the Ellis Island Immigration Museum and will tell the complete story of immigration to America and the important role immigrants have played across the generations in the making of this great nation.

This is significant because there is no other place where this story is told. There are museums of great art, of natural history, and of many other topics, but there is no other museum that tells the total story of the populating of America, as this one will.

The center will be on Ellis Island to complement the Ellis Island story and because, in the mind's eye of America, Ellis Island stands as the symbol of welcome, freedom, and opportunity—even though there were other ports and other periods of immigration.

Fig. 2. The Main Building at Ellis Island as it looks today. In 2012, the museum will be renamed Ellis Island: The National Museum of Immigration and will tell the complete story of American immigration, including America's "new immigrants," who came to this country after 1954, when Ellis Island closed its doors. Photograph used by permission of the Statue of Liberty National Monument (National Park Service).

This expansion significantly broadens the scope of the museum's content. It will start with the days of the Native Americans and early Europeans and will continue through the establishment of the nation, the Civil War years, and into the existing exhibits on the Ellis Island era itself (1892–1954). Then we will encounter those people who came to America after Ellis Island closed, millions of people whose arrival has had an enormous impact on our nation and its future. Their stories will now be told, and as a result, Ellis Island will remain a relevant and evolving center for chronicling the ongoing story of the peopling of America. To reflect this

Cleveland, was finally, after two years of immigration hearings, granted a waiver of deportation in May 2010 and became a legal US resident. It didn't hurt that her nephew happened to be president of the United States.

Most immigrants are not so lucky.

In the post–Ellis Island era, we have experienced unprecedented technological advances that have changed the nature and speed of communication, transportation, and how we look at our world, which has gone from agrarian to Internet, from analog to digital, from the village crier to the global village.

The stories have changed, too. These are not the same nostalgic tales of Grandpa Giuseppe or Aunt Sadie coming to America in search of "streets paved with gold." During the Ellis Island era, immigrants came predominantly from countries within Europe. In the post–Ellis Island era, there are not just countries but entire continents of people to consider—Asia, Africa, North America, South America, Australia—and so the stories and experiences are as rich and as varied as the cultural differences among the countries and the continents themselves. While Europe still plays an important role in terms of present-day immigration flows, it now ranks sixth overall, and it is Mexico, not Italy, that tops the list in immigration. In short, there is the rest of the world to consider now.

In addition, the sheer scale of immigration has changed in the modern era. While more than twelve million legal immigrants came through Ellis Island in the sixty-two years between 1892 and 1954, more than thirty-seven million legal immigrants came to America in the fifty-six years between 1954 and 2010. Factor in illegal immigration, conservatively estimated at more than twelve million, and you can see how the numbers in the modern era have dramatically increased—more than quadrupled—since immigrants to America started coming from all over the world, not just predominantly from Europe.

What keeps people coming to America's borders and shores?

During the Ellis Island era, the drivers of freedom were numerous: political, social, legal, medical, educational, economic, religious, and more. Today, in this modern era of tolerance, economic freedom is by far the principal motivation of immigrants to America in all modes of transportation, not just by boat, but by plane, car, truck, foot, helicopter, even Jet Ski®. Many people have the mistaken impression that America's new immigrants are principally uneducated Latinos. Not so. America's new immigrants include the well educated and the affluent, as well as the middle-class who come from good families and are here to study at our universities or earn higher-paying jobs, such as brilliant young Indian computer programmers or the burgeoning ranks of technology whiz kids from Asia.

Others, at the lower end of the economic spectrum, are frequently migrant workers seeking a better wage and a better life. Many are illegal, crawling under high-watt border fences, or digging tunnels in the middle of the night, selling drugs for cash, and then giving cash for freedom. Other, less fortunate souls come by boat from China or South America hiding in cargo holds—women, mostly, but also children, many of whom are lured by the promise of good jobs and instead will end up working off a $40,000 ticket to freedom as prostitutes, part of an elaborate global network in the human flesh trade. And though many immigrants, from all walks of life, have come here to work hard and send money back for family members to join them as their Ellis Island ancestors did, most illegal ones will be caught and deported. Some will try again. Others will give up. A great many immigrants, however, have successfully assimilated into society, improving their lives with each new generation and thus strengthening the materials that make up the great mosaic that is America.

But what really changed immigration to America in the modern era and eliminated the need for Ellis Island altogether was the transfer of responsibility for alien processing, which was gradually assigned to US consulates or embassies abroad at the beginning of the 1930s. In this way, all immigrant processing was completed *before* a visa was granted to enter the United States. These hundreds of consulates in countries all over the world became like mini–Ellis Islands.

America's new immigrants are different in many ways from their Ellis Island ancestors. They, too, seek a better life, but many of them today are more educated and offer more in the way of professional knowledge in science and technology, fields that have also made coming to America easier for all immigrants. During the Ellis Island era, the overall commitment to immigrate was a huge deal. Leaving your homeland entailed the likelihood that you would never come back and never see your relatives again, a complete cutoff—this on top of a boat trip that could last over a month. There's a great quote from former Israeli prime minister Golda Meir in her autobiography, *My Life* (G. P. Putnam's Sons, 1976), in which she writes as a Russian Jewish immigrant coming to America in 1906, "I can remember only the hustle and bustle of those last weeks in Pinsk, the farewells from the family, the embraces and the tears. Going to America then was almost like going to the moon."

Today an immigrant can board a plane and be in the United States in less than twenty-four hours from virtually anywhere, and usually the trip is much shorter than that. So the level of commitment in immigrating to America is far less today. In addition, the expectations upon arrival are minus the fear of the unknown felt by Grandpa Giuseppe and Aunt Sadie. Today's new immigrants can click on the Internet and see exactly where they're going. They also have the solace of knowing that they can readily travel back and forth, which was not really an option before the mid-twentieth century. As a result, many of today's new immigrants plan to go back to their homeland; the emotional commitment is further reduced because cell phones allow people to stay in touch in a way that didn't exist before, and international calls, once prohibitively expensive, have become relatively cheap.

The world has changed. The game has changed. Immigration has changed. It is no longer just an American phenomenon, but a global issue that touches scores of nations, each with at least one underclass: the French have the Algerians; the Germans have the Turks; the Turks have the Kurds; the Italians have the Chinese and Latin Americans (many of whom find work as domestics); the Spanish have the Moroccans, Romanians, and Ecuadoreans (in that order); and so it goes. The Canadians? They have American liberals. Overpopulation and overdevelopment on a global scale have forced people to scatter to all corners of the globe in a desperate search for the diminishing returns of economic opportunity. Historically, much of the United States's immigration—and its "golden promise"—was part of the quest to conquer the frontier: the great westward march and migration to settle the land; build cities and towns, homesteads and railroads out of prairie dust; and mine the mountains for gold and silver in the inexorable push to reach the orange groves of California and the sweet salt air of the Pacific, first encountered by Meriwether Lewis, William Clark, and the Corps of Discovery in 1805. This later inspired newspaper editor Horace Greeley, who supported liberal policies toward settlers, to famously exhort in a July 13, 1865, editorial in the *New York Tribune*: "Go West, young man, go West and grow up with the country."

Well, we've done that. In a little over two hundred years, the country *has* grown up. The West *has* been settled. There is no more "California Dreamin'." With the country conquered from sea to shining sea, there is precious little land left to develop. The great westward push has turned inward to the few remaining open spaces left in middle America. This once holy ground, traversed by native Americans across the Great Plains and European settlers forging blindly ahead in rickety Conestoga wagons and on horseback, is now the growing domain of new immigrants: Latinos (mainly Mexicans), but also Bosnians, Sudanese, Iraqis, Laotians, and others from all walks of life who have come to America's heartland in search of the same "golden promise" once extended to their predecessors. This promise was best symbolized by the Statue of Liberty after its October 28, 1886, unveiling in New York Harbor. Today, as open land slowly recedes and economic opportunity with it; as ethnic enclaves that gave neighborhoods their distinctive character and charm disappear; as whole towns become annexed, gobbled up with Pac-Man-like efficiency, to form the endless suburbs of cities; as America's once mighty manufacturing economy has become a hollow service sector led by low-wage jobs and an endless loop of mind-numbing strip malls and disingenuous corporate brands, which have homogenized the face of America—from Pasadena to Maine, it all looks the same—new immigrants, for the first time, have begun to question whether coming here is still the answer. After the start of the economic crisis in 2007, we experienced for the first

Fig. 3. An 1890s advertisement exhorting immigrants to join in the great westward push to the promised lands of California, Oregon, Nevada, and Utah. Photograph used by permission of the Statue of Liberty National Monument (National Park Service).

time "reverse immigration," whereby many immigrants returned home unable to find work, and the unprecedented trend of "reverse revenue," in which Mexican families actually began sending money north to the United States to help support relatives who could not find employment. Have the light and luster from the original promise of Lady Liberty begun to dim?

Yes, the world has changed. The game has changed. Immigration has changed. But the fact remains that for many, America is still their best bet.

What has made life harder for new immigrants is their difficulty in obtaining a visa at a US consulate. US visa laws have changed significantly and become much more complex since the days of Ellis Island. The visas today are, by and large, limited to the educated, the affluent, or those who have parents or spouses in the United States. "If the ancestors of most Americans had tried to immigrate to America under today's rules," said one immigration attorney, "their American Dream would have ended at the docks because they wouldn't have been able to get on the boat."

Fig. 4. The only known photo of the dedication ceremony for the Statue of Liberty, held on October 28, 1886. The smoke is from cannon fire. Photograph used by permission of the Statue of Liberty National Monument (National Park Service).

This has consequently created a huge surge in illegal immigration that involves risks many are prepared to take to escape poverty, exit the Third World, and enter the First World. There's a never-ending stream of customers waiting to take their chances. They may go on their own or pay guides known as "coyotes." In 2009 alone, more than three hundred thousand people were arrested for crossing the sixty-mile stretch of California–Mexico border known as the "Tortilla Curtain." US border patrols sit and wait: each patrol truck armed with guns, helicopter backup overhead, and state-of-the-art night-vision surveillance equipment with which patrols can easily spot illegal immigrants crouching in the dark because their body heat appears luminous on the surveillance screen. Like moths to flame, the immigrants don't have a chance, except to scatter and hope that there's enough distraction so that one or two can slip through undetected.

Save sneaking across the border or hiding in the cargo hold of a boat, plane, or tanker ship, the usual scenario (for those lucky enough to get a US visa) is for a visitor to come here as a student or on holiday and simply stay. Then, over time, the new immigrant finds a sponsor to get a permanent resident alien card ("green card"), marries an American citizen, or pays someone to be their spouse. In the latter scenario, the husband and wife appear at the immigration interview for the green card, providing all the necessary paperwork to make it appear that they are a loving, married couple living under one roof. Once the green card is in hand, the "couple" go their separate ways.

In recent years, illegal immigration at the Mexican border has escalated, though statistics vary widely; one number puts illegal immigration at more than two million people entering the United States in 2009. The migration is largely influenced by the drug trade. "Drugs are the Microsoft of Mexico," said David Cardoza, a senior California Border Patrol agent for more than twenty years. "This trade has infiltrated into the United States at a massive rate with many of the illegal immigrants stuck in the middle and some getting involved." Drug cartels and gang killings have turned border cities and towns into war zones, but some operations are sophisticated. In a recent bust, US authorities discovered thirty tons of marijuana that were part of a smuggling operation using a

Fig. 5. The United States–Mexico border is approximately two thousand miles long. By 2008, more than 190 miles of federally enforced barriers and fencing were at strategic points on the border in Texas, New Mexico, Arizona, and California. Here, a US Border Patrol car keeps watch along the "Tortilla Curtain," a sixty-mile stretch of border that separates California (on the left) from Mexico (on the right). Photograph by the author.

tunnel under the California–Mexico border. The 600-yard tunnel, like something out of a James Bond film, featured a high-tech rail system, lighting, and ventilation; it connected a warehouse in Tijuana with one in an industrial area south of San Diego. The problem has become epidemic, to the extent of spawning a reality show called *Border Wars* on the National Geographic Channel. But it wasn't until a wealthy Arizona rancher, along with his dog, was shot dead by an illegal alien on his property near the Mexican border that push came to shove: in 2010, Arizona governor Jan Brewer signed SB 1070 into law. The controversial measure requires Arizona police officers to question anyone they reasonably suspect of being an illegal alien as to their immigration status, and to detain them if they cannot provide proof of their status. Critics of the legislation said it encourages racial profiling; supporters said the law simply enforces existing federal law. Either way, this was not exactly immigration's finest hour.

I hope you will find that taken as a collective, the stories in *Toward a Better Life* form a moving elegy of the human longing for freedom. In one sense, this book is the ultimate reality show, with stories of love and loss, sorrow and sacrifice, inspiration and success—a poignant meditation on the ebb and flow of the hopes and dreams of immigrants everywhere who decided to gamble it all and come to America in their quest for a better life.

My inspiration to write this book came from readers. During public speaking engagements and book signings over the years, people often came up to me, asked when I was going to write a book about today's immigrants, and expressed how they are nothing like our Ellis Island ancestors.

It wasn't until modern-day immigration stampeded my own backyard that I became motivated. I had recently married for the second time, and though I had already personally lived through the immigration process with my first wife in the 1980s, I did not remember any of this being the nightmare undertaking I was about to endure while helping my second wife get her green card in 2008. I well understood that Immigration and Naturalization authorities had always been concerned that new immigrants carry their weight so as not to become public charges, but what I encountered was ridiculous. There were rigorous background checks and seemingly endless requests for paperwork, substantiating not just income, but ample income plus savings, investments, you name it. The necessary fees, including the attorney's, were absolutely egregious!

In the past, when people came through Ellis Island, all they needed, by and large, was a ton of courage, somebody to vouch for them, and maybe some cash stashed in their shirt.

What had changed?

After experiencing the excruciating journey through the immigration process with my second wife to get her a green card and permanent legal status, I thought: This is insane. My wife and I are well educated and reasonably OK financially; what do people without such wherewithal do? How is the new immigrant experience different from the Ellis Island era?

I had to find out.

To best understand America's new immigrants, one must first understand America's old ones. As a result, *Toward a Better Life* is written in two parts. The first part covers the Ellis Island era (1892–1954); the second one, America's new immigrants in the modern era (1954–2010). In this way, the book seamlessly bridges the old world of immigration with the new one and tracks 120 years of American immigration, decade by decade, through the first-person accounts of the immigrants who actually lived it. The book tells their stories in their words—sometimes sad or angry, other times joyous, tragic, or bittersweet, but always honest, candid confessions told straight from their heart and their lips. These come from ordinary people doing extraordinary things like fifteen-year-old Ava Rado-Harte's late-night escape to Austria during the 1956 Hungarian Revolution and the bittersweet story of New York City doorman and Austrian immigrant Steve Keschl, and they come from celebrities like the von Trapp family portrayed in the movie *The Sound of Music* and Cesar Millan, the "Dog Whisperer," and his dramatic story of blind determination to cross the border from Mexico.

Each chapter covers a decade in American history, with firsthand immigrant stories representative of that decade. The immigrant stories contained in each chapter appear chronologically in order of the year of emigration and essentially answer three fundamental questions: Why did they leave their homeland? What did they endure in coming here? And what subsequently became of them and their family?

The immigrants selected for this book were chosen because their stories were representative of their nationality for their decade, but also because their stories were both unique and compelling. Since 120 years of immigration is being covered, the goal was to be not comprehensive, but rather representative, and provide a balanced mix of stories across nationality, gender, geography, occupation, and time lines—for both the famous and common folk alike—to give you, the reader, a real sense of the complexity of American immigration and how it has changed over time. This is important because each decade has experienced a different immigration profile, and so migration flows are researched on a decade-by-decade basis (see appendix).

There were dozens of wonderful stories that did not make the final cut for the book. So what you have here, as part of the distillation process, are the very best stories. Rather than providing shorter stories and more of them, I chose quality over quantity, and decided to focus on providing fewer stories that went into greater length, depth, and detail about the lives of each immigrant. Stories where the emotion was strongest tended to be the most accurate and telling. I therefore let the stories go where the emotion took them. Some stories centered on the "old country" or "homeland"; others ended soon after arrival here, while still others extended through the assimilation process in America. It depended on the material. I edited to avoid redundancy, and I moved material only when necessary to preserve chronology so that their stories would make sense. At all times, I preserved their voice. Some of the immigrants chosen for the Ellis Island era came from interviews originally done by National Park Service personnel for the Ellis Island Oral History Project, with follow-up interviews by me during the 1990s to confirm facts and gather additional information (which invariably jarred their memory, however faded, for another anecdote or two). Many of these immigrants were advanced in age *then*, and virtually all have since passed away; these were not issues (old age, memory loss) when I interviewed the new immigrants of the modern era.

If there was any personal indulgence on my part in writing this book, it would be my love of cooking, French cuisine in particular. So I particularly enjoyed sharing immigrant stories of some of the world's great French chefs. I permitted myself this opportunity only because the food industry is a natural entry point for new immigrants, both legal and not, to earn a living, and for employers it's an opportunity to save money by hiring cheap labor "off the books."

I would like to thank several people in connection with this book. Usually this is the part where the author overzealously, and sometimes disingenuously, thanks everybody involved with the project or not so involved with the project, or even those who had nothing to do with the project, turning a two-paragraph exercise into three pages of pretentious hyperbole. I have been guilty of this in the past, and I promised myself I would not do it here. No mothers-in-law. No fifth-grade history teachers. No thanking people who don't deserve to be thanked. So, out of respect to you, the reader, here goes:

I would like to thank all of the immigrants who so kindly cooperated to be interviewed for this book, in particular Cesar Millan, Jorge Munoz, Iris Gomez, Yakub "Jay" Shimunov, Gail Boliver, Martha Garcia, Johannes von Trapp, Maria von Trapp, Jacques Torres, Alain Sailhec, Ariane Daguin, Jacques Pépin, Ava Rado-Harte, Steve Keschl, and legendary French chef André Soltner. I would also like to thank Jeff Dosik of the Ellis Island Museum; Peg Zitko of the Statue of Liberty–Ellis Island Foundation; Michelle Mittelstadt of the Migration Policy Institute; Patricia Brennan for her meticulous copyediting of the manuscript; photographers Cengiz Ozdemir and Mustafa Kizilcay; my literary agent, David Fugate at Launch Books, for his consummate professionalism and infectious enthusiasm; the whole crew at Prometheus Books, especially editor Linda Regan; and, of course, Ellis Island historian Barry Moreno for writing the foreword; Stephen Briganti, president and CEO of the

Statue of Liberty–Ellis Island Foundation for writing the preface; and my family: to my wife, Nur, for her love and inspiration, to Harry Weinberg and Rhona Liptzin, and to my daughters, Melissa and Sara, for joining me on some long car trips.

Finally, and perhaps most importantly, I would like to thank new immigrants everywhere, who have made the decision, for one reason or another, to take a leap of faith and come to America in search of a better life. Welcome!

Peter Morton Coan

PART 1

ELLIS ISLAND–ERA
IMMIGRANTS

1892–1954

Chapter 1

1890s

This decade was dominated by the depression of the 1890s, which was on par with the Great Depression of the 1930s. A deep agricultural crisis hit Southern cotton-growing regions and the Great Plains. The shock waves reached Wall Street and urban areas by 1893 as part of a massive worldwide economic crisis. A quarter of the nation's railroads went bankrupt; in some cities, unemployment among industrial workers exceeded 35 percent.

KEY HISTORIC EVENTS

Immigration to America began in 1607 at Jamestown, Virginia. In the pre–Ellis Island era, traditional large-scale immigration began with the Irish potato famine in the 1840s, leading up to the 1890s, the Ellis Island era, to present day.

★ 1846: Irish potato famine triggers large-scale emigration to the United States.
★ 1848: Chinese immigration spikes with start of California Gold Rush.
★ 1855: Castle Garden opens as an immigrant reception station in New York City to accommodate mass immigration.
★ 1861– 1865: During the American Civil War, large numbers of immigrants serve the military on both sides.
★ 1880: US population exceeds fifty-one million; more than 6.4 million immigrants enter the country between 1880 and 1890.

★1882: Chinese Exclusion Act curbs Chinese immigration; first federal immigration law bars "lunatics, idiots, convicts" and those likely to become "public charges."

★1886: The Statue of Liberty is dedicated, ironically, just when resistance to unrestricted immigration begins to escalate.

★1890: New York is home to as many Germans as Hamburg, Germany, is. Pogroms in Russia trigger significant Jewish immigration to the United States.

★1891: The Bureau of Immigration is established to administer immigration laws. Congress adds health qualifications to immigration restrictions: "the insane, paupers, persons with contagious diseases, polygamists and persons convicted of felonies or misdemeanors of moral turpitude are barred from entering the United States."

★1892: Ellis Island replaces Castle Garden as the reception station for immigrants; Chinese immigration to the United States is prohibited for ten years.

★1893: Economic depression widens.

★1894: The restrictionist movement emphasizes the distinction between "old" (northern and western European) and "new" (southern and eastern European) immigrants.

★1897: President Cleveland vetoes literacy tests for immigrants. A fire on Ellis Island destroys buildings; no lives are lost, but many years of federal and state immigration records are burned along with the pine buildings, so the US Treasury orders that all future structures on Ellis Island be fireproof. During reconstruction, immigrant processing temporarily moves from the island to the Barge Office in New York City until the new "fireproof" Ellis Island buildings are built, of stone instead of wood, in 1900.

MIGRATION FLOWS

Total legal US immigration in 1890s: 3.7 million

Top ten emigration countries in this decade: Italy (603,761), Germany (579,072), Russia (450,101), Ireland (405,710), United Kingdom (328,759), Austria (268,218), Sweden (237,248), Hungary (203,350), Poland (107,793), Norway (96,810)

(See appendix for the complete list of countries.)

FAMOUS IMMIGRANTS

Immigrants who came to America in this decade, and who would later become famous, include:

Gus Kahn, Germany, 1890, lyricist
Annie Moore, Ireland, 1892, pioneer
Antonín Dvořák, Czechoslovakia, 1892, composer
Rudyard Kipling, England, 1892, writer
Irving Berlin, Russia, 1893, composer
Francis Hodur, Poland, 1893, priest
Knute Rockne, Norway, 1893, football coach
Warner Oland ("Charlie Chan"), Sweden, 1893, actor
Frank Costello, Italy, 1893, gangster
Mary Antin, Russia, 1894, writer
Felix Frankfurter, Austria, 1894, Associate Justice of the United
   States Supreme Court
Asa Yoelson ("Al Jolson"), Lithuania, 1894, actor/singer
Kahlil Gibran, Lebanon, 1895, writer
Al Dubin, Switzerland, 1896, lyricist ("We're in the Money")
Samuel Goldwyn, Poland, 1896, producer
Moses Teichman ("Arthur Murray"), Austria-Hungary, 1897, dancer
James Naismith, Canada, 1898, inventor (basketball)

Fig. 6. Steerage deck of a steamship bound to New York in 1898. Photograph used by permission of the Statue of Liberty National Monument (National Park Service).

Fig. 7. Dutch Boys from Friesland at the Barge Office near Battery Park in Manhattan, 1890. Photograph used by permission of the Statue of Liberty National Monument (National Park Service).

FAYE LUNDSKY
BORN JULY 2, 1893
EMIGRATED FROM RUSSIA, 1898, AGE 5
SHIP UNKNOWN

She was born in a small border village near Bialystok, Russia (now Poland). Her family escaped the pogroms to America; her father came first, and the rest of the family joined him later. An only child from an Orthodox Jewish family, she grew up in Boston and eventually married a man who became a successful real estate developer. They would go on to have three children, six grandchildren, and five great-grandchildren. They were married sixty-three years. "It's been a wonderful life," she said. She passed away in 1994 at the age of 101.

I remember just a little of my life then. I was so young. I remember I was told that my father was in the service and my mother was, at that time, pregnant with me. However, at that time it didn't matter if he was a soldier; he had to serve whether he had a wife to support or not, and I was born while he was in the army. He was in the army three or four years, the usual time that they had to serve, and then he was supposed to be discharged, but they didn't let him go.

Well, he had a sister in New York, and he wrote to her, told her that if she didn't send him a ticket that he would surely be killed. They were close. His sister had very little money, but when the people came over from Poland and Russia in those years they always had jewelry, watches they had accumulated somehow. Well, she pawned everything to send him a ticket to come, and he paid off the guard, and that's how he escaped the army. And that's why I never knew my father. When I was born he was in America.

I was living with my mother. She had no way of supporting me, and I think she was a cook or did cooking for people, and at that time she told me that she gave me to a wet nurse. That's what they did in those days. However, one day she came and found me in a deplorable condition, not very clean and she was heartsick, so she took me with her, and I think I stayed with her. I was maybe two or three years old. I was an only child. My mother didn't have any parents. They had already passed.

But my mother had a sister, and she lived with us in one room. I remember it, one room, one great big room where there was a bed and there was an oven where they baked; a great big oven they used to bake bread or challahs, and sell them to the peasants there. They were very good cooks.

My mother was very religious, very orthodox, and very observant. She went to services. She would hire a horse and wagon and drive to the city to observe the holidays because there was no synagogue in our village. A man would drive them, a Gentile man. Mother was extremely religious. My aunt was, too. They always kept a strict kosher home and observed the holidays as best they could.

We had no running water in the house and there were no such thing as toilets, those were outside. For water we used pumps from the well. My aunt had two boys, one a little older than me, and one younger. And the younger one, I remember a cradle, and I used to rock him in the cradle. So it was me, my mother, my aunt, my aunt's two sons and my uncle.

I was very close to the two boys. They were more like my brothers as we grew up. We came to America first. Then they came, and they lived with us for quite a while. There were no handouts, no aid of any kind.

I was too young to go to school in Poland. My mother wasn't able to go to school so she couldn't read or write. But my father was very well-learned. He spoke about four languages. He knew Polish, he knew Russian, he knew Hebrew, he knew the religion very well. He was very well-learned. And my mother, they never allowed her to go to school. It was true for many women then, especially Jewish women, so you will find that many of the elderly Jewish people that came, they were illiterate. They didn't know how to read or write. But she knew how to pray because she went to shul all the time.

America. It was a custom in those years for men to come first, but sometimes they met a woman who they liked, and he just wouldn't send for his wife, or divorce his wife. My mother felt this. She felt since my father was already in America, he'd never send for her. So she had two brothers in Boston, and she wrote to them that she'd like to come to America, and they sent her a ticket. And she told me, this is one thing I remember so distinctly, "If anybody asks you your father's name, say he died." Because she felt he wouldn't come to take her off the boat. So if he wasn't there she'd have no problem. But he did come.

Fig. 8. An affluent Scottish family having arrived from Aberdeen, 1895. Photograph used by permission of the Statue of Liberty National Monument (National Park Service).

I don't remember the boat or where we left from, but I remember we went steerage, way down, and I must have been very sick. Everybody was puking down there, and I contracted the measles on the boat, so when we landed at Ellis Island I was separated from my mother. They took me to the hospital where they kept those that were detained, and it was very frightening. I didn't know the language, and I didn't know what happened to my mother. They wouldn't allow her to see me for some reason. I was isolated, and she couldn't come to see me. But my father came to visit me as soon as he heard I was there, and he came every single day. And he always came with some kind of a toy or a doll or something. He was a wonderful father, very lovable. And when I got better he took us to New

York, and we lived on Cherry Street. He had a little apartment for us on Cherry Street on the East Side of New York.

Years later I went to Ellis Island through the hospital where people that got sick stayed, and where the parents stayed, and I said to my daughter, "Can you imagine what they did to me?" I says, "They might have told me that I was sick, I was going to stay there, but I wouldn't understand. I didn't speak anything but Yiddish."

In America, my father was a sheet-metal worker, and he worked on roofs. He was jack of all trades and master of none. He was a very handy man; he could do anything. He got any kind of a job he could, and he struggled; it was very rough, but he made it on his own. I remember we always had somebody living with us. One person brought over somebody else; it was an uncle or a cousin, they had no place to go. Everybody at that time had a boarder, if you know what I mean. Most were relatives. My father had a young brother and he had no place to go. Well, he came with us. There was always room somehow, even if it was on the floor.

We were close with our neighbors. If anybody was sick, they would bring chicken soup. And as I said, we always had somebody stay with us. Everybody had boarders, either to help pay the rent or give somebody a chance to get on their feet.

My mother's sister and my cousins stayed with my aunt. The sister who sent a ticket to my father pawned all her jewelry, everything she ever had, and to add to her plight, she had five children. She lived on Ludlow Street: five flights walk-up, three rooms, five children. And when my father came to America, she was so delighted to see him, and he saw her plight, he says, "I'm going to get myself a room."

She says, "No, you're not. We'll move."

They all slept on the floor. They all had these feather comforters they took with them, and he stayed there one night and he got himself a room because he realized that she was in bad circumstances, that she pawned everything she had to send for him. All his life, he said, "My sister-in-law saved my life."

Fig. 9. Ellis Island as it looked when it opened in January 1892. On the night of June 14, 1897, a great fire burned down the entire immigration complex. To this day, no one knows for sure how it happened. Photograph used by permission of the Statue of Liberty National Monument (National Park Service).

And he did pay her back for the ticket so she could get her jewelry back, and my mother used to say, "You paid her back." He says, "I could never pay her back." There was such love, and I loved her so dearly. She was my favorite aunt.

For school they put everybody in one class. Most of the children in the school were immigrants. I learned English right away. You know, you pick up those things. The children came from everywhere, not just Poland. But they were mostly Jewish immigrants.

My father was quite a smoker. He smoked a real Russian cigar, and I said to him one day, "Papa, why do you smoke so much?"

He said, "Well, I had a rabbi who said if we learn this passage, the one that learns the passage first will get a cigarette."

And that's how he got sick: he got hooked on cigarettes in those days. He said, "I got more cigarettes than anybody else." And unfortunately he died of lung cancer. . . .

My mother said, you know, there's an expression in Europe: "America, the golden land." She comes here and says, "Where's the gold?" She saw people struggling, you know, and it was a letdown for her. But as soon as he was able to, my father became a citizen and he would go and vote. He would drag me along. Women didn't vote then, and there were suffragettes and I remember saying to him, "Pa, please vote for the women to vote." He said, "Yes, I certainly will." Well, I remember when the women got the vote and we were all elated. And I was glad that he voted for the women, because I begged him to, and he said he would.

So he was very broad-minded, and he was so very proud of his citizenship papers that he had them framed and he always looked up at it. My daughter has it framed today as an heirloom. She kept it. It was falling apart, and she had paid eighty-five dollars to have it put together because she wanted that as a remembrance of her grandfather.

My mother was a good soul, very honest, very devoted to my father. She was a wonderful wife. She always did things that would please him. In those days the man or the husband was the head of the household, the king. I remember never eating until Papa came home. We all ate together as a family to show respect.

She always begged him to become more religious, and she always begged him not to work on the Sabbath, and she always said to him, "No matter how much you make, I'll manage. I don't care. I don't want you to work on the Sabbath." My father wasn't as religious as my mother. He was more liberal, more Americanized. But as they got older he became active in the temple and served in the capacity of a president. And he was very capable as a leader, I would say. He was either the president or the secretary or head of something.

My parents were extremely honest. If a bill was due on the first, it was paid on or before. We were never allowed to buy anything paying out [on credit]. We always had to have the money before we bought. Those are the values, I would say, that I have always held to this day.

Since I was an only child, my cousins were almost like brothers. We lived together for years when they came. Then when we all accumulated a little money and we did, we bought a house together on Grove Street in Boston. We couldn't afford a house by ourselves. It was a three-family house, so we had one apartment, they had one apartment, and there was a store downstairs, and my father had the store. He was a plumber, did all kinds of fixing, a handyman. And that's how he went into business for himself. He didn't work for anybody when he came to Boston.

I met my husband one summer. In my day we didn't go away for the summer; we couldn't afford to. So what we did as young girls, we ran a dance and made money and we rented a cottage. We made about $300 selling tickets, and we rented a cottage for the summer near the beach in Winthrop, north of Boston. We went there weekends, and boys did the same thing. And that's how I met my husband. They had cottages nearby, and we'd meet on Saturday nights and have dances with a Victrola, and we had a lot of fun. [*She pauses, nostalgic.*] He was very attentive to me and he was very much in love with me and he said, "You'll never be sorry if you marry me because I'll always adore you." Something like that—and we got married.

He went into the real estate business here in Boston. He was born in America. He was born in Chelsea, a suburb of Boston. And he went into business for himself. His father died when he was four years old, but he had an uncle that he was very close to, so he got a lot of advice from his uncle, and he became very successful in buying property and sort of followed in his uncle's footsteps.

My husband and I had three children, six grandchildren, and five great-grandchildren. We were married sixty-three years!

I remember we had planned to go to Florida for a month, and I had gone into town to get a new jacket and I came back and he had a stroke.

He was rushed to the hospital and I nursed him for about five years. Near the end, my children wanted me to send him to a nursing home because they felt it was way too much for me, but I thought about it: his mind was clear, very sharp, and I could never in a million years do that, and so I handled him. It wasn't easy, but I did. So I say life has its ups and downs; we have to make the best of the situation.

Fig. 10. Immigrants in legal detention having a meal on Ellis Island, 1893. Photograph used by permission of the Statue of Liberty National Monument (National Park Service).

I feel very grateful and blessed to have three wonderful children, and they're very caring and very interested in me. And I'm concerned about every day because my health is failing and I recognize it and I sometimes see the writing on the wall that I may go into a nursing home, but they say, "No way," so I'm holding my own. I'm living one day at a time. What else can you do?

Chapter 2

1900s

After the depression of the 1890s, immigration to the United States more than doubled in the first decade of the new century with an unprecedented wave of immigration, mainly from eastern and southern European countries. Swedes and Norwegians escaping poverty and religious oppression settled in the Midwest, especially Minnesota and the Dakotas, while many Danish immigrants who were Mormon converts moved to Utah.

KEY HISTORIC EVENTS

★1900: The new "fireproof" Main Building on Ellis Island is opened, and 2,251 immigrants are received that day as immigrant processing resumes there.

★1900: US population nears seventy-six million.

★1903: As a result of President William McKinley's assassination in Buffalo, New York, by anarchist Leon Czolgosz, immigration law denies entry to anarchists or persons believing in the overthrow by force or violence of the US government.

★1905: Japanese and Korean Exclusion Movement formed on the West Coast by organized labor in protest against the influx of cheap "coolie" labor and the perception that they are taking jobs from American workingmen.

★1906: Bureau of Immigration and Naturalization established.

★1907: Immigration peaks, with more than 1.3 million immigrants arriving this year alone.

MIGRATION FLOWS

Total legal US immigration in 1900s: 8.2 million

Top ten emigration countries in this decade: Italy (1,930,475), Russia (1,501,301), Hungary (685,567), Austria (532,416), United Kingdom (469,518), Ireland (344,940), Germany (328,722), Sweden (244,439), Norway (182,542), Greece (145,402)

(See appendix for the complete list of countries.)

FAMOUS IMMIGRANTS

Immigrants who came to America in this decade, and who would later become famous, include:

Pauline Newman, Lithuania, 1901, labor organizer
Anzia Yezierska, Russia, 1901, writer
Vincent Impellitteri, Italy, 1901, politician
Philip Murray, Scotland, 1902, union leader
Joe Hill, Sweden, 1902, activist/writer
Antonio Moreno, Spain, 1902, actor
Edward G. Robinson, Romania, 1903, actor
Ricardo Cortez, Austria, 1903, actor
Frank Capra, Italy, 1903, film director (*It's a Wonderful Life*)
Angelo Siciliano ("Charles Atlas"), Italy, 1903, bodybuilder
Max Factor, Russia, 1904, cosmetician
Hyman G. Rickover, Poland, 1904, admiral
Enrico Caruso, Italy, 1904, opera singer
Edward "Father" Flanagan, Ireland, 1904, priest
James Wong Howe, China, 1904, cinematographer
Louis Nizer, England, 1905, lawyer
Johann "Johnny" Weissmuller, Romania, 1905, Olympian/actor
  (*Tarzan*)

Leopold Stokowski, England, 1905, conductor
Golda Meir, Russia, 1906, fourth prime minister of Israel
Mary Pickford, Canada, 1906, actress
Lily Chauchoin ("Claudette Colbert"), France, 1906, actress
Henny Youngman, England, 1906, comedian
Abraham Beame, England, 1906, politician
Sol Hurok, Ukraine, 1906, producer
Charles Luciano, Italy, 1906, gangster
Ben Shahn, Lithuania, 1906, painter
Arthur Tracy ("The Street Singer"), Russia, 1906, singer/actor
Giacomo Puccini, Italy, 1907, opera composer
Sidney Hillman, Lithuania, 1907, labor leader
Frances Winwar, Italy, 1907, biographer
Irène Bordoni, France, 1907, singer/Broadway performer
Bob (Leslie Townes) Hope, England, 1908, actor/comedian
Gustav Mahler, Germany, 1908, composer
Frank Puglia, Italy, 1908, actor
Bartolomeo Vanzetti and Nicola Sacco, Italy, 1908, anarchists
Lee Strasberg, Austria, 1909, director
Donald Crisp, Scotland, 1909, actor (*How Green Was My Valley*)
Erich von Stroheim, Austria, 1909, actor/director

Fig. 11. Bob (Leslie Townes) Hope, one of Ellis Island's most famous immigrants, sailed with his family from England aboard the *St. Louis* in 1908 and passed through Ellis Island when he was five years old. He grew up in Cleveland, Ohio. Photograph used by permission of the Statue of Liberty National Monument (National Park Service).

Fig. 12. Mulberry Street, 1900. Photograph used by permission of the Statue of
Liberty National Monument (National Park Service).

PATRICIA FITZGERALD
BORN AUGUST 21, 1894
EMIGRATED FROM IRELAND, 1907, AGE 13
SHIP UNKNOWN

One of eight children, she came to America with her older brother when she was thirteen. They lived with relatives who had already settled in Rhode Island in the wake of the Great Famine of 1845–1852, which sent more than one million Irish to America's shores. Like many Irish women of her day, she found work as a domestic. Good-natured with a sweet disposition, she eventually married and raised a large family of her own. She passed away peacefully at the age of ninety-nine.

I was born in central Ireland in a small village south of Tullamore. We lived in a cottage, no upstairs, and there were two big bedrooms and a kitchen and parlor. Fireplaces heated the house. There were three of them, one in each room, and one in the kitchen, of course. The kitchen had two big windows in it.

There were six windows in the cottage, three in the back and three in the front, and visitors would walk up to the house from the road down below. There was a large table in front of the window where we ate.

For water, there was a pump outside not far from the door. We'd bring water in from the pump. We had a farm with cows and chickens and turkeys, but not for selling anything, just to live. My father was a gamekeeper, you see. He used to shoot different things—pheasants, birds mostly. There was a large family that lived next door to us and he worked for them. They had a big farm. They had money, they were well off, and so my father was a gamekeeper for them. And he was a happy man with his family and my mother. He was a good-looking man, medium height, dark brown hair.

In this cottage it was me, my mother and father, one brother, and six sisters. That's a lot of people for such a small space. Each of us had chores to do. I had to wash the dishes and sweep the floor and maybe sometimes help pick potatoes. We had our own little plot of potatoes. We also grew turnips, cabbage, and onions, not to sell but to eat. My mother used to make good sturdy bread. She'd mix some bread in a pan, put it in there, pat it all around and bake it, bake it over the hangers, you know, in the kitchen. And there was a hanger down with a hook in it, and that's where she put it, there. She boiled potatoes and cabbage and turnips. We didn't store any kind of food for winter, just the potatoes. Occasionally we did canning.

For special meals, my mother made chicken; if she had a big crowd, it had to be a turkey. We raised them. We raised chickens and everything. We only had a small place, though.

In my school there were two teachers and a big room and a smaller room and outside toilets. They taught us the basics: reading, writing, arithmetic. That's about all. They didn't teach Gaelic. I couldn't speak a word of it; neither could my parents. Just English. Later on, my husband—his folks came from the south of Ireland where they used to teach Gaelic, he could speak it.

We were a very religious family, my father especially. We had to go to church, and you had to be good. Caught swearing or anything and we'd get a good whipping for it, or a "good clout," as they say. [*She laughs.*] We used to say the rosary in Lent time and special times. We went to church every Sunday; it was three miles away, and we walked it. The church and the school were in Tullamore. It was a nice little town with a tavern. Of course, my father went there to get a drink occasionally, but he'd always come home. [*She laughs.*] He was a good father. My brother Rex, he used to work outside with Father, but the girls didn't. We all stayed home, indoors, with Mom, helping her.

We came to America because my father had two brothers and their families were already here. They had originally come after the famine in the 1850s. My older brother Rex and myself—he was one year older—came to America together. I was thirteen, he was fourteen, so we came. We were the eldest children. My uncles in America paid [for our passage]. I went to live with the one in Pawtucket, Rhode Island, and his wife, and Rex went to the other aunt and uncle in Providence.

The day we left for America, the farm neighbors and all the school kids came to see us. We somehow got a jaunting car and a horse. [*She laughs.*] We had a long ride to Queenstown [now called Cobh, its

Fig. 13. Jewish immigrants receiving a medical examination from US Public Health Service doctors, October 1907. Photograph used by permission of the Statue of Liberty National Monument (National Park Service).

original name]. My father went with my brother Rex and me, and one of our neighbors joined us. My mother couldn't come because she had all the other children to take care of. We stayed overnight there in Queenstown in a pension [hotel or boardinghouse] and then got the boat the next morning. I don't remember the name.

I remember we had to get on a tender [supply ship] to go out to the big boat. It looked to me like a million dollars, it was so big, so grand, and they were playing music on board. It was great. I could see my father waving from the deck, as we were on the tender going off. Rex and I went steerage, third-class. The boat ride took over two weeks and I was sick all the way. I nearly died, but Rex didn't get sick. He took care of me. I wasn't able to get on my feet the whole time. It was terrible. I remember there were a lot of kids and their families, a lot of people sick, vomiting, crying. . . .

I remember seeing the Statue of Liberty for the first time when we came into the harbor. It looked like a big statue of a man. [*She laughs.*]

When we arrived at Ellis Island we had to take a physical. My aunt and uncle, the ones that lived in Providence, they came with a cousin, and they were waiting for us and took us right off the boat. It was crowded, jam-packed. And I saw all the people that were all around. It was dizzying. [*She laughs.*]

I had never seen a black person before. I never saw a black child till we came off the boat in New York, and I saw a bunch of them, you know, on the sidewalk, playing ball and skipping. I thought it was great. And Rex was, of course, with me, and my aunt and my uncle to bring us home.

We took the train north. I remember looking out the window amazed at America, such a big place, so many tall buildings, so different than Tullamore and the life I knew back in Ireland.

My uncle took me back to his brother's house in Pawtucket, Rhode Island. Rex went to the aunt and uncle in Providence. My aunt and uncle in Pawtucket had kids about my own age. I lived in the house with them and they treated me like one of their own, all very loving, everybody helped each other. I went to Catholic school. There were nuns. I think they put me in the third grade. And I was older than most third graders, but it didn't bother me a bit. [*She laughs.*] I was a pretty happy-go-lucky kid anyway. I was almost fourteen. And I loved it there. I was used to living in a cottage in Ireland.

Well, the house in Pawtucket was big, and it had electricity, which was a first for me. There was the kitchen and three bedrooms, two on one side of the kitchen and one on the other. And then we had a couple of cots for anyone that wanted to stay if they came to visit. We lived right in the city. My uncle was a real estate man. His wife, my aunt, she was Irish, too. But they were born here. I didn't have to work or pay them anything at all. I had room and board, but my uncle would never have taken anything from me. Never. Neither of my uncles. We were family. Everybody helped each other.

I stayed with my aunt and uncle for a little over a year, and then I wanted to work. I wanted to go and make money. I also missed my brother. So after one year I went to Providence to be with Rex and my other uncle and his wife. He was a policeman. Then my uncle got me a job in Providence Hospital in the linen room where they used to put away the clean linen. I got a job there. My uncle knew the laundress there, and she said, "Bring her in and I'll give her a job somewhere here." [*She laughs.*] Rex got a job working with my uncle in real estate, a good job.

We both sent money back to Ireland. The job paid me eighteen dollars a week or something like that, and that was good money then, but we sent most of it back to Ireland because that's why we came to America: to help out, as we were the eldest children, the first in line, so my sisters could come. And so that's why my uncle brought us here. As time went by, all the sisters came here except my father and mother; they stayed in Ireland. They were happy there. But they wanted a better life for my brother and me and the rest of my sisters, and America was where the opportunity was. . . .

Rex eventually got married. I became a domestic for a rich lady. I did housework. She was a rich old lady, and she could be mean as a hungry dog, but she was good to me. She also had another girl working for her, from Donegal, from the north and west of Ireland. She would do the cooking, and I'd do the rest of the housekeeping and such. A lot of Irish women did domestic work in those days.

I met my husband at church. I remember that was the first time I ever saw him. I was about seventeen. He came from Providence. He was a bus driver, or a motorman, as we used to call him. He came from the south of Ireland, near Cork. He had been in America before me. Not too long before me. I forget now. We had a boy and three girls. . . .

Fig. 14. Bavarian immigrant, 1906. Photograph used by permission of the Statue of Liberty National Monument (National Park Service).

I love America. I'm glad I came. I'd be a farmer's wife digging ditches in a little garden over there. [*She laughs.*] They didn't have much work for girls then, not in the rural country where we came from. They were all farmers. And that means lot of digging, and I never could do that. I didn't like it much either.

BETTY DORNBAUM
BORN FEBRUARY 12, 1903
EMIGRATED FROM ROMANIA, 1909, AGE 6
SHIP UNKNOWN

She traveled with her sister and maternal grandmother to America. For reasons unknown, she was processed at Castle Garden, not on Ellis Island, where she met her mother for the very first time. "I remember seeing the Statue of Liberty when the boat was coming into the harbor and saying to my grandmother, 'That is not my mother.' What did my mother look like? In my imagination as a child I thought, 'Well, maybe that's her {the Statue of Liberty}, made in her honor,' because my grandparents told me she looked like a queen. . . . And then I saw her! She was a beautiful lady. She had on a big fancy hat with a feather and, of course, a long flowing dress. She certainly looked like a queen to me!"

I was born February 12, 1903, in Iasi, Romania. I never knew my father. He died of pneumonia before I was a year old, and I was brought up by my maternal grandmother and grandfather. I remember where we lived, you came into a yard and there were apartments on the ground floor and there was a balcony with apartments overhead. On the right side as you came in from the gate was the toilet, and it had two foot marks in ceramic and a hole. It was a big yard, and maybe once a month gypsies would come, and if you had copper pots they used to shine them for you.

My grandfather was a sexton for a big temple, the biggest temple in Iasi. In America you would call him Gerald, but his Jewish name was Gedalia. My mother's parents' last name was Markowitz. And they raised us, my sister and myself. My sister was two years older than me. It was just the two of us.

I remember that we lived in the middle of the block and at the end of the block was an avenue and a lot of stores. I remember there was a hayloft across the street. There was a store where they had a big window where I saw them make matzos. And on the corner there was a bar, and opposite that was a big fruit store.

I got in trouble at the bar. It was Passover and my grandmother and grandfather were at temple, and my sister and I were supposed to be very nice young ladies. And somehow or other I found a gold piece, and I went into the bar, and I said it belonged to Grandpa and I asked him if he could change it. And then I took all my friends on a binge.

Of course, we were only supposed to eat certain foods at that time. And I don't remember how many blocks away was a square, and around that square they had a movie, and they had a two-tier merry-go-round, ice cream soda, they had a sideshow, so I took my friends. We went on the merry-go-round. The show was a snake that sleeps in a bed that is almost human, and we were screaming because we thought the snake wouldn't go where it was supposed to. But the snake went up on the bed and, with its head, pulled the cover over. And we bought a lot of candy, which I wasn't allowed to eat. And while we were on the merry-go-round, I saw my sister and her friends. And I called them over and I told them they could have a ride, too. But when I got home, she snitched on me, and I got a beating. [*She laughs.*]

My grandfather was very strict. He was worse than a general in the army. Everything had to be just so. We couldn't do anything wrong. But he liked to tease us, too. That was all right. Like putting hot pepper in our soup. We weren't allowed to pick up our spoon before he did, so it was safe, you know, when he picked up his spoon, and then he just got a kick out of seeing us run around with cold water trying to put the fire out in our mouths!

In our school, the Christian children had one period for them and the Jewish children had a period to learn Hebrew. But I got in trouble all the time because I used to love sugar. And at that time they used to eat those square sugar lumps. So I used to take a bunch of them to school, and it would crunch, and the teacher would always punish me for that because it was crunching and would disturb the class. So, in order to punish you, they took a paper and they cut it, folded it, and then cut out the center a little and left like two horns and then they, with a string, they tied it on your head and you had to walk through all the classes. So you ended up in the principal's office. If my grandfather didn't catch me there, then my sister would tell him.

Fig. 15. Dwarfs from Asia outside the Main Building, 1900. Photograph used by permission of the Statue of Liberty National Monument (National Park Service).

I don't even remember my mother because when I was one year old my aunt was supposed to go to America to marry a man. The man was going to America to get a job because he couldn't get one in Romania, and he sent her a ticket. But my aunt had trouble with her eyes and was sent back from Ellis Island or Castle Garden or wherever she was—and my mother went in her place, so I don't even remember my mother. I never even saw a picture of her!

Since she was a widow and being that it was so hard for a man to get a job, let alone a woman, she had no way of making a living, no way of paying my grandmother and grandfather for her staying home and doing nothing and taking care of the children. But when my aunt was supposed to go to America to marry and was sent back, my mother figured maybe she could get a job in America.

So she came to America, and she got a job in a factory and she worked for seven years and saved up money that my grandmother should bring my sister and me to America. My mother bought the tickets and sent it to us, but my grandmother decided with my grandfather that she, my grandmother, would stay in America for a year and then go back to my grandfather, so as not to leave him alone for too long—that she was coming just to bring us over.

My grandparents didn't tell me and my sister that mother worked in a factory and things like that, but that she was very well off and that the streets in America were paved with gold, and so they tried to paint this beautiful picture for us. I remember that we were worried about going because my sister got sick with typhus.

At that time we lived in a different house. It was a private home that was divided into four apartments. And there was a cellar where we kept barrels where the people who lived in the house made sour pickles, sauerkraut that I stole a lot of. The other half of the block was like an orchard. So I remember that my sister got typhus and they had to take her away in a wagon to the hospital. And I missed her very much, and I remember running after the wagon as they were taking my sister away. And when it got too far away, I ran back to the house and got into her bed and covered myself with her covers and eventually landed in the hospital with her! But they didn't have enough room, so they put me at the foot of her bed, so that she was at one end of the bed and I was at the other. I was maybe about five or so.

I remember from Iasi we took a wagon with all our possessions and that led us to a train. It was me, my sister, and our grandmother. I don't remember packing anything. I know that we didn't go to stores to get a dress or a coat or anything—it was always made by hand. My grandmother made it. And I don't remember too much about the train, but I remember that we went to Le Havre in France to get the boat to America, and while we were on the train in the station there, I remember a man putting his hand through the window and handing me a box of cookies. Whether they knew that these people were going to America or not, waiting to board the boat, I don't know. But that I remember very vividly.

I remember being very seasick on the boat. I remember eating delicatessen salami and bread and upchucking a lot. We were in steerage. We went to Castle Garden, I distinctly remember, not Ellis Island, and we were there overnight.

I remember seeing the Statue of Liberty when the boat was coming into the harbor and saying to my grandmother, "That is not my mother." What did my mother look like? In my imagination as a child, I thought, "Well, maybe that's her, made in her honor," because my grandparents told me she looked like a queen. So naturally that's the attitude I took. Then, when I came into Castle Garden and I saw all these people who came to pick up the immigrants, they didn't look like rich people to me. And then I saw her! She was a very beautiful lady. She had on a big fancy hat with a feather and, of course, a long flowing dress. She certainly looked like a queen to me!

At Castle Garden all I remember was that they looked at my eyes and somebody put something to my chest, so I gathered it was the doctor. And we passed our examinations, which was the next day.

This was the first time my grandmother had ever been to America either. But she tried to calm us down, that our expectations shouldn't be more than we see. Evidently when she was younger she had gone to large cities and saw things, so she knew.

But my mother was there to meet us, and I don't know whether the baggage was sent to the house or what, but my mother took us to an apartment. To get there, we rode an elevated train. I was sitting by the window, and my mother met us with a box of chocolate-covered cherries, which I had never tasted before and I ate like a pig. And I remember putting my head out the window, and my mother said, "You don't do that!" The train seemed to be so close to the buildings, the houses, that at times it scared me that if I put my hand out I could touch the house. But then I was afraid my hand or arm would fall off because the train seemed to go so fast. But then it stopped and I looked and everything looked so dingy, so dark. And then we walked to the house.

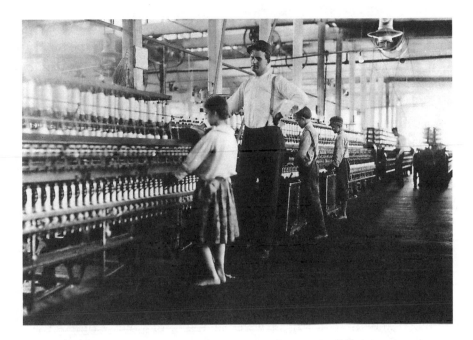

Fig. 16. Immigrant children working in the spinning room of a New England textile mill in North Grosvenor Dale, Connecticut, 1902. Photograph used by permission of the Statue of Liberty National Monument (National Park Service).

I remember it was 117 Avenue C between Seventh and Eighth Streets on the Lower East Side of Manhattan. It was a tenement. When you walked in you came to a large kitchen. To the right was a living room, to the left was a bedroom, no windows. She got it [the apartment] just before we came. It was in the same building that my aunt lived in. And I remember there was a couch that was contoured so you could sleep on it, and my mother had two boarders besides us—a brother and sister. I think they were Romanians. My mother and this sister, she was a young girl, slept in one bed. The brother slept on a folding bed in the living room. My grandmother slept on the couch. In the kitchen there was a coal stove, and two chairs were put together in front of the coal stove, and feather pillows and things were put on there, and that's where I slept.

There were two toilets on each floor. There were four tenants on each floor, so two tenants used each toilet. We had gaslight. The bathtub was next to the sink, and it had an enamel cover on it. Every Friday my mother cleaned the house. And because Saturday would be the Sabbath, she made what some people jokingly referred to as "Jewish rugs" and put newspaper on the floor on Friday so it should be clean for Saturday.

I was enrolled in Seventh Street School. My mother worked in a factory and she worked sometimes nine hours, sometimes ten hours, sometimes eleven hours. She made $3.50 a week. She spoke some English, but it was broken English because she only worked with immigrants. And she didn't go out very much so it was very hard for her to learn. Grandma would've liked to learn, but she said it didn't pay for her to try at her age, that she was too old to learn a new language.

I wanted to be an American, and fast! So I learned the language, but I also went with a bad bunch of cliques in the street. If they stole a banana, I did the same thing. If they shimmied up the pole, I did the same thing. And the horses drew the trolley cars, so if they went up the lampposts and threw a bag of water at them, or flour, I did the same thing—to be an American!

Chapter 3

1910s

This decade marked the high point of Italian immigration to the United States. Immigration inspectors had decided to divide the influx into two groups: southern and northern Italian. In 1910, the Mexican Revolution began south of the border, the twentieth century's first modern social revolution. The resultant economic and social chaos pushed many Mexican natives north. The railroads hired most of them for construction and maintenance. While more than 185,000 Mexicans came here legally, it is conservatively estimated that more than one million Mexicans actually crossed the border.

KEY HISTORIC EVENTS

★ 1910: Mexican Revolution results in the first major wave of Mexican immigrants to America.

★ 1911: The Triangle Shirtwaist Factory fire in New York City kills 146 people, most of them immigrant women and children, and leads to legislation requiring improved factory safety standards for sweatshop workers.

★ 1912: The maiden voyage of the RMS *Titanic* from Southampton, England, to New York ends in tragedy when the ship, with hundreds of immigrants aboard, strikes an iceberg; 1,517 people perish.

★ 1913: The Alien Land Law passes the California legislature, effectively barring Japanese, as "aliens ineligible for citizenship," from owning agricultural land in the state. The Bureau of Immigration and Naturalization was divided into two separate bureaus—the Bureau of Immigration and the Bureau of Naturalization—and was placed into the new Department of Labor.

★1914–1918: World War I affects mass immigration to the United States from Europe.

★1916: Madison Grant's popular book *The Passing of the Great Race* calls for exclusion, on racist grounds, of "inferior" Alpine, Mediterranean, and Jewish "breeds," preferring Scandinavians or the "Nordic race."

★1917: Persons of "psychopathic inferiority," men and women entering the United States for immoral purposes, vagrants, alcoholics, and stowaways are added to the exclusion list. A literacy test for immigrants is finally adopted after being defeated in Congress seven times when Congress overrides the second veto by President Woodrow Wilson.

★1919: Antiforeign fears and hatreds shift from German Americans to alien revolutionaries and anarchist radicals; thousands of alien radicals are seized in Palmer raids and hundreds deported.

MIGRATION FLOWS

Total legal US immigration in 1910s: 6.4 million

Top ten emigration countries in this decade: Italy (1,229,916), Russia (1,106,998), Canada and Newfoundland (708,715), Austria (589,174), Hungary (565,553), United Kingdom (371,878), Greece (198,108), Mexico (185,334), Germany (174,227), Ireland (166,445)

(See appendix for the complete list of countries.)

FAMOUS IMMIGRANTS

Immigrants who came to America in this decade, and who would later become famous, include:

William O'Dwyer, Ireland, 1910, politician
Spyros Skouras, Greece, 1910, film producer
David Dubinsky, Russia, 1911, labor leader
Alfred Levitt, Belarus, 1911, painter
Meyer Lansky, Belarus, 1911, gangster
Charles "Charlie" Chaplin, England, 1912, actor/comedian
Arthur Stanley Jefferson ("Stan Laurel"), England, 1912, actor/comedian
E. E. Clive, Wales, 1912, actor
Ludwig Bemelmans, Italy, 1912, writer/artist
Ruby Keeler, Canada, 1912, dancer
Jule Styne, England, 1912, composer
Claude McKay, Jamaica, 1912, writer/poet
Barbara West, England, 1912, *Titanic* survivor
Rodolfo Guglielmi ("Rudolph Valentino"), Italy, 1913, actor
Mike Mazurki, Ukraine, 1913, actor/wrestler
Louis Adamic, Slovenia, 1913, writer
Elia Kazan, Turkey, 1913, film director (*On the Waterfront, A Streetcar Named Desire*)
George Zucco, England, 1913, actor
Ettore Boiardi ("Chef Boyardee"), Italy, 1914, cook
Jean Hersholt, Denmark, 1914, actor
Harry Houdini, Hungary, 1914, magician
Xavier Cugat, Spain via Cuba, 1915, bandleader
Juano Hernandez, Puerto Rico, 1915, actor
Marcus Garvey, Jamaica, 1916, ethnic leader
Sergei Rachmaninoff, Russia, 1918, composer
Emma Goldman, Russia, 1919, anarchist
Igor Sikorsky, Russia, 1919, inventor (helicopter)
Lilly Daché, France, 1919, hatmaker/fashion designer

Fig. 17. The Registry Room, or Great Hall, which had a capacity of five thousand people. The metal dividers were eliminated in 1911. Photograph used by permission of the Statue of Liberty National Monument (National Park Service).

SISTER MARY TESAR
BORN DECEMBER 7, 1903
EMIGRATED FROM AUSTRIA, 1914, AGE 10
SHIP UNKNOWN

Her story is reminiscent of the von Trapp family from the movie The Sound of
Music. *(See page 115 for the story of Maria Franziska von Trapp.) Born in
Vienna, raised in a rural village, she escaped Austria before the outset of World War
I and came with her family to America in 1914 via Hamburg, Germany. Trained
in a Baltimore seminary as a nun and a teacher, she found peace in the church and
satisfaction teaching schoolchildren, which she did for sixty-seven years at the School
of the Sisters of Notre Dame in Wilton, Connecticut. "I love my life," she said,
ninety-three at the time. "I'm very happy that I came to America. America gave me
everything. There was no living in Austria. I went back in 1972. The village was
now part of Czechoslovakia. My old house was gone. Everything was destroyed.
And I saw this big field of roses and I asked someone, 'What is that?' and they
said, 'Those are all the boys and girls killed by the Russians.' Every time I see* The
Sound of Music, *it reminds me of what we went through."*

We were living in a remote village outside of Vienna called Cejkovice, my
mother's village. My father was a cabinetmaker. He had his big shop, and
there he made his furniture. He made beautiful engravings on the furniture. And then when the furniture was finished, it was shipped to the city
of Hodonin. My father had a warehouse there. And the furniture would
be sold from there.

My father also made things for people in the village—chairs, tables,
things like that. And off and on he went to the priest's house, and if the
priest needed anything to be done, my father would help.

My mother died of tuberculosis when she was thirty-two. I was eight
years old at the time. Her sisters also died of the disease; one was twelve,
one was sixteen. My father made the coffin for her funeral. Many people
came and paid their respects. In fact, the whole village came and prayed and
the body was put on a big wagon and taken to the cemetery. I remember
all of us standing there. I remember my little brother and me crying.
Momma was going down into the hole. And they gave us a shovel of dirt
to throw in, and it was very sad, but we knew that Mother was in heaven.

About two years later, my father had business in Hodonin, and when he got there he found out that the husband of his former fiancée, who was married with two little children, had suddenly died of appendicitis. So my father proposed, and she immediately accepted.

They were married in the morning. But in the afternoon my grandmother put us into a big wagon pulled by a farmer, and the farmer took us to a village to meet my stepmother. My father greeted us and said, "Now look, you're going to see your new mother. And be sure you say 'mother.'" That was hard for me. My brother didn't care, he was too young. He was three years younger, so he was five years old.

Then she came out, and she was a lovely lady with beautiful brown hair. And she smiled. And she handed me a beautiful dress and said, "This is for you," and gave me a kiss. And that big, big heaviness from my heart went because in that village, there was a woman who adopted a child, and afterward she threw the child into a ravine, and from that day forward the ravine had the name of the mother, "Machosa." I always thought if I had a stepmother, I'd wind up in the Machosa. Then she gave my brother a gift too, kissed us, and said, "Now, come and meet your little brother and sister." So we went into the garden of the house where she was living, and there was a little girl about two years old, and a baby boy in a cradle. And we were so happy because now we had a bigger family. Such joy!

By 1914, it all changed. The war was brewing, and everybody was restless. It was a very bad time. Men were being enlisted, and we heard about a buildup of soldiers in Vienna. Suddenly, people were too afraid to buy anything. Furniture that my father made, nobody would buy. And, in fact, soldiers even damaged furniture in my father's warehouse in Hodonin. So he knew his business was going down, down, down.

Then, one day, the military police came and told my father he must pay for wood he already bought. It was harassment. Extortion. And my father said, "I don't have any money because I don't have any sales."

So they said, "If the money is not here by tomorrow morning, you will be put in jail." And we stood there watching these police. I remember my father had a few bags of flour and sugar, so they stuck their bayonets in and ripped them open. Then they put "For Sale" signs on our property.

We just stood there: my mother holding one child, my father holding the other, and we were all crying. We didn't know what was going to happen. Where would we live? Where would we find a home? My father had a brother who lived in America who helped us later on. He lived in Brooklyn with a wife and seven children. He, too, was a cabinetmaker like my father, and they used to correspond. Would we find my uncle? We had the address, but there were no telephones.

So, being a good churchman, my father went to the rectory and told the priest. The priest said, "Don't worry, you were a good helper to me in my church. I shall give you enough money to escape." And my father said, "Don't worry, I will return every penny after I get in my betters."

When my father came home with the money that evening, my mother took a bedsheet and wrapped our clothes in it. My father took his tool chest and asked a farmer if he would please take it to his father's village because it was too big. The village was called Uherské Hradišti. And late that night, all packed, we covered ourselves with hay in a wagon so nobody would see us. There were not that many homes in the area, but we had to be careful. It was the six of us. And we went to Uherské Hradišti and stayed overnight.

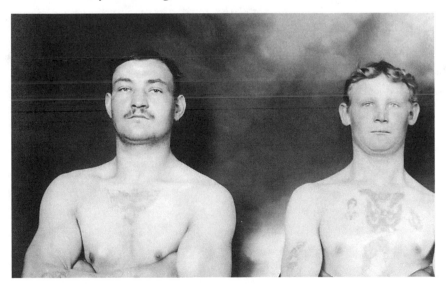

Fig. 18. Tattooed German stowaways, May 1, 1911. Photograph used by permission of the Statue of Liberty National Monument (National Park Service).

Early the next morning, before dawn, we made our getaway. Later on my grandmother told me the police were looking for us in Vienna because they thought my father went there. But no one knew where we went. It was very, very difficult because we were in such a hurry. We had no time. We had to go quickly. But we didn't know where to go. We knew the police would be looking for us. My stepmother cried and cried and cried. She said, "I thought this would never happen to us." And she put her arms around my father. I remember the two of them just cried on each other's shoulder. She clung to him—talking, whispering with tears. And she loved us. And she put her arms around us and said, "Don't worry, don't worry, God will take care of us." Then my father said to me, "When we get to Vienna I'll buy you a dancing doll."

But we never got to Vienna. About a week later we arrived in Hamburg, Germany. It was summer, and we were staying in a hotel. My father had bought boat tickets—steerage, third class—and I said to him, "Papa, are we going on that boat?" And he said, "Yes, we're going to America." I said, "Papa, you said we were going to Vienna. Does that mean I don't get my dancing doll?" I remember that as clear as day. We boarded the boat, set to leave, when my stepsister disappeared. She had been playing with my brother and she ran off. We couldn't find her. Everyone was hysterical. The boat was already whistling away, and then the captain found her, and we went to America.

GIACOMO "JACK" UBALDI
BORN SEPTEMBER 16, 1910
EMIGRATED FROM ITALY, 1918, AGE 7
PASSAGE ON THE *DANTE ALIGHIERI*

*He is from the country village of Bevagna near Perugia. His father was swin-
dled out of his business, so he immigrated to America, to Scranton, Pennsylvania. Jack and his mother and three sisters came later. They eventually settled
in Bethlehem.*

I was born with the name Giacomo. But nobody seemed to be able to say
Giacomo when I came here, so I took Jack. I think it was because Jack
Dempsey was champion and I thought that was a great name to take.

My father was a butcher. He owned a delicatessen. He had the largest
store in town. He sold meat, cheese, wine, things like that. In our town,
either you owned a small business or you worked on a farm. There was no
industry really. People were tenant farmers. The owners never did the work.
The tenant farmer and his family were given a house, and they lived on the
property and they did the work.

My father was a large man. He weighed about 220 pounds, six foot.
He was like a god to me. At one point, he went into business with a group
of people to start a supermarket—a bunch of supermarkets, actually—but
his store was the only one that was worth anything. After a year's work,
the money disappeared and he lost his store. He was so angry. He had a
passport already and the war was starting. So he left for America in 1914.
He had been to France. He had traveled to Luxembourg and Germany and
he didn't like them. There were some of our countrymen, you know,
townspeople who had come to America, and so there was a ship coming to
New York, and he just went on it. I was four and a half.

He found a job in Manhattan on Thompson Street as a butcher, and
he didn't like it. He was a man already about thirty-eight, and they used
to poke fun at him because he couldn't speak English. They paid him very
little, five dollars a week. He couldn't live on it, even in those days. What
helped was that he could have a free lunch. He'd go to a bar to have a mug
of beer. They had a smorgasbord of food, and you ate. All you had to do

was buy a nickel's worth of beer. America was a very disappointing experience for him.

Then someone mentioned he should go to Pennsylvania. He went to Scranton. At first, he worked in the mines. That wasn't his work. He couldn't do it. He lasted about three months. While he was there, someone mentioned there was a job available as a butcher. He applied for it. This husband and wife, they had two stores, a meat market, a general store, and they liked him and they said, "Well, look, if you can't speak we'll help you. My wife will help you." He took over the meat market, and he built a nice business for them. He was making about twenty-five dollars a week.

He was with them for three and a half years when we came here. Me, my mother, my two older sisters, and one younger sister. Five.

My mother was an angel. She always took care of me as if I was the only one. She was a hardworking woman. She ran a little store. And she made sure that my two older sisters were able to go to school. There was a big age difference between me and my sisters because in between us, there were five other children who died at birth. Nobody seemed to know why at that time.

Just before we left for America, I was gathering wood, twigs, for the fireplace, what we called "fornelli"—little burners that you made with bricks, and you put a pot over it, you know. So we needed little sticks. There was no charcoal or anything like that in those days. So I was with a friend, and he started chasing me and I tripped over a stump, then right across a wheelbarrow with a shovel, and I split my eyelid. I started bleeding. I was afraid to go home because I would get a beating besides. So I was packing it with dirt to stop the blood from flowing. I was about seven.

Well, I finally got home; they took me to the pharmacist. In those days, the pharmacist did as much work as the doctor. And he cleaned it. He patched it up. The following morning, my face was like a balloon, and we went to the doctor, who took our physical for the boat, the *Anconia*. He says, "The boy cannot go." So my mother says, "If my son doesn't go, none of us go."

Two weeks later, we found out that the *Anconia* was torpedoed and sunk. Then I became a hero. I have always said, "I have St. Francis on my shoulders. He's been watching me." Because St. Francis of Assisi used to live only about four miles from our town.

We finally got on board the *Dante Alighieri* in Genoa, and we went as far as Gibraltar. We were there for four or five days. They refueled us, and we were supposed to go out in a convoy, one behind the other. But our captain decided he wouldn't do that because he had no cargo. The boat was very light in the water, and he went in a different direction where he figured the German submarines wouldn't be hiding underneath. Midnight, after we left Gibraltar, they called everybody to the lifeboats and we huddled there. No lights on. There were two cannons, one at the bow, and one at the stern.

At dawn, all I could hear was screaming, crying, people, mothers calling for their children because they got lost. The ship was mostly women whose husbands were in America. No men. I look overboard and I see lifeboats one after another going toward shore. The convoy had been attacked by submarines.

We were in one of two big salons, no cabin. Just bunk beds, one after another, three high. The toilets were in the open. I remember we ran out of sweet, fresh water halfway through. There was only fresh water for drinking. So if you washed, you had to wash with saltwater from the ocean. There was a shower in the open on deck. I never took a bath for the whole twenty-three days on board ship because it was too cold. It was February. I wasn't going to take a shower in the middle of the Atlantic in February. . . . We were black from coal dust [because the ship ran on coal].

The food was lousy. My mother used to go with this dishpan, and they used to put this slop into it. After a while, we couldn't eat it no more. But if you had some money, you could buy rolls, little oval rolls they used to sell. They cost a lira. A lira at that time was about twenty cents. So we couldn't afford too many of those with five people to feed.

New York had a lot of ice floes in the bay. They had an icebreaker ship. That's was how cold it was. I saw the statue, but America, the statue, meant nothing to me. I knew nothing about it.

Fig. 19. Very few blacks came through Ellis Island. Those who did invariably came from the Caribbean, such as these Guadeloupe women, who arrived at Ellis Island on the SS *Korona*, April 6, 1911. Photograph used by permission of the Statue of Liberty National Monument (National Park Service).

We expected my father to be at Ellis Island to claim us but he wasn't there. Nobody came to claim us. And my mother was frightened because he wasn't there. My sisters, too. There was some sort of communication snafu.

We spent six days at Ellis Island. We had to be washed to get the coal dust off. We went through physicals. Doctors checked us all over. The first day I got big glasses of milk and white bread, which, to me, was like manna from heaven. I was treated very nicely, but you live on rumors. People were being sent back. And you never knew what was happening. My mother was crying her heart out. My sisters were worried, crying, because the trip coming over wasn't a cruise. And to go back and go through the same thing, or be blown up, you know, it was a horrible thought for them.

My father finally came to Ellis Island. He had been waiting for us in Scranton, it seems. He looked like a stranger to me. It had been years.

We took the ferry to Battery Park and went directly to Scranton, Pennsylvania. He had found a house. A private house. He was working in the meat market. I was enrolled in school. . . . I used to get beaten up by the other kids because I couldn't speak English. They called me "Guinea," "Wop," you know. I got over that, then things began to get a little bit better.

But it was always work. Work was the main thing in my family, with my father. He was not happy here because he came here against his will. He didn't find happiness in any possible way, whether in his work or anything. And he always wanted to go back. He wanted to go back to show those people who conned him that they couldn't hurt him. Something like that.

My parents and my younger sister went back to Italy in 1930. I was twenty years old. They left me in charge of a business, a little restaurant in Bethlehem, Pennsylvania. We had moved there. And I kept it going for almost four years. The last year and a half things got so bad because of the Depression, I finally had to give it up.

In the years since, I traveled quite a lot. I was always looking for a Shangri-La someplace. I traveled all over Europe, South America, Central America, and I didn't find any Shangri-La. Once, when I came back from a trip, I was so happy when I saw the Empire State Building on Thirty-Fourth Street, I said to myself, "I'm home."

The closest I've come to any Shangri-La are my children. I was married in 1941, and my wife, Mary, and I had two sons and a daughter. They're all grown up now. The oldest one is getting his master's at Harvard. The second graduated from the University of Chicago. My daughter is a senior at Cornell.

I became a teacher. In fact, I teach cooking now. But I never wear a white toque because when I was in the first grade, the teacher in Scranton called on me. She had a picture of a tree and the number "three."

So she says, "What's this?"

Well, I knew what a tree was so I said "tree."

"No, three," she said.

But I didn't know about the "th" sound. I couldn't pronounce it. So I kept saying, "tree, tree."

She got so mad. She pulled me out of my seat, put me in a corner, and put a dunce cap on me.

Now, every time I see a chef's hat, I think of that and I won't wear one—and that was seventy-five years ago.

Chapter 4

1920s

The "Roaring Twenties" continued America's economic growth and prosperity, as the incomes of working-class people increased alongside those of middle-class and wealthier Americans. The major growth industry was car manufacturing, as Americans fell in love with the automobile, which radically changed their way of life. On the other hand, the 1920s also saw a decline in immigration as the result of new quota-law restrictions.

KEY HISTORIC EVENTS

★1921: Immigration Restriction Act sets temporary annual quotas according to nationality and emergency immigration quotas heavily favoring northern and western Europeans, all but slamming the door on southern and eastern Europeans and causing an immediate drop in immigration.

★1923: The Ku Klux Klan, virulently anti-immigrant, reaches the peak of its strength.

★1924: National Origins Act sets a ceiling on the number of immigrants and establishes discriminatory national racial quotas, ending the period of mass migration to America.

★1929: The stock market crash and resulting economic crisis pressure the Hoover administration to further reduce immigration and to order rigorous enforcement of the prohibition against admitting immigrants who are liable to be public charges.

MIGRATION FLOWS

Total legal US immigration in 1920s: 4.3 million

Top ten emigration countries in this decade: Canada and Newfoundland (949,286), Italy (528,133), Mexico (498,945), Germany (386,634), United Kingdom (341,552), Poland (223,316), Ireland (202,854), Czechoslovakia (101,182), Sweden (100,002), Norway (70,237)

(See appendix for the complete list of countries.)

FAMOUS IMMIGRANTS

Immigrants who came to America in this decade (not all through Ellis Island), and who would later become famous, include:

Archibald Alexander Leach ("Cary Grant"), England, 1920, actor
James Reston, Scotland, 1920, journalist
Karl Dane, Denmark, 1920, actor
Gregory Ratoff, Russia, 1920, actor
Alan Mowbray, England, 1920, actor
Mischa Auer, Russia, 1920, actor
Arshile Gorky, Armenia, 1921, painter
Bela Lugosi, Hungary, 1921, actor
Pola Negri, Poland, 1921, actress
Vernon Duke, Russia, 1921, composer ("Autumn in New York")
Hannah Chaplin, England, 1921, Charlie Chaplin's mother
Douglas Fraser, Scotland, 1922, union leader
John Kluge, Germany, 1922, billionaire/businessman
Simon Kuznets, Ukraine, 1922, economist
George Papashvily, Georgia (Caucasus), 1922, sculptor/writer
Isaac Asimov, Russia, 1923, writer
Greta Garbo, Sweden, 1925, actress

Willem de Kooning, Netherlands, 1926, artist/abstract expressionist
Ayn Rand, Russia, 1926, writer
H. T. Tsiang, China, 1926, actor/writer
Sir Charles Kingsford Smith, Australia, 1928, aviator
Gian Carlo Menotti, Italy, 1928, composer/librettist
Colonel Tom Parker, Netherlands, 1929, music manager
    (Elvis Presley)
Louise Nevelson, Russia, 1929, artist/sculptor

Fig. 20. Immigrants in steerage upon arriving in New York Harbor, November 1920. Photograph used by permission of the Statue of Liberty National Monument (National Park Service).

BERTHA RENNER ZEICHNER
BORN JUNE 8, 1901
EMIGRATED FROM AUSTRIA, 1920, AGE 19
SHIP UNKNOWN

Her family was torn apart during World War I, then reunited for the boat trip to America. When she was ninety-five years old, she lived alone in an apartment in Franklin Square, New York, near the seven grandchildren and six great-grandchildren who "are my pride and joy," she said. "I have one great granddaughter who is twenty-one years old. So who knows? If God lets me, I can stay a little bit longer and maybe become a great-great-grandmother."

I was born in Kolomea, Austria. Now it's the Ukraine. It was a very beautiful place, and we had a very lovely family, and I was very happy. But my mother was always sick. She had problems with her gallbladder, diabetes, different things. My father was a peddler. He had a horse and a wagon, and he bought and sold dishes, earthenware. He would go away for a whole week to make a living, stop in different places, and come home for the weekend. Saturday was family day. All the children went to shul, and it was very beautiful. In the afternoon, we had dinner, and we went for walks near a river in the woods. Saturday nights, neighbors would stop by to visit, and they would talk and plan and dream and tell stories about what's going on in America, what they would do if they ever got there. Occasionally a person came from New York for a visit to see relatives, so they knew of New York and America from these visitors. We knew because my eldest sister had already left for America and she would write us. She came to America in 1914, just before the war broke out.

I lived in Kolomea till 1916 and the Russians occupied the city. We were told to emigrate. When the Russians come in, they said, they do horrible things to girls. So we made up our minds to leave. But they had no trains, so we had to walk. For four weeks we walked by foot and slept near the waters because on the main roads soldiers marched toward battle.

You could see houses off to the side of the road that were burned down by the soldiers. And city by city, my parents, my brother, my younger sister, and me, we walked until we reached the biggest city,

Stanislaw. And then we were separated. My father got drafted into the army to fight the Russians. He was fifty years old, imagine! My brother was about fifteen. He was sent to the Italian front, near the Piave River, where thousands of soldiers got slaughtered, drowned. My mother, my sister, and I became refugees. We were put on a train by the government and taken to Yugoslavia. It was a train full of mothers and their children. Yugoslavian families would then come to the train and adopt you as laborers. Of course, they picked us because we were the cleanest, you know. [*She laughs.*]

I remember well a very wealthy family took us. But we didn't understand them because they spoke a different language. They had a big house with a little house behind it where we lived, and they had a gazebo with grapes and vines growing over it, and they had a farm. We would pick string beans, bushels of them. And in the evenings, even the meals, they didn't take us in their house. They served us outside—but delicious meals. We were there for several months, until we contacted my aunts in Vienna and this Yugoslavian family took us to Vienna by train. We lived there from 1916 to 1920, and I worked. I worked in a military factory, working machines that made uniforms. And we would sing. All these young Viennese girls. I was about sixteen years old then. And we got paid. I don't remember how much. They say you sing when you're hungry. Well, we sang all the time because there wasn't enough food.

They would give out ration tickets. My mother got up, as sick as she was, at four o'clock in the morning to stand in front of a dairy store where the government sold milk and butter and eggs. She would stand in line, and the line was long with poor people, and sometimes the food was sold out, so you got nothing. But most of the time she came home with a little food. When the war was over, we got in touch with my sister in America. She made affidavits and got us visas to come here; otherwise, we would have had to go back to Kolomea.

A few weeks before we were going to leave Vienna and go to America, I met William, my husband. He also came from Kolomea. We met through my brother, who was back from the war in Italy; my father was back, too. But William—we fell in love. So I promised him when I'd come to America I'd send for him, and I did.

Fig. 21. German immigrants traveling third class, or steerage, on the SS *Bremen,* March 1925. Photograph used by permission of the Statue of Liberty National Monument (National Park Service).

I remember the day I left William and left for America. I was crying the whole night on the train. We went on the train through the different countries to the ship. We stopped in Innsbruck, Paris, a night here, two nights there, until we came to Le Havre in France. I even remember the dress I wore. I kept it for years. It was a nice flared skirt that I made myself. It went below the knee, and a blouse with a navy blue sailor collar and bow. I have pictures of it.

The voyage was hell. They gave us food, if you want to call it that [*laughs*], but we were so seasick we couldn't eat. We were not in first class. We were with the luggage in steerage. I remember the rats climbing over our limbs, and I would cover myself from fright . . . but we survived. We slept in bunk beds. There were a lot of different people. Lots of Italians. And they sang. I sang. We made the best of it.

I was very happy when we arrived in New York. I don't know how long the voyage took, maybe fourteen days. When you're on the ocean, you think you'll never see land. We passed the eye examination, all the tests, and a day or two later, my sister came to pick us up at Ellis Island. We were very happy to see her.

She brought us to a three-room apartment in Williamsburg, Brooklyn. She had a husband and two little children by then, plus us: my mother, father, sister, brother, and me, five people. Of course, we brought few belongings with us, clothing and bedding mostly. In Europe, bedding was important, and we would spread it out on the floor to sleep. It was crowded, but at least our whole family was together . . . and we managed. My younger sister started work in a millinery. I worked in a clothing factory. My brother worked in pocketbooks. So we made a little money.

We started to look for a place to rent for ourselves. So many people could not live in three rooms. And we found one a few blocks away. In the front was a cleaning store and in the back were two rooms with a kitchen, so we rented it. And then my mother found a better place and we could afford a little bit more rent, like eighteen dollars a month from fifteen [dollars]. And we kept moving up until the time William, my boyfriend from Vienna, was supposed to come.

He was twenty-two when he came here, a year after me. And we got married. Got an apartment. He learned a trade. He became a furrier, and had ambition, and always reached higher and higher to become, from the machine, a cutter, you know, to make more money. When we got married, he was already making sixty-five dollars a week, which was a lot of money in 1923. I remember Saturday used to be payday. So he would come home with the envelope and let me open it if he knew there was a raise in it. And he was always getting raises. William was the type who always tried to learn. Long after everybody went home, he would help clean up and sweep the floor. Ambitious. Years later he went into the furrier business for himself, did very well, and we raised three beautiful girls together. [*She pauses.*] I'm tired now. I need to rest. [*She smiles and closes her eyes.*]

Fig. 22. German mail-order brides, or "picture brides," meet their future husbands in Brooklyn after arriving on Ellis Island July 3, 1922. Photograph used by permission of the Statue of Liberty National Monument (National Park Service).

DAVID SALTMAN
BORN OCTOBER 25, 1912
EMIGRATED FROM SCOTLAND, 1922, AGE 9
PASSAGE ON THE TSS *CAMERONIA*

Born in Glasgow, he immigrated to America with his mother, brothers, and sisters when he was nine years old. He served in the tank battalion during the invasion of Normandy and was part of General George Patton's Third Army, which helped liberate Europe from the Nazis.

We lived at 184 Main Street, Glasgow. It was an apartment house. I remember Queens Park, where we went as children. We were six children. I was the youngest. Of course, I went to school. I remember getting lost in Glasgow as a youngster, just wandering off, not knowing where I was or how to get home, but I got there.

My father owned a wholesale lumberyard. By trade, he was a carpenter. He always suffered from asthma, and it was very damp there. He was thinking about coming to the United States or going to South Africa. He preferred South Africa, but my mother had relatives in the New York area, so we came to the United States, for which I'm glad. He continued as a carpenter after he came here. He had a fair amount of money. He built a couple of small apartment houses in Staten Island. Actually, he built three of them, and then during the Depression of the 1930s, he went broke completely.

My father came with my older sister as a visitor to see how he would like it, and he stayed with relatives in Staten Island. Later, we followed, my mother with the other five children, including me.

We took the TSS *Cameronia*, sailing from Glasgow to New York. It was my mother and five children. She bundled all of us, and off we went. It was very ordinary accommodations, and that's about all I can remember. It certainly wasn't in first class. My father was here about nine months when he sent for us. He decided this was the place where he would settle. It was with my mother's relatives in Staten Island.

Of course, when we got to Ellis Island it was very, very crowded—I mean, the Great Hall. A lot of hustle and bustle and luggage and people milling about. I don't know how long we stayed. I'm sure it was a couple of days. I thought Ellis Island was horrible, and I couldn't wait to get out of there. I remember that. Then somehow or other my father came and got us and brought us to Staten Island. That's where I stayed and went to school.

I recall my father had sort of run away from the military service in Russia. I say Russia because he was born in Brestlatovsk and so was my mother. I say Russia because that was the area between Poland and Russia as the map changed over the years. But they were all trying to escape military service. There was also an awful lot of antisemitism in Russia and a lot of persecution, and I'm sure that had a lot to do with it also. Why he settled in Scotland I don't know, except that I heard many stories of people who came over, went on a boat and it seemed forever, and the first port that the boat stopped, they thought it was the United States [immigrant profiteers told them Scotland was America]. My father had come with my mother because my oldest sister was born around 1902 in Russia. So they had to come together. They had the one child. They were in Scotland for about eighteen or nineteen years. So the trip to the United States was really a second resettling for my father and mother. I don't think they came because of antisemitism. As far as I knew, there was none. The reasons were mainly economic.

My parents hated anything military, and when I wanted to join the Boy Scouts and put on a Boy Scout uniform, they didn't like it a bit. They called that military, and they were very much against it. But I still stayed as a Boy Scout in Staten Island and grew up there.

They did talk Yiddish a lot, and then, of course, they learned English. My father read the Jewish paper called the *Jewish Daily Forward*. That was his main newspaper. But when we were in Scotland, we learned English and spoke it with a Scotch accent. They did talk Yiddish at home, but I did not.

When he came over here, besides doing this building, my father was quite a cabinetmaker, a little more on the refined side, a little more on the artistic side. He worked on the Staten Island ferries when they were building those in Staten Island. He had his own business.

Financially, we were comfortable at the beginning, especially after my father started building those small apartment houses when he came in 1921. I went to elementary school, PS 16 on Staten Island, and graduated Curtis High School. Then I went to City College, CCNY, for a couple of years. Then came the Depression, and it got the best of me, and I had to go out to work. It was very difficult finding a job. I managed to get odd jobs. My first job was as a messenger for Western Union on Staten Island. I went back to CCNY for another year and then left it again, and that was the end of it.

My father had a partner, and he lost it all [his business]. He also suffered from asthma quite severely. He started a grocery store. That was his livelihood—not great by any means, but that's what he did.

I finally joined a publishing company in 1940. I left them to go into the service in May 1941 and, of course, left the service at the end of 1945. I was in the European theater. My mother died in 1928, and my father died in the 1930s. He was not alive when I went into the service.

On December 7, 1941, I went to Jacksonville, Florida, to buy a return ticket on the train home. The radios were blasting away about the Japanese attack on Pearl Harbor. When I heard that, I knew this was the day that I had been long waiting, expecting, and I turned around, didn't buy a ticket, and went right back to camp and just waited. I did the right thing because the MPs [military police] were rounding up all soldiers in the town and sending them back to camp, and everybody who was over twenty-eight was sent right back to the unit promptly.

Immediately after that, they started an officer candidate review board, and I went on the first group from the artillery brigade and was examined, graded, and so forth. Rather peculiarly, I was not in the first group. I was not in the second group. I was not in the third group. By April 1942, I was getting a little restless, and I went to my commanding officer, regimental commander Colonel Barnes, and asked him why I had not gotten a call to leave. He took out the lists of the brigade's three artillery regiments, and he looked up and down the list, and I was number ten on a list of 150.

Fig. 23. Irish immigrants being checked for glaucoma in the early 1920s. Inspectors are wearing their new army-green uniforms; the old ones were blue and gold. Photograph used by permission of the Statue of Liberty National Monument (National Park Service).

I went to officer candidate school at Fort Sill, Oklahoma, in June 1942. I graduated from Fort Sill in ninety days—what they called the "ninety-day wonders"—became a second lieutenant, and they assigned me to a tank destroyer battalion. I asked them why I wasn't assigned to a field artillery unit, and they said, "You're too old for field artillery, so we had to put you with the tank destroyers." Actually, the tank destroyer command had just started the school. It was a new concept. They needed officers. So I went through most of the war with the tank destroyer battalion in Europe.

When we went across, it was a very memorable journey. We went across on one of the so-called liberty ships. I was quite impressed by the amount of armament, and there was a navy officer on board, and I said, "What is this? What's going on? This seems peculiar." He told me he was there on a guard ship for a troop convoy. I worked out a deal with him, since he had limited personnel, that we would take some of the personnel from the tank destroyer battalion and put them on watch at night for submarines. We had our submarine alert practices at dusk because that's the time when submarines generally surface.

We started out from New York Harbor with a convoy, and we had a right lead ship. Three days out, another convoy came out of the dusk from Boston and joined us to form a large convoy, which I understand was the largest convoy that ever went to Europe [for the Normandy invasion]. Our ship was still the right lead ship of the convoy. Along the line, we started dropping depth charges when we suspected submarines below. We didn't see any evidence of any, but I understood later on that somewhere a submarine had penetrated the heart of the convoy and sunk at least one or two ships.

When we got to the British Isles, the convoy peeled off to different ports. Our ship went directly to Cherbourg, France, and that was our first sight of what the war was about, all the wreckage that we saw. We debarked on a smaller landing ship and went to the coast of Normandy, and that's where we started our campaign.

I was finance officer for the trip, which is a menial job. I got rid of a safe that had been entrusted to me, which I never even looked at. I got rid of that at Cherbourg, and, of course, the unit was put on sort of guard duty against German attacks from the neighboring Jersey and Guernsey Islands until they decided to deploy us. Then we were moved north to the town of Geilenkirchen in northern Germany, near the border with Holland.

We were attached to the British Second Army at the time because they were right on the border of the American Ninth Army. And, of course, the activity, when we got up there, was very heavy. It was just a strange sight to see German planes flying over, strafing, dropping bombs. I saw American planes flying over, and for some reason you never saw the two get together. One came, one went, and you don't know why the two didn't meet each other in midair somewhere.

I recall as we were being led into Germany to the beginning of the Siegfried Line, the motorcyclist that came to us just got lost. He was leading a whole group. So I stopped the motorcycle and said, "Do you know where you're going?" He said, "No." I said, "Then get behind me and I'll try to figure out where we're going."

I was riding in a jeep. Behind me were a whole bunch of tank-destroyer vehicles mounted with seventy-five-millimeter guns or ninety-millimeter guns. It was Thanksgiving Day 1944 and we were on the Siegfried Line, and I had my first hot meal standing up inside of a German pillbox. The word "pillbox" is what they described as a very strong concrete fortification built by the Germans, which was certainly capable of thwarting any direct tank shells, it was that strong. But we fought our way slowly, bit by bit, and we penetrated the Siegfried Line.

I remember I had gone to take a shower at a coal mine, and as I came back, I checked into my radio, just to check in. My commanding officer barked, "Silence your radio and return immediately." I wondered what happened. As I was heading back to the battalion area, I found out the Germans had invaded Belgium, and our mission was to reinforce First Army and contain the attack.

We got into the town of Marche, Belgium, in the Ardennes Forest. It was very cold. There was plenty of snow on the ground. This was the first time I saw the American army on the defensive. Division headquarters pulled back. We stayed forward, and the Germans had been in that town the night before. All civilians were sleeping in the cellars because of shelling, and, in fact, I took an upstairs place. You can't very well pitch tents in congested areas, but there was plenty of shelling, and it got so heavy that the glass in the room just shattered right in front of me. So I went down to the cellar for the rest of the night, more like on a stairway, because it was too crowded down below.

Slowly we repelled the German attack and straightened out the front line. It was very hectic. Everything was moving very fast. Tank destroyers got hit, were immediately replaced. It was so cold that the water in my canteen froze. The temperature was about twenty degrees below zero in the Ardennes Forest in Belgium. We straightened out the line, and when we did that I went back to Ninth Army, 13th Corps, and I was transferred to the Sixth Tank Destroyer Group. This was a break for me because I had always wanted to get out of the battalion. You couldn't get a promotion there. You just had to do what you could.

The corps commander decided that he would try to do what had been done in Third Army successfully, so I was chosen, as one of the liaison officers, to be attached to the Fifth Armored Division in a final push to the Elbe River in eastern Germany. I asked for Combat Command A, because I figured that would be the one which got the most action, and I was correct. It was commanded by a brigadier general, while the others were full colonels.

We moved along across the rivers Ruhr and Rhine. There were no bridges, so we built pontoon bridges. The bridges were manned by combat engineers. They were told to shoot any floating mines that may be in the river, or any other suspicious object. This was a one-way bridge, twenty-four hours a day, crossing the pontoon bridge into the main area of Germany, from which we would launch the final and main attack for the end of it.

Combat Command B and Combat Command C moved forward. My Combat Command A was in reserve, and I was rather unhappy because it was just too far behind. Then Combat Command B and Combat Command C stopped, and Combat Command A, we just roared up our tanks and off we went, passing through B and C, and took the lead to the Elbe River. We were the armored spearhead for the corps unit, followed by two infantry divisions, anywhere from twenty to forty miles behind us.

We were very successful in moving fast. We never stopped. We just kept on going, and German soldiers were passing alongside of us with their hands over their heads. They had gotten rid of their helmets and their guns, but we couldn't take them because we were not equipped to take prisoners any more than those in Desert Storm. Our tactics were to get to the objective as quickly as possible, and prisoners were out of the question. We just couldn't do that. That was not part of our mission.

I recall when we got to an airfield, there were six German planes during a two-hour period that were trying to land, never dreaming that the American forces had moved so fast to that area. We shot down every one of them. It was a huge brand of fire. One plane caught fire, careened out of sight, and crashed into one of our armored vehicles, killing all of the crew.

We reached the Elbe River and waited for the Russians to meet us. The Germans were on the other side. Day after day I would stroll up to the river, look at it. I still saw no sign of activity, no sign of the Russians. There was a bridge. I remember my commanding officer said, "You can be sure they [the Germans] won't let us take that bridge. They'll blow it up." And sure enough, as I was turning my radio on, there was a loud explosion. The general's aide came rushing up to me. They had blown the bridge right in our face.

Later on, the able-bodied Germans, rather than surrender to the Russians, swam across this wide river, about as wide as the Hudson River, to surrender to the Americans. But in about a week or ten days, the Russians finally caught up and stayed put. We could easily have gone on to Berlin in this situation. Winston Churchill said, "Let's shake hands with the Russians as far east as possible." But [General] Eisenhower held up the entire front, knowing that we would give up this sector of Germany to the Russians, according to the agreement of Franklin Roosevelt, Churchill, and Stalin at Potsdam.

So we sat there, a large area that later became East Germany. It could have been a lot shorter if we decided to hold the ground that we had taken. But political agreements take precedence over any military tactics. Eventually we gave this area over to the Russians. We moved further west, further back, and then we occupied our sector in Bavaria, which was the mission of the American forces.

At that time, of course, all units were disbanded, and I was given an assignment with the provost marshal officer, Third Army, which was commanded by General George Patton.

The job I took over was as a security officer for the Third Army at the prisoner of war hospital. It was an area of German military hospitals ranging from Munich south to Salzburg, Austria. The headquarters was in Bad Tölz, and General Patton took over the headquarters that had been held by the German Wehrmacht. He made that his headquarters in the town of Bad Tölz.

My mission was security control, to supervise these prisoners of war who were in the hospitals and disabled—typical enough. During that time, I went over to Dachau, that infamous camp where they had a lot of American DPs, or displaced persons. As I went through that camp, I went into one of the furnace areas where they burned bodies; you could see footprints on the wall. I repeat, on the wall, not on the ground, where they had stacked bodies high. I had the mistaken impression that one of the reasons why the Nazis had starved Jewish people was so they could get them so skinny they could fit into those very narrow furnaces. It just happened that those were the narrow furnaces that I saw, but there were others that were much larger. But, of course, starving them to death meant that they could cremate them easier after they gassed them.

We cleaned out Dachau and got all the displaced persons out of there, and we filled it up with German SS troops. I had gotten to the commander of the hospital, who was a full colonel in the German army, and he spoke very good English, so we were able to talk.

As we got friendly, he told me a story that I have never yet seen in any of the history books: how Germany started World War II. It was not started by Adolf Hitler. World War II was started by some elite Germans who were never satisfied in the Athletic Club in Berlin. They were plotting to revive Germany as a military power. This full colonel, a medical doctor, was offered the job of being chief of all the German medical forces. He refused. Instead of being a full colonel, he could easily have been a major general, but he turned it down.

When they chose Hitler, that was their mistake. He was supposed to be a front man. But he so fired up the German people that he pushed everybody else to the background, and of course the rest is history when you have a madman who thinks he can conquer the world and was not able to do so.

I retired as a reserve officer, which was compulsory at the age of fifty-three. I was a lieutenant colonel. I was forced to retire. That was the law. I have stayed in it as a retired officer subject to recall in case of any national emergency, and it still continues to this day.

Chapter 5

1930s

Immigration patterns in this decade were greatly affected by the 1929 stock market crash and the resulting Great Depression. In addition, quota-law restrictions, first enacted in 1921, finally took full effect. For immigrants in foreign countries seeking visas, this meant that immigration processing was now slowly shifted to US consulates abroad, thus turning them into mini–Ellis Islands. While the US population reached 125 million in 1930, for the remainder of the decade it would only see seven hundred thousand new immigrants arrive, the lowest number since the 1830s. Many of the immigrants who came were Jews fleeing the persecution of Nazi Germany and Hitler's mounting war machine. At home, Americans were hurting economically, as one in four workers were unemployed and many families went hungry. Deporting illegals now became a viable solution as a nation built on growth turned to subtraction to help solve its problems.

KEY HISTORIC EVENTS

★1931: Anti-immigrant campaign begins as the US government sponsors a Mexican repatriation program intended to encourage people to voluntarily move to Mexico, but thousands are deported against their will; more than four hundred thousand Mexicans, both illegal aliens and legal Mexican Americans, are pressured through raids and job denial to leave the United States, many of them children who were US citizens—a similar situation faced today by DREAM Act students (see chapter 12, page 329).

★1932: Hitler's antisemitic campaign begins, as Jewish refugees begin fleeing Nazi Germany to the United States and other nations.

★1933: Hitler becomes German chancellor; Jewish refugees from Nazi Germany come to the United States, though barriers imposed by the quota system are not lifted. The Immigration and Naturalization Service (INS) is formed by a merger of the Bureau of Immigration and the Bureau of Naturalization.

★1934: The Tydings-McDuffie Act, also known as the Philippine Independence Act, is approved by Congress and strips Filipinos of their status as US nationals and restricts Filipino immigration to an annual quota of fifty.

MIGRATION FLOWS

Total legal US immigration in 1930s: 700,000

Top ten emigration countries in this decade: Canada and Newfoundland (162,703), Germany (119,107), Italy (85,053), United Kingdom (61,813), Mexico (32,709), Ireland (28,195), Poland (25,555), Czechoslovakia (17,757), France (13,761), Cuba (10,641)

(See appendix for the complete list of countries.)

FAMOUS IMMIGRANTS

Immigrants who came to America in this decade (not all through Ellis Island), and who would later become famous, include:

Sidor Belarsky, Russia, 1930, singer/composer
Primo "The Ambling Alp" Carnera, Italy, 1930, heavyweight boxer
Lin Yutang, China, 1931, writer

Albert Einstein, Germany, 1933, physicist
Billy Wilder, Austria, 1933, film director
Jack "The Gorgeous Gael" Doyle, Ireland, 1934, boxer/actor
Nigel Bruce, England, 1934, actor ("Dr. Watson")
Ieoh Ming (I. M.) Pei, China, 1935, architect
Desi Arnaz, Cuba, 1935, bandleader
Hans Bethe, Germany, 1935, Nobel laureate in physics
Edward Teller, Hungary, 1935, nuclear physicist
    ("father of the hydrogen bomb")
Wenceslao Moreno ("Señor Wences"), Spain, 1936, ventriloquist
Subrahmanyan Chandrasekhar, India, 1937, astrophysicist
Dick Haymes, Argentina, 1937, singer
Pauline Trigére, France, 1937, fashion designer
Georg and Maria von Trapp and family, Austria, 1938, singers
Henry Kissinger, Germany, 1938, political scientist/diplomat
Enrico Fermi, Italy, 1938, nuclear physicist and Nobel laureate
Lucien Aigner, Hungary/France, 1939, photojournalist
Richard Krebs ("Jan Valtin"), Germany, 1939, spy
Elizabeth Taylor, England, 1939, actress
Mike Nichols, Germany, 1939, film director
Thomas Mann, Germany, 1939, writer
André Previn, Germany, 1939, pianist/conductor/composer
Anne Elisabeth Jane "Liz" Claiborne, Belgium, 1939, fashion
    designer

TRIPLICATE
(To be given to declarant)

No. 1442

UNITED STATES OF AMERICA

DECLARATION OF INTENTION
(Invalid for all purposes seven years after the date hereof)

United States of America
District of New Jersey

In the District Court
The United States *at* Trenton, N. J.

I, Dr. Albert Einstein
now residing at 112 Mercer St., Princeton, Mercer, N.J.
occupation Professor, aged 56 years, do declare on oath that my personal description is:
Sex Male, color White, complexion Fair, color of eyes Brown
color of hair Grey, height 5 feet 7 inches; weight 175 pounds; visible distinctive marks none
race Hebrew; nationality German
I was born in Ulm Germany, on March 14, 1879
I am married. The name of my wife is Elsa
we were married on April 6th 1917, at Berlin Germany; she or he was
born at Hechingen Germany, on January 18, 1877, entered the United States
at New York, N.Y., on June 3½ 1935, for permanent residence therein, and now
resides at with me. I have children, and the name, date and place of birth,
and place of residence of each of said children are as follows: Albert born 5-14-1905 and
Eduard born 6-28-1910 both born and reside in Switzerland

I have not heretofore made a declaration of intention: Number, on
at
my last foreign residence was Bermuda Great Britain
I emigrated to the United States of America from Bermuda Great Britain
my lawful entry for permanent residence in the United States was at New York, N.Y.
under the name of Albert Einstein, on June 3, 1935
on the vessel SS Queen of Bermuda

I will, before being admitted to citizenship, renounce forever all allegiance and fidelity to any foreign prince, potentate, state, or sovereignty, and particularly, by name, to the prince, potentate, state, or sovereignty of which I may be at the time of admission a citizen or subject; I am not an anarchist; I am not a polygamist nor a believer in the practice of polygamy; and it is my intention in good faith to become a citizen of the United States of America and to reside permanently therein; and I certify that the photograph affixed to the duplicate and triplicate hereof is a likeness of me: So HELP ME GOD.

Albert Einstein

Subscribed and sworn to before me in the office of the Clerk of said Court,
at Trenton, N. J. this 15th day of January
anno Domini 1936. Certification No. 3-120742 from the Commissioner of Immigration and Naturalization showing the lawful entry of the declarant for permanent residence on the date stated above, has been received by me. The photograph affixed to the duplicate and triplicate hereof is a likeness of the declarant.

George T. Cranmer
[SEAL] Clerk of the U. S. District Court.
By Deputy Clerk.

(The seal of the court will be impressed so as to cover a portion of the photograph)

Form 2202-L-A
U. S. DEPARTMENT OF LABOR
IMMIGRATION AND NATURALIZATION SERVICE

Fig. 24. Albert Einstein's Declaration of Intention to become a US citizen. Concerned about growing Nazi aggression, Einstein immigrated to the United States, accepting a faculty position at Princeton University in 1933. He traveled from Southampton, England, to New York on the steamship *Westerland* with his wife, his secretary, and an assistant. Photograph used by permission of the National Archives.

Fig. 25. Albert Einstein takes the oath of allegiance to become a US citizen on October 1, 1940, in Trenton, New Jersey. Photograph used by permission of the National Archives.

RENATA NIERI
BORN NOVEMBER 14, 1919
EMIGRATED FROM ITALY, 1930, AGE 11
SHIP UNKNOWN

She came to America during the Depression from Renazzo, thirty miles north of Bologna. Her father was a stonemason who helped build the subways, highways, and bridges of New York City. Her family settled on Long Island. She had three children and five grandchildren and celebrated her fiftieth wedding anniversary with her husband, George, in Hawaii. "I'm very proud to be interviewed by you," she said. "I would like to dedicate this in loving memory of my mother and father, Albano and Argia Ardizzoni Nieri, for the sacrifice they made to give us a better life in the United States."

We lived in a courtyard on a farm. My father had come here in 1923. A friend of his had come to the United States and kept after my father to come here. He became a foreman in a brick-making factory. I remember when he left. My mother was very sad; we were all crying. She was left there, twenty-six years old with three small children: one at ten months old, I was four, and my other brother was three.

I couldn't quite grasp the reason. I knew that he was going to America. And although my grandparents on both sides of the family didn't live very far, we were still isolated. My grandparents were tenant farmers, and they couldn't take off any time they wanted. They had a horse and buggy, and once in a blue moon they'd come to visit. Fortunately, the other tenant family that lived in the same courtyard with us was very friendly with Mom, and they kept her company and so on because we just couldn't do any traveling.

So we lived on this farm, and you can imagine my mother being very sad because we had no money. Pop had to borrow the money from my mother's father to come here. It was October, just the beginning of the winter setting in. Fortunately, all the supplies had been already bought and provisions made for the winter. We had to do that because we had no form of transportation whatsoever. Mom had my father's bicycle. We had a lot of snow. Renazzo is about the same latitude as New York and Long Island, so we had very severe winters.

We went to school from eight in the morning till two in the afternoon, and then from two to five we'd go to the nuns, the Catholic school, to learn religion, and to learn our prayers, which were taught to us all in Latin, and the masses. During summer vacations, my mother kept us in the Catholic school. We lived right near the church. And the nuns would teach the girls mending, crocheting, knitting, a little cooking.

The boys were taught, besides religion, farming and a little carpentry, which came very handy later on in life. The nuns were very strict with us. There was a boy sitting behind me in class and he was pulling my hair, so I turned around to tell him to stop, and the nun came and she gave me a whack across the face. But it was OK because everybody else got treated the same way.

The first year I went to school, I had never been apart from my mother and my brothers, and I just didn't want to go to school. So I didn't pay any attention to the teacher, and I would be put in the corner. Every day I wanted to be home with my baby brother and my other brother. I was a little mommy to them because Mom used to work on the farm whenever she could to earn extra money. We raised corn, wheat, hemp.

Our house, I went to see it in 1973. It was still there, but now it was a little store because it sat on the main road that led into town. We had four rooms, the downstairs kitchen and fireplace—that was our heat— and a utility room with a dirt floor. The second floor had one big bedroom and a smaller one where we put our winter supplies, the corn and wheat and everything, because we had to get all that stuff in before winter set in.

We had no glass windows, just shutters, wooden shutters, and you could put your finger through the cracks in them. So upstairs Mom would have to put rags in the cracks so we wouldn't get snow or rain in. Downstairs, Mother used a certain kind of brown paper to glue on to the windows and then put oil on the paper so it would be somewhat translucent to let light in. And if we forgot to put up the paper before a rainstorm or a heavy wind, the glue—which was made with flour and water—would tear up and we'd have to do it all over again.

When it was really cold, the well would freeze in the courtyard. There was no pump. We'd drop a pail down and bring the water up. We had a water pail in the kitchen. So we used to melt snow and use that for cooking and for drinking. It wasn't polluted like it is today.

We had a little box which held about six chickens, but we kept them upstairs on the second floor so they wouldn't be stolen or the eggs stolen. We had no property, just this little house that we rented from the farmer. I remember the chickens would walk up the rickety stairs to the second floor. Little rickety stairs about six inches wide, and to train them to go up there, when we got a new batch of chickens, we would put corn feed upstairs and they'd learn. To make them come down, Mama would call them in the morning and put the corn on the ground, and they would come. After three or four days they did it automatically.

We had delicious brown watermelon, and sometimes that would be our supper. Our meals were very simple. We had our own eggs, so we ate eggs all the time. We'd take a sack of wheat and go down to the mill and have it ground into flour. We had cornmeal, from which we made polenta. And we made it in many different ways. Our staples for the winter were beans and rice. We never had any vegetables. Even in summertime, the only vegetables we raised were celery, lettuce, and peppers, which we dunked in olive oil. We had a nanny goat for milk. We drank very little milk. We didn't drink milk like we do here. I can remember when the nanny goat had babies they would jump on my mother's back, stomp on her back, while she was milking the goat.

For holidays, Mama's specialty was tortellini or cappelletti, little dumplings filled with meat. Now they make them with all kinds of fillings, but we made them with meat and then cooked them in chicken broth. It was a family affair. We'd all help Mom to make it. I remember standing on a little stool trying to make the homemade noodles and I couldn't reach the table.

My mother was a very loving but stern mother. If my baby brothers got into trouble, I got a spanking because it was up to me to keep them out of trouble. She was the oldest in her family, a family of seven. She had to help with her [mother's] children, so that's the way she brought me up. So I have nothing but praise for my mother. She never left us alone.

In the fall, there were a lot of festivals and feasts in honor of the patron saints. Fireworks at night, flea markets, games of chance, loads of food, and all the young ladies would have their dates. We had two of them living in the next-door tenant house with us. They used to come in and wait for their boyfriends, and they would meet at our house and then change into better shoes. They'd come with their old working shoes through the small streets all full of mud, and then change. They used to play with us children. I have very pleasant memories.

I can remember having these big racks with trays of silkworms. Hundreds of silkworms. And you think a worm is quiet? When they're feeding, what a humming sound they made! Mom would climb the mulberry trees early in the spring, when the leaves were nice and tender, to feed these worms. We would have them until they went into the cocoon stage. We would raise them in our homes. I presume my mother got paid for taking care of them. Then the farmer would take them and send them to be processed for silk.

We had no candy. When we wanted candy, Mom would say, "What do you want with candy? This is no good. When we get to America, Dad has a big bag of candy for you." We were so disappointed when we got here. [*She laughs.*]

When my father left, he told my mother that as soon as he could, he would send for her. However, after he got here, the law was changed in 1924, and he had to become a citizen. So he went to night school and learned the history of the United States, and in 1929 he got his citizenship papers and he sent for us.

We came here August 13, 1929. From our little town, we had to go to the railroad station in Ferrara. We left about four o'clock in the morning. My grandfather came with his wagon where we put our trunks in. Pop had told Mom to bring her feather mattresses because here they only had mattresses with corn husks and they were uncomfortable.

We took the train to Genoa. That took eight or nine hours, and we were exhausted. We went to the hotel. We had a guide with us because Mom was afraid to go by herself. She'd never been away from Renazzo. So we had a tour guide from the travel agency accompany us to Genoa.

The next day we had our papers checked. A doctor examined us all, although we had been examined at home and we were all OK, and then we were reexamined [on the boat]. They told my mother that she'd have to bathe us. We fiddled with the faucets. We didn't know what the faucets were for, only that we saw this thing dripping. So we fiddled until the water came out. Mama says, "How am I going to give you a bath? The water keeps going down in the hole there!"

We were fourteen days on the boat. We were in a cabin, the four of us. At night, the steward, a woman, would come around with evaporated milk. "You must drink it," she said. "This is good for you." But we didn't drink it because we didn't like it. Mama was always so afraid that we would fall overboard. We always had to stay by her skirt. So we didn't explore the ship at all. We'd go up on deck, and she'd hang on to us for dear life.

The night before we arrived, they told us if we wanted to see the statue we'd have to get up early in the morning. We were up at four o'clock. We went up on deck, and everybody was up. And, oh, my God, when she came into sight I got gooseflesh, and to this day, I've been out there six or seven times. The last time was a year and a half ago. I took some cousins of mine who came from Italy. We went to Ellis Island, and I still get gooseflesh. I love that lady. She's beautiful.

When we came in, we saw my father down on the docks. We recognized him. Then we went into the big hall, and it was all brown and dreary, and everybody was crying. We were like sheep in there, all so crowded. My mother started to cry because she was sure my father wouldn't find us. We were examined again. I read where some people had terrible experiences. But they just looked in our hair, our teeth, our eyes, and that was it. It took about four or five hours before we got out of there.

My father tried to grab all of us. He was a big man, all right, and hugged us and kissed us. He was so happy we were here. Then he took us home.

MARIA FRANZISKA VON TRAPP
BORN AUGUST 28, 1914
EMIGRATED FROM AUSTRIA, 1938, AGE 24
PASSAGE VIA THE *BERGENSFJORD*

She was part of the world-renowned Trapp Family Singers, who inspired the 1959 hit Broadway musical and the 1965 Academy Award Best Picture winner The Sound of Music. *She was the second-oldest daughter of Baron Georg von Trapp and Agathe Whitehead von Trapp, who had seven children. When Agathe died in 1922 from pneumonia, the forty-seven-year-old Baron (portrayed in the movie by Christopher Plummer) remarried in 1927 to twenty-two-year-old Maria Augusta von Trapp (portrayed in the movie by Julie Andrews). Maria Franziska sang second soprano in the choir but spent most of her adult life in Papua New Guinea as a missionary. Besides her elder sister Agathe, she is the last of the original seven von Trapp children. "In the movie, I was Louisa," said Maria, who was ninety-six years old at the time. "I was the third one. I had brown hair."*

I had two mothers. My birth mother died of pneumonia in 1922. I was eight years old. My [birth] mother, she was not religious. I remember when she was very sick she asked my father, "Where will I go when I die?" She had no knowledge about eternity or anything.

My second mother, my stepmother, her name was also Maria—we were not close, sometimes maybe. [*She makes a face and smiles.*] She was a very strong, a difficult person. My second mother was religious. My father, Georg, was very kind. He was a Protestant. When he remarried to Maria, she wanted to raise the kids Catholic. So when we were growing up, we were told not to talk about religion with our father. So we're not really Catholic. Am I Protestant? I don't know what I am. [*She laughs.*] I'm a believer, I guess. I'm just a child of God. . . .

In Austria growing up I remember the Nazis. They were scary—not a nice memory. . . . We didn't have Austrian passports. We had Italian passports, and so the Nazis couldn't do anything. They couldn't touch us. Hitler and Mussolini were aligned—but because we had Italian passports we could leave. We didn't have to sneak out of Austria and over the mountains like it showed in the movie. Also, we had a contract to sing here in America. They wanted us to come here for concerts for six months, and while we were away the Nazis came and took over our home. Many years later I went back to Austria, to the house, and it's still there. It's now a bed-and-breakfast hotel, very nice.

Fig. 26. Maria Franziska von Trapp at her home in Stowe, Vermont, in June 2010. Photograph used by permission of Melissa K. Coan.

When we left Austria I remember we went by train to Italy and took the boat to America from Genoa. We came to this country on the boat, the *American Farmer*. Funny, in the end we became farmers, we became American farmers. [*She laughs.*] The boat sailed to New York. Upon arriving I remember being amazed at all the skyscrapers—they seemed to rise out of nothing. It was the first time for me. Seeing such a thing. . . . Later we went back to Europe, to Scandinavia. We toured, we sang.

Then the second time we came to America we waited for the boat from England, from Southampton, and we came back to New York. We were detained at Ellis Island for one or two days. I was 25 at the time. We went to the Big Hall [Registry Room]. They separated the men from the women. I remember babies crying. . . . Once in New York we stayed at the Wellington, Hotel Wellington. We came to do a concert north of New York, I don't remember where. . . .

Then, in the 1960s, I went to Papua New Guinea as a missionary. Actually, I wanted to go to Africa, but we were in Australia at the time. There were missionaries there, and then we went to New Guinea. I went all by myself. I was all alone. I was a teacher. I taught [*she gestures with her hands*] everything! [*Broad smile.*] I taught elementary school students— but they knew more than me! [*She laughs, then becomes serious.*] I loved it there. I was there for thirty years! Very few visitors. I think my stepmother came once or twice in that time. I was very happy there.

Before I left New Guinea, I adopted a boy. He's from Africa. He's black. He lives here [in Vermont] with me. I adopted him several years ago. I met him in New Guinea. He had nothing to eat. . . . Our bond is our faith in God. I don't go to church. I'm too old. My church is here, my home. I pray with Kakooly, who I adopted [now in his fifties], my adopted son. We pray together. We pray at home. . . . I was never married. I never found anyone. God didn't bring me anybody—so I never had children, although I had plenty of nieces and nephews. More than enough! [*She laughs.*] But I'm happy with that. I'm not angry with God. Anyway, I feel uncomfortable about marriage. It's a risk, you know? My younger brother Werner, he was born after me. [*She points to a picture of him on the wall.*] We were very close. Then he got married and they went away, his wife took him away. I'm sure when I meet God he's not going to ask, "Why didn't you get married?" [*She laughs.*]

So why did I come back? [*She pauses again.*] The Lord called me back. That was about fifteen years ago I came back to America. I would have stayed in New Guinea. That was the happiest time of my life. I did not know what it was going to be like before I went, but [*pauses*] it was paradise! [*She smiles with joy.*] I had friends there. We had such wonderful times in Port Moresby [capital of Papua New Guinea and its largest city]. I don't know why the Lord called me back. I'm not sure why, but he did. I would still be there, even though the life in New Guinea can be very hard and it became very dangerous at the end of my time there. I would still go back there, but I'm too old now. . . .

Fig. 27. Original movie poster from *The Sound of Music*. Photograph used with permission, Barry Moreno, *Ellis Island's Famous Immigrants* (Charleston, SC: Arcadia Publishing, 2008).

I'm surprised by the popularity of *The Sound of Music*. People still talk about it. They watch it in Russia and Japan. I think people love it because it's a good story, but mostly because the children are in it. . . . I met the actors in the movie, but Julie Andrews—she didn't want anything to do with us. I think she didn't like my [step]mother. They didn't get along. The children actors in the movie, they came here recently [2008] for a reunion. But Julie Andrews didn't come or Christopher Plummer. I never met them. They were both invited, but they didn't show up. [*She pauses, looks straight away.*] I'm glad we came here. I'm glad we came to the United States. But it would be nice to go back to New Guinea. I was happy there.

JOHANNES VON TRAPP
BORN JANUARY 17, 1939,
PHILADELPHIA, AMERICAN BORN

His mother, Baroness Maria Augusta von Trapp, was pregnant with Johannes when the von Trapp family came by boat to America for the second time in September 1938. They were detained at Ellis Island for several days after his mother exclaimed to an immigration inspector, "I'm so glad to be back, I never want to leave again!" Johannes was one of three children born to Maria, played by actress Julie Andrews in the movie The Sound of Music, *and his father Georg, "The Captain," played by actor Christopher Plummer. Georg had seven children from his previous marriage, ten in all. The family sang and toured extensively until they performed their last concert in New Hampshire in 1956. They settled in Vermont, opening a twenty-seven-room Austrian-style ski lodge on 2,400 acres in Stowe, run by their mother, in 1950. Although trained as a forest ecologist, Johannes found himself pressed into service to help his mother run the lodge. In December 1980, a tragic fire forced forty-five people, including his mother, to flee in their nightclothes, leaving behind the body of a thirty-year-old Illinois man, who was later found in the rubble. The Trapp Family Lodge was rebuilt. When his mother died in 1987, America's most famous immigrant family endured internal turmoil of their own involving lawsuits over stock, with Johannes eventually buying out thirty-two family members in 1994. Today, his son, Sam von Trapp, manages the lodge, with Johannes's goal to completely turn over the reins to him one day so he can travel and hunt and ranch, his passions. "As I get older, I realize that life is not a dress rehearsal," said Johannes. "You've got to do it and enjoy it while it's happening, because we don't get to do it again."*

I was born January 17, 1939. We came over in September 1938 into New York Harbor. We came to New York by ship. The first time we came, we took the train from Salzburg to Genoa, Italy, and took the boat the *American Farmer*. For our first visit we were perfectly legal, and so there was no reason to send us to Ellis Island because we came as "visiting artists." I was born a few months after we arrived. Then we traveled, performed, sang. We were living in Philadelphia. The following June, when I was five months old, our visas were not renewed, and we had to go back to Europe. So we spent the summer in Denmark and Sweden. We couldn't go back to Austria, obviously, because of the war, and Sweden had been very welcoming to my family earlier when they had a concert tour there. Sweden was officially neutral, but it had certain Nazi sympathies, and we were not all that welcome.

Fig. 28. Johannes von Trapp in front of his Trapp Family Lodge in Stowe, Vermont. Photograph used by permission of Melissa K. Coan.

We finally got the visas straightened out, and we returned to the United States on the *Bergensfjord*, the Norwegian ship. We had spent the summer in Scandinavia and came to New York, but when my mother spoke to the immigration officer on board the boat in New York Harbor, he asked, "How long do you plan to stay?" and my mother said, "I'm so glad to be back, I never want to leave again!" which is not the right thing to say to an immigration inspector, so he sent us to Ellis Island, and we spent several days there.

My mother was a very strong-willed person. She was much more complex than her film portrayal in *The Sound of Music*. She had an unhappy childhood, and that kind of childhood either makes you very strong or you end up homeless somewhere. And she ended up very strong. She had a really fine mind. She had a gift for languages. She had incredible charm when she chose to exercise it. Great persuasive powers. She loved being outdoors. She loved to walk and exercise. After a childhood in which she was not at all religious, my mother underwent a conversion and became very religious, I would say to a fault, too much, but that's just my opinion. She wasn't a fundamentalist; she didn't claim that everything written in the Bible happened the way it was written. But her life was built around what she felt God wanted of her. [*He smiles.*] I once said as a kid in an argument with her, "Your will or God," implying that it was her choice, not God's, and there was that element too, you know. But we got along very well. I was raised as a Catholic. Religion was an important part of her life, but it wasn't everything. I mean, she loved music, history, art, all sorts of things. She really had a great appreciation for Western culture and enjoyed life tremendously.

I was eight years old when my father died in 1948. He was a much warmer person than he was portrayed in the film. I have lots of good memories of him. He drove very fast, I remember that. He was just a really kind, strong figure. But he lost his fortune [inherited mostly from his first wife, Agathe Whitehead von Trapp] and got depressed over it. I think my father was not a businessman in any accepted sense. He was a leader. A natural leader. He fought in the Boxer Rebellion in China in 1900. The thought of sitting down and figuring margins was sort of foreign to him. But he was a fine leader, and I think the whole family really missed him when he died. There's a small cemetery on the grounds of the lodge, and he's buried here beside my mother, along with other family members. She died in 1987.

We were ten children. Agathe is the eldest. She's ninety-seven and lives in Baltimore. Maria [Franziska] will be ninety-six, and she lives here on the property in a little house about half a mile down the road. Then my sister Eleanor lives in Waitsfield, Vermont, twenty-seven miles south of here, my sister Rosemary lives in Stowe, and I live here.

Our estate in Austria was taken over by [Heinrich] Himmler [Hitler's right-hand man] after we left. It was his headquarters during the war. The estate was in the American occupation zone, so it was given back to us shortly after the war. And we decided—I say "we" even though I was very small at the time—we decided that we wanted to stay here [in America] and didn't want to go back to Austria, so it was sold by us to a religious order, and it became a seminary for many years, and now it's a bed and breakfast. I don't think Hitler had an office there, but he visited several times. There were bomb shelters built in the garden. There was a brick wall around the property with an electric fence on top.

We initially settled in Philadelphia because after one of our concerts a gentleman came backstage and introduced himself. He was a lover of baroque music and he said, "I have an empty house across the street from my own where my mother used to live and she recently passed away—would you like to live there?" He said, "It's a large enough house," and my mother said, "Well, we probably can't afford the rent." And he said, "No, no—the rent will be singing Bach with me once a week *all day!*" [*He laughs.*] His hobby was in translating the choral works of Bach, so we moved there and lived there, except Philadelphia in the summer is very hot, and in the fall, winter, and spring, we were traveling and performing—so it wasn't an ideal place for us.

We wound up here [Vermont] because we had been lent a house in Stowe for the summer, and while we were here, we found this hillside, and my family fell in love with the view and the feeling of space and openness. And I really think that this is one of the few places in the East where I could be happy. I feel really claustrophobic elsewhere. But here you can see twenty miles north and twenty miles south. There's a feeling of open space.

We bought this property in 1942 and moved up here and lived here and farmed the property, and my mother quickly realized that there was no way this was going to support a large family, even though we had bought two farms. The ground was too rocky and stony, and the growing season was too short, and the hills were too steep. At that time, the ski business was just getting started in Stowe. The lifts had been built, and skiing was becoming a popular activity, so when we were away singing, our rooms were rented to skiers. And that's how we got into the lodge business. We began renting rooms in 1950. It was after my father died in 1948. We hired a lady to be a caretaker. My mother was the guiding force but she didn't check people in and out. We also had a music camp down the hill.

I started singing when I was four years old. But then from seven years old on I was full-time with the family singers. Our last concert was in 1956 in New Hampshire. My brothers and sisters had gotten tired of traveling and singing. They just didn't want to do it commercially any-more. They were tired. My brother had six kids, and he didn't want to travel throughout the year. My mother would have happily gone on for another ten years, but my brothers and sisters had pretty well had it.

Most people don't know this, but I'm a forest ecologist. I studied forest ecology. I got my master's and then took two years off to straighten out the lodge business. [*He sighs.*] My mother, for all her tremendous energy and entrepreneurial ability, was a terrible manager and adminis-trator, so that every person who spent thirty dollars here cost us thirty-five. And so I needed to get some things straightened out. I was going to hire a professional to run things and go back and finish my doctoral work and be a scientist, but that didn't work out. I got married, and we had children, and after a while I realized that this was going to be my career. But I was not into this at all. This is not what I wanted to do. My mother didn't want me to take over. We had a huge battle, although I sometimes wonder whether she staged all that, thinking that if I didn't fight for it I wouldn't care about it. She really had no idea how to run a business. When I took over, we had seventy-five employees, and I cut it to twenty-seven. This was 1969. There were just a lot of people here who weren't doing anything. They were here because they needed this place, not because we needed them. So I, for better or for worse, cleaned that up and we started making money! [*He pauses.*] It's been a challenge. It's a tough industry, and Vermont's a tough state to have a business because it has a low population base and we have to bring all our visitors up from the eastern megalopolis. But I've been able to do some fun things on the side as well. For instance, we've just launched a new line of draft lager beers with the name "Trapp Family Lodge, Stowe, Vermont." Is the brand of the von Trapp name still strong? I think we'll find out with this beer.

It's been more than forty-five years, and people are still drawn to the movie. It's sort of a phenomenon. There are a whole bunch of different themes in it I think that resonate with people. It was, for example, not only popular in the English-speaking world—it was popular in Japan. It was extremely popular in China. Now, if you've ever expected a movie to be censored by the Chinese authorities, it would have been *The Sound of Music* because it highlights resistance to authority and all sorts of sensitive themes, but the film was tremendously popular in China. I think there are certain themes in it that are timeless, such as love of family, pursuing freedom, following your conscience, and doing what you like.

I met Julie Andrews and Christopher Plummer. Christopher Plummer, interestingly, was here as a guest with his grandmother when he was a little boy. They came skiing and stayed in the old lodge, long before any film stuff. Actress Mary Martin and my mother had a very nice relationship. [The original Broadway production of *The Sound of Music* opened in November 1959, starring Mary Martin and Theodore Bikel.] They got along very well. Julie Andrews and my mother didn't get along quite as well. They respected each other, but Julie Andrews definitely wanted to do her thing and not what my mother wanted. But then, we didn't have creative control over the movie. My mother made a very bad deal a long time ago and sold our rights away. The *Sound of Music* company was generous enough to say, "Hey, you made a bad deal—we think you should have some participation in this," and so they gave my mother some participation, both creatively and financially. They needn't have done that, which was very kind. I never met Robert Wise, the director, but my mother knew him quite well. My mother even went to Austria, and she was involved in the making of the film, but the rest of the family were not involved. . . .

The greatest difference between the film and real life is first of all the time scale—my parents were married in 1927 and the film is set in 1938. So the children are all eleven years older. Another one is that the film downplays a very important personality, the priest who was our conductor, our musical director, Franz Wasner [portrayed by the character named Max Detweiler in the movie], and without him the family would have never had great success. He was a gifted conductor and arranger. He knew how to select music and arrange it so that it built on the family's strengths and minimized its weaknesses. [Arturo] Toscanini listened to one of our recordings and is supposed to have said, "They have a good conductor." [*He smiles broadly and chuckles.*] Wasner returned to Austria and died there in 1992, I believe. He never became an American citizen. My family all became Americans, although my father did not. But my brothers were in the American army, and they fought their way up through Italy and drove into Salzburg three days after the war ended, wearing their American army uniforms in the jeep—it was quite an emotional feeling for them. . . .

I'm a big-game hunter. I love to hunt. I've been to Africa a few times, traveled all over North America. I want to go to Asia. I've had ranches out west. One was in southwestern Montana, a beautiful property, about twenty-seven thousand deeded acres and another seventy-five thousand acres leased. It was a huge operation. We ran six thousand sheep and two thousand cows and it was hard work. I've never worked harder in my life. I was up at 5:30 every morning, and I hate getting up in the morning. I have trouble going to sleep in the evening. For me, the day should be thirty hours long rather than twenty-four. I had the ranch for three and a half years. But I had a property in Arizona for ten years before that and one up in British Columbia for three years before that. I'd love to get another ranch.

After my mother died in 1987, her stock in the business was widely distributed among nephews and nieces, etc., and people who had been bought out years earlier once again got stock—so suddenly we went from five stockholders before she died to thirty-two stockholders, and it just wasn't a workable thing. Everybody was pulling in different directions, and I ended up buying most of them out. Actually, I bought them all out. So I own it now with my kids, Sam and my daughter Kristina, who lives on the property in a house with her husband. But in the process, unfortunately, my ranch had to get sold, so I would like to buy another one out there. . . .

Regrets? I was having breakfast with my son, Sam, the other morning and I thought, "This is something that I would have liked to have experienced with my father." Just sitting there, talking about various things. That's something I didn't get to do because I was eight when he passed.

But what I really miss is my family singing. That was a fabulous thing. If we were together working, doing something, one of us might start a song and the others would chime in, and we sang together so much, we were so rehearsed, we knew all the harmonies—and were immediately singing in four-, five-, or six-part harmony—and it was just huge fun.

Chapter 6

1940s

America's involvement in World War II limited immigration in the early 1940s, which had become not just a matter of economics but a matter of national security. National fears about foreign-born individuals continued to bubble up and were handled poorly, as when the Immigration and Naturalization Service (INS) organized internment camps and detention facilities for enemy aliens, even when they were not actually enemies or aliens. After World War II, INS programs addressed the needs of returning GIs and the conditions in postwar Europe as immigration slowly started to increase again, and has risen steadily ever since.

KEY HISTORIC EVENTS

★1940: President Franklin D. Roosevelt moves the INS from the Department of Labor to the Department of Justice. The task of securing our borders against enemy aliens is added to the INS's wartime responsibilities; its workforce doubles during the war years, from approximately four thousand to approximately eight thousand employees.

★1941: The United States enters World War II, and Ellis Island serves as a detention center for enemy aliens.

★1942: Japanese Americans along the Pacific coast are detained and sent to internment camps or "War Relocation Camps" by the US government in the wake of Imperial Japan's attack on Pearl Harbor, even though 62 percent of those detained are American citizens; Ellis Island is enlisted for use as a detainment facility, holding seven thousand Japanese, Germans, and Italians.

★1943: The Chinese Exclusion Act is repealed. By the end of the 1940s, all restrictions on Asians acquiring US citizenship are abolished.

★1945: Large-scale Puerto Rican migration to escape island poverty causes many to settle in New York. The War Brides Act provides for admission of foreign-born wives of US servicemen.

★1948: The Displaced Persons Act allows four hundred thousand refugees fleeing persecution to enter the United States during a four-year period.

MIGRATION FLOWS

Total legal US immigration in 1940s: 857,000

Top 10 emigration countries in this decade: Canada and Newfoundland (160,911), United Kingdom (131,794), Germany (119,506), Mexico (56,158), Italy (50,509), France (36,954), Cuba (25,976), China (16,072), Ireland (15,701), Netherlands (13,877)

(See appendix for the complete list of countries.)

FAMOUS IMMIGRANTS

Immigrants who came to America in this decade (here, not all through Ellis Island), and who would later become famous include:

Angela Lansbury, England, 1940, actress
Ricardo Montalbán, Mexico, 1940, actor

Vladimir Nabokov, Russia, 1940, writer
Yoko Ono, Japan, 1940, artist/John Lennon's wife
Bill Graham, Germany, 1941, music producer
Yul Brynner, Russia, 1941, actor
An Wang, China, 1945, cofounder of Wang Laboratories
Ann-Margret, Sweden, 1946, actress
Yma Sumac, Peru, 1947, singer
Tom Lantos, Hungary, 1947, politician (California)
Madeleine Albright, Czechoslovakia, 1948, diplomat/
   US Secretary of State
Charles Trénet, France, 1948, singer
Max Frankel, Germany, 1948, journalist
Frank Oz, England, 1949, film director/puppeteer

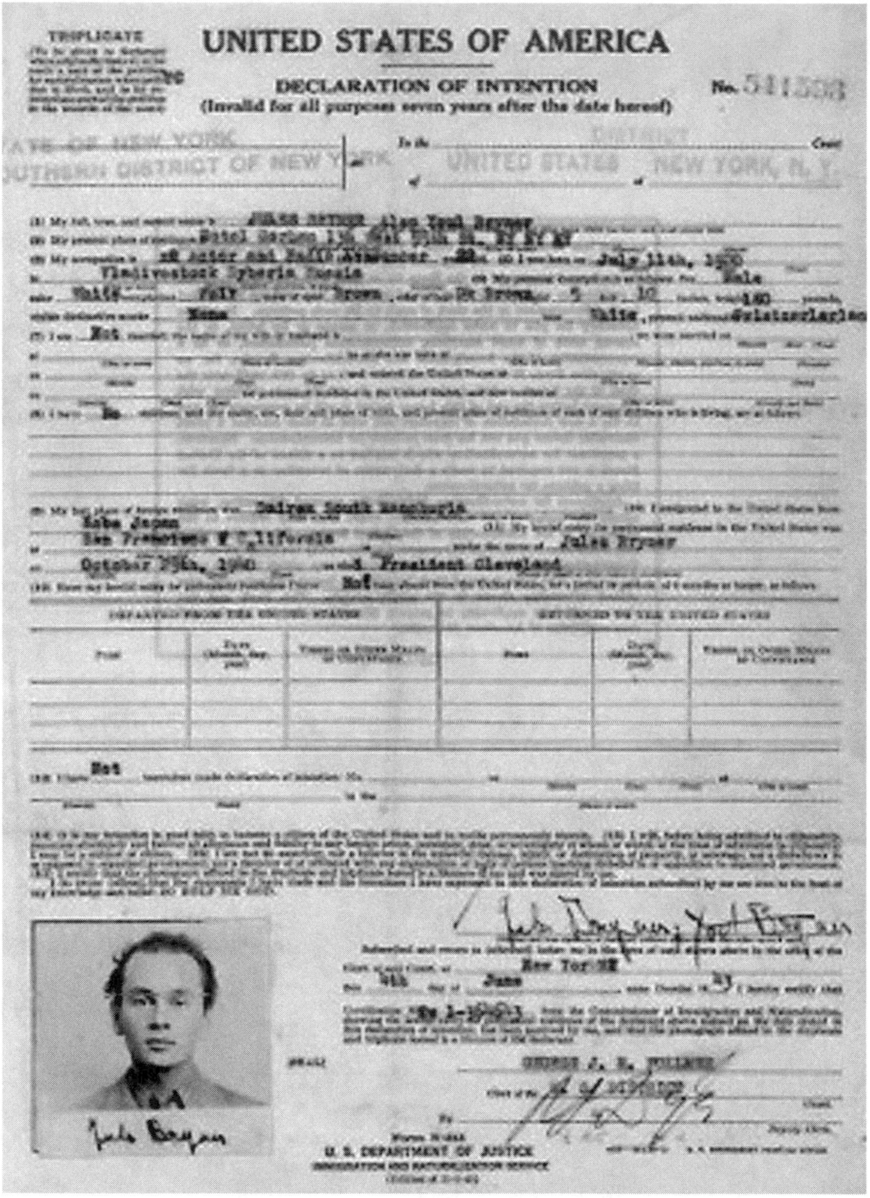
TRIPLICATE

UNITED STATES OF AMERICA

DECLARATION OF INTENTION

(Invalid for all purposes seven years after the date hereof)

STATE OF NEW YORK
SOUTHERN DISTRICT OF NEW YORK

In the DISTRICT Court of the UNITED STATES at NEW YORK, N. Y.

U. S. DEPARTMENT OF JUSTICE
IMMIGRATION AND NATURALIZATION SERVICE

Fig. 29. Actor Jules "Yul" Brynner (*The King and I*) arrived at the Port of San Francisco, California, in 1940. He filed his Declaration of Intention to become a US citizen on June 4, 1943. Photograph used by permission of the National Archives.

PAUL LARIC
BORN MARCH 20, 1926
EMIGRATED FROM YUGOSLAVIA VIA INDIA, 1940, AGE 14
PASSAGE ON SS *POLK*

The son of a prominent Jewish industrialist, his is an E. M. Forsteresque journey to America via Asia, India, and South Africa. He traveled with his brother, mother, and father, who left Yugoslavia to escape the Nazis. Their journey took many months, circumnavigating nearly half the globe, only to arrive in New York, find out his brother's visa had expired, and then spend nearly another month in detention on Ellis Island. This interview was conducted on Ellis Island itself for the Oral History Project in February 1991. It was the first time Paul had been back to Ellis Island since 1940, when his family first arrived. "I realize now that I should have come back sooner," he said, "because there are so many memories attached."

I was born in Vienna, although we lived in Yugoslavia at the time. My parents thought the hospital in Vienna was better than the hospital in the little town of Maribor, Slovenia. It's close to the Austrian border. We also had a better hospital facility in the town of Graz, Austria, where my brother was born. His name is Ivan. He is two years older.

My father's name was Vilko. He was a textile manufacturer. In fact, he was one of the founders of the textile industry in Yugoslavia. And he had both weaving and knitting mills in Maribor, and then he continued in that career when we came to this country. He started again and had textile mills here.

Our town was in a valley on the Drava River, beside a mountain that is actually the last in the Alpine chain. The name of the mountain is Pohore. The town at the time when we lived there had a population of about fifty thousand people. Now it's three times that size, and the people were, of course, Slovenian, but prior to World War I, that area was part of the Austro-Hungarian Empire and German was the second language. So almost everyone knew German quite well, but Slovenia tried to keep its language going, and therefore all schools and all official functions were strictly in Slovenian.

My father actually had his apprenticeship in the textile industry in Czechoslovakia. Czechoslovakia was quite advanced in that area, much more, of course, than Yugoslavia, and when he moved to Yugoslavia, he thought this would be a good area to develop the industry because of the availability of a labor force. But he had to bring some experts with him from Czechoslovakia who would run certain parts of the mills, so that it was a matter of training many of the employees, and this is just what happened, and it became a flourishing industry.

My mother's name was Margaretta. She was also Czechoslovakian and came to Yugoslavia after marrying my father, when he decided to move his business there. So they met while he was in Czechoslovakia. In fact, he was in business with my mother's mother, my grandmother, who was an importer and exporter and merchant in textiles in Prague and in other towns in Czechoslovakia. She was quite prominent in that business. This was unusual because women were primarily housewives then, but she had both a housewife career and a business career, and she met my father as a business associate, and that's how he met my mother. She actually worked together with her husband, but when he passed away she just continued the business.

My grandmother was a wonderful person. I remember her as being particularly generous and indulgent. She absolutely adored her grandchildren and spoiled us rotten every time she came to visit. She was a marvelous cook and we always looked forward to her arrival, not just for the cooking but for all the gifts she was always bringing. Her specialty was a preparation that involved a goose liver. It's taking the liver of a goose and treating it in some way, chilling it, and I remember the liver itself being in the middle of a sea of fat—all this, of course, solid after it's been chilled, very similar to the French foie gras. She made it for the holidays, for Christmas and Easter or whenever she would visit us.

My father's family was originally from Stupava, Czechoslovakia. My grandfather died before I was born. He was also a merchant. I don't know exactly what business he was in, but he had eight or nine children and kept a very close rein on everyone's doings and instilled in each a sense for business because they all have followed in his footsteps in that area.

When my father moved and established his first factory in Yugoslavia, on the factory grounds was a residential house, and we lived there a number of years. I was quite small, but I do remember it because it also had a garden and we had various pets to play with, ponies and, I think, a lamb. I still have photographs of that. I don't remember their names. [*He laughs.*] I do remember the dog's name that I got in Czechoslovakia. His name was Bonzo. [*He laughs.*] I don't know why I should remember that.

Fig. 30. After the United States entered World War II, President Roosevelt ordered the evacuation of approximately 110,000 Japanese Americans from their West Coast homes to ten relocation centers. This photograph, taken July 3, 1942, shows the barrack-type housing of the Manzanar War Relocation Authority Center in California during a dust storm. Photograph used by permission of the National Archives.

However, after a number of years we moved to the center of town and actually occupied an apartment from then on in Maribor. That was one of the most modern buildings at the time, and I think we had something like eight or nine rooms plus a kitchen and two bathrooms. I was about six. So it was just Mother, Dad, me, and my brother. And I was just starting school the year we moved in.

My brother and I shared a bedroom, but we had other rooms that remained empty. We also had a room for a cook and a room for a cham-

bermaid. These were live-in help. My father was one of the most prominent individuals in town and financially very comfortable. He was not
involved in politics—only in that, from the beginning, he drastically
opposed the Nazi movement in Germany and made it well known
throughout the town what his position was. And that was really the
reason for our leaving Yugoslavia when we did. He knew that with a
German takeover he and his family, and his property, would be the first
victims if it came to pass. The fact that there were so many German-
speaking people in the town—many with families in Austria and Germany—meant there was a considerable contingent of Nazi sympathizers.
He knew this was a dangerous situation for us.

My parents were Jewish, but we became Catholics in the thirties. As
far as the Nazis were concerned it didn't matter [*laughs*] because it was
Jewish origin they were concerned with. My parents were not particularly
religious. They did not observe many of the Jewish customs and obser-
vances. And since Yugoslavia was predominantly Christian—that is,
either Roman Catholic or Serbian Orthodox—we wanted to conform
pretty much to the rest of the population, so rather than stand out, we
changed our religion.

So we went to church. We had two churches in Maribor. Church
played a big part in everyone's life, particularly for children because religion was one of the required courses in school. And we had to go to church
on Sundays and conform to all the various practices.

I enjoyed sports a great deal. Maribor is situated, as I mentioned, near
a mountain, and in the winter we would go skiing. I began skiing at age
four. My mother was the instigator there because she began to ski, and we
enjoyed it ever since and went on ski vacations for Christmas and to Austria and other parts of Yugoslavia. Skiing was a very big part of our lives
in the winter. In the summer we went to a little island in the middle of
the Drava River which had swimming pools, and the rest of the time we
would go on hikes and we also had horses. My brother and I became very
fond of riding, and so every spring, summer, and fall we would be with
our horses. We had a stable that was right in the middle of town, and
many people in town knew us for galloping through the streets and
holding up traffic once in a while.

My mother went to the Music Conservatory in Czechoslovakia but unfortunately didn't keep up with her piano, but she did ask me to take lessons, which I did at the same time I started school. I was not particularly fond of my teacher, who was a very demanding older gentleman. He required a great deal of my exercise time and I didn't always perform very well, as much as I enjoyed music. Many years later, I picked up the clarinet, and I still doodle around once in a while. But that's about as far as my musical education went, except that my brother and I were very fond of American jazz.

When the war began in September 1939, my brother and I were in England. My parents had sent us to Switzerland to learn French and then to England to learn English. We were about to return to England from Yugoslavia after our summer vacation when the war broke out and we didn't return, so we spent one more year in Yugoslavia. This was a touchy time because my father expected an invasion of Yugoslavia at any moment. And, in fact, we made various trips out of Maribor, which is so close to the Austrian border, to Zagreb and to other towns whenever he suspected something was happening at the frontier.

We spent the next summer, 1940, on the Adriatic at a resort, but by this time our papers were in order and we had received visas. My brother and I had student visas. My parents had visitors' visas. And without even returning to Maribor, we left from our vacation place to Zagreb and picked up our personal belongings, which we had with an uncle, an aunt, and cousin of mine who lived there. The aunt was my father's sister.

We said our goodbyes and took the train from Zagreb to Belgrade, then Belgrade to Sofia in Bulgaria, then Sofia to Istanbul. We stayed in Istanbul for about ten days awaiting papers that would allow us to spend some time in Bombay because we knew that we would have to wait for a ship there. My father had preplanned it all. By that time, the war had started. The Italians had occupied the southern part of France, so to go west, for instance, to reach Spain or Portugal where we might have gotten passage to the States, would have been very difficult.

So he decided on a longer but safer route, and that was to go through India and then take a ship. It could have gone west to New York or east and ended up in California. We weren't particular. We took the first one that came and ended up in New York. My brother and I were absolutely delighted. We were very pro-American in many respects, listening to a lot of jazz records, but we were also fond of American films, American books. We read Jack London a great deal, and we were very eager to come to this country. We knew very little American history. The schools in Europe, particularly Yugoslavia, were much more preoccupied with European history, particularly the history of Yugoslavia, which was difficult enough, the country having been first the kingdom of Serbs, Croats, and Slovenes and then united as one country with three basic ethnic groups— the Slovenes, the Croats, and the Serbs—and a few minor groups such as the Montenegrins and the Macedonians. There was a great deal to be studied there. Also, there were periods under the Ottoman occupation from the Turks and the occupation under the Austro-Hungarian Empire. So we had to know this pretty well. America was a far-off land that we knew about only as the "great democracy" in the world and a land that "promised progress and freedom" and all the good things that we read about and wanted to be a part of.

My parents studied English. They took private lessons from professors in Maribor, but their English was never particularly good. They spoke well, but they both had very heavy accents.

In Istanbul we were staying at a hotel on the Bosphorus, a place called Tarabya, which was a beautiful Turkish resort place, and we had a wonderful time. I remember going fishing in the Bosphorus and the Black Sea and waterskiing and visiting Istanbul and the various places of interest: Topkapi Palace, the mosques, the Hagia Sophia. For two teenage boys, this was absolutely fabulous. Both my brother and I kept diaries. Just recently I rummaged through some papers and I found my brother's diary. I reread the story of our journey and he sketched some of the sights that we had seen, such as the minarets in Istanbul and later on some of the sights in Bombay and South Africa.

Then, one day, we crossed the Bosphorus by boat to the train terminal on the Asian side of Istanbul and from there took a train to Baghdad, which was a very long journey. It took two days and two nights. I remember the train compartment was not particularly well ventilated.

This was September and it was hot, and I remember looking out the windows as we went through Turkey and later on Iraq on our way to Baghdad and [seeing] the extreme poverty of the people, some living under wooden planks made into a living area and maybe a goat as their only possession. Having come from a rather privileged background, this was the first time we were confronted with this kind of poverty.

Fig. 31. Ryohitsu Shibuya (top left) made his fortune as a flower grower (chrysanthemums, mainly). He is shown here with his family at their Mountain View, California, home on April 18, 1942. The Shibuyas were US citizens. Nevertheless, a few days later—just because they originally came from Japan—they were all arrested and taken to the Heart Mountain Relocation Center in Wyoming. The family eventually returned home in April 1945 after the war, but without Ms. Shibuya (top right), who died at the internment camp. Photograph used by permission of the National Archives.

We were in a first-class compartment, which was upholstered, but the ventilation was nonexistent so we had to open the window, and this was a coal-fired locomotive so we received a lot of soot. [*He laughs.*] It was a very uncomfortable trip. We had a dining car, which was adequate, I suppose, in terms of the food that was being served, but that was also hot and uncomfortable. And we were sitting next to people the likes of which I had never seen before up to that point. Some of them were Arabs, others were Turks, and they all looked very fierce to me.

I think we felt bewilderment, going through unknown places and into a bigger unknown as far as the future was concerned. I'm sure my parents were wondering if they had done the right thing. Did they take a step that was really necessary? We had left family and friends behind. What was going to happen to them? So knowing that we very likely would not see them again, certainly not very soon, there was a mixture of excitement in terms of seeing new things. but also sadness in leaving many things behind.

We were in Baghdad I think two days. I remember arriving after this long, tedious, and boring journey. Then, all of a sudden, we were surrounded by a mob of people who were trying to outshout one another, each one telling us they represented the best hotel in Baghdad. And so they were grabbing our luggage and beginning to load it on their various taxis, and finally we decided to go with the one who was the most aggressive because he had already gotten half our luggage and we ended up in a hotel that was not the best in Baghdad. But so be it. We had no other choice.

The hotel was, too, very warm. In Baghdad the temperature was something like 120 degrees Fahrenheit in the shade and there really was not very much shade anywhere. [*He laughs.*] The hotel was ventilated primarily by fans. The hotel rooms also had fans. Some of them were working, others were not. But we were so tired that we decided to make the best of it. I remember my brother and I shared a room and couldn't sleep because of the heat at night so we filled the bathtub with cold water and took turns lying in it. Then around five o'clock in the morning the sun came up and we walked out into the garden of the hotel and I remember some employees were lying on the benches in the garden and flies were all over them, going in and out of their mouths and noses. [*He laughs.*] It's a memory I still keep to this day.

The next day we all bought *topees*, tropical hats, to try to keep cool under the hot sun and we also went to a doctor to get shots. I think it was for diphtheria and various other diseases that we would likely catch in the Orient. Then we took a train from Baghdad to Basra and spent a couple of days there. Basra was a port city heavily involved in the oil industry. But we stayed in a hotel constructed by Germans and that was our first exposure to air conditioning. It was a wonderful change from what we had gone through the last few days.

I remember my brother and I went to a movie theater in Basra that showed a Tarzan film [*laughs*] with one of our heroes at the time, Johnny Weissmuller. The movie was interesting in that the film had some African natives fighting Arabs who were trying to capture natives for the slave trade. And when some of the Arabs were beaten by the African natives, the audience was not particularly pleased and started to heave things at the screen. [*He laughs.*] But then the theater manager gave a little speech in Arabic, which I didn't understand, and everything was much better.

After two days we boarded a ship from Basra to Bombay through the Persian Gulf. The name of the ship was the *Barpeta.* It was a British cargo ship, and the major cargo it carried was dates. It had maybe twenty passengers; half were American and English. They were all involved in the oil business in Iran, Iraq, and Arabia. The other half were Arabs. I don't know what nationality, but they all looked the same and they all dressed the same. One was a sheik who was traveling first class. His attendants, however, traveled second class, and my brother and I were in second class, so we got to know the attendants. The boat ride must have lasted a week.

We stopped in many ports in the Persian Gulf. We were able to go ashore in the ports. We saw Bahrain and a few ports on the Iranian side, and I remember the morning we spent in Karachi, Pakistan, which was a fairly large city, but half the traffic in the city was people riding camels or leading them! And it was very hot, so we didn't spend too much time in town. We went back to the ship, which then continued down to Bombay. The cabin was fairly ordinary. It had bunk beds for my brother and me, a small cabin. My parents had a much larger stateroom, which was quite comfortable, and the shipboard life was fairly ordinary.

In the morning we would get up early. Sometimes we slept out on deck because it was cooler. However, we had to get up very early in the morning because they started sweeping the deck around five or six in the morning. And then we spent the rest of the morning lounging in deck chairs being served bouillon. [*He laughs.*] I remember there was even some skeet shooting.

At night all the lights were out because of the possibility of U-boats [military submarines operated by Germany in World Wars I and II], so the crew was very attentive. There were English officers, and I got to know the captain, who had me up to his cabin because he said he had a son who was my age who was in England—in fact, who went to school very close to the school that I had gone to when I was in England, which was Brighton College. And so he wanted to know a bit about us. I guess he wanted to know who we were with Yugoslav passports going to India, which was sort of unusual.

India was another revelation to us. We had never seen anything like it. Bombay was a huge town with low buildings, crowded streets with people and cows wandering at random. These were holy animals and therefore were admitted anywhere. We arrived in Bombay about the middle of October, I would say, and it was still very warm. The monsoon season was about to start, and we were fortunate in obtaining an apartment rather than a hotel because we were waiting for a ship to take us to the States, to California or the East Coast. And we made some friends, my brother and I, in Bombay. We had met a Hindu couple on the ship, and they said we had to meet their children, and so we had a crowd of friends that we spent time with, both bicycling and going to a swimming place with pools both indoors and out. And we spent most of our time there.

In the evening my parents and I would sometimes, if it wasn't too warm, walk the various parts of Bombay, visit Malabar Hill and various restaurants, especially if they were European. There were some fairly good

French and Italian restaurants in Bombay. The population was enormous, and all the people were Hindu. The European population could be seen primarily in some of the newer apartment buildings and some of the better hotels—the one we stayed at had four o'clock tea, including dancing, and they had their own swimming pool. We were in Bombay close to a month.

I remember many trips with my father to the American Express office and the American consulate in Bombay, so by the time the ship arrived we were ready to go. At that point we didn't know that our papers were not in order. For some reason or other, the American consulate didn't realize that my brother's visa was about to expire, and that's what really brought us to Ellis Island.

The boat was the SS *Polk*, for President Polk, part of the President Lines. The trip was from Bombay to Cape Town, South Africa, where we stayed for a day, and then to Trinidad and then New York. That trip was also long. It took about a month, from the beginning of November to the beginning of December.

The SS *Polk* was much larger than the *Barpeta*, and it was very comfortable. It was primarily a passenger ship with all kinds of distractions including a jukebox, which we had never seen before. There was dancing; there were games on deck such as deck tennis and shuffleboard. And we had our [jazz] records, and we immediately had a crowd around us because they all wanted to listen to the same music.

There were mostly Americans and many people from the Persian Gulf region who were in the oil business, either returning from a tour there or maybe just back from a visit with the family. Others were refugees like us. We had a Turkish family on board, some people from Greece, some people from Poland, all escaping the war in Europe.

The ride was quite smooth, except as we approached Cape Town. I remember huge waves, and there were some people who were seasick. We had regular updates as to what was happening in the world. Every morning a news sheet was posted on the bulletin board so we could read the events of the war, and again we were reminded of how fortunate we were to be on our way to America.

I remember one morning my brother woke me up very early and said, "You've got to come out and see this!" and he dragged me up topside. I was still in my bathrobe, and in the distance he said, "Now take a look," and there was the Statue of Liberty, and it was a beautiful sight. We had, of course, seen pictures of it, but you really have no concept of size and grandeur, so that was just marvelous. Of course, beyond the Statue of Liberty was the Manhattan skyline, and that was equally impressive, if not more so. We had seen that in various films in the past, and to be there was just a terrific experience!

At this point we didn't realize that my brother's visa had expired. We thought this would be a formality and it could just be renewed because my visa was intact and we thought the authorities would take a look at this and say, "Well, since everybody's papers are in order, just the expiration of one visa is not going to be a major problem." It turned out to be quite the opposite.

On arrival, as happy as we were to be in New York and a new life for all of us, we were disappointed almost immediately when the immigration officers looked at our papers and realized that my brother's visa had expired and that he would have to be taken to Ellis Island to await processing of a new application.

The rest of us were permitted to land in Manhattan, but my brother was only sixteen years old and we didn't want to leave him on Ellis Island by himself, so we joined him. We spent a little over three weeks there.

Most of our time was spent in the Great Hall. The day we arrived, we were given a physical exam. We were told that my brother's papers would be processed and that we would be advised as to the outcome "in due time." We were given no time frame whatsoever as to when this would happen, so we had no idea how long we'd be detained. We entered the Great Hall and found someplace on a bench that also had a table, and we set up our headquarters there for the next three weeks. [*He laughs.*]

The place was filled. There were people in similar circumstances who had their papers looked at and processed. There were others who had been there for weeks, some for months. Some as much as a year. And there was a feeling of desperation because we had no idea when we would get out, and neither did anyone else. The other feeling was that this being wartime, and the influx of immigrants at such a high level, it was understandable that the United States would be very careful in screening the people that it admitted. And so there was a great deal of suspicion as to who was being admitted, and for that reason also, there was a feeling of privacy that you wanted to observe and not mingle with too many of the other detainees because you had no idea who they were, what their political persuasions were. There were rumors that half the people in the Great Hall were Axis spies or infiltrators so that we kept pretty much to ourselves, except my brother and I had met people our own age and we mingled quite a bit, playing various games such as Monopoly and exchanging pictures we brought along showing what Yugoslavia looked like. And the people we met showed us what various parts of the globe looked like where they came from.

The sleeping arrangements were highly regimented in that women had to sleep in their own dormitory and the men and boys in the other. I think it was the first time that my parents were separated. So it was pretty much a prison atmosphere I would say. And a fairly gloomy atmosphere most of the time.

There really wasn't much to do. We were given permission to walk outside in the courtyard twice a day if the weather was so inclined and even then we had to walk single file and for one reason or another we were not allowed to talk to one another, which was almost like a prison courtyard.

They fed us quite well though. We had not been used to many of the things that we received. I remember that most of the people, being from Europe, had never seen Jell-O before, and when Jell-O was served for dessert hardly anyone touched it, not so much because they didn't like the taste but because they didn't like the wobbly texture of Jell-O. [*He laughs.*] I remember the dining area had long tables where you just sat wherever you could as you marched in. But even that was under supervision. There were people standing around telling us when we had to be finished and leave. We were fed three times a day. Breakfast quite early, I think, because reveille was around seven o'clock or so with breakfast following shortly thereafter. And then lunch I guess maybe at noon, and dinner also quite early, maybe sometime between five and six.

The medical examinations were quite cursory because we all looked in fairly good health and therefore we didn't go through any extensive exams. Others who did not look healthy were checked more thoroughly.

I remember shortly before Christmas they put up a Christmas tree that was already decorated, somewhere near the center of the Great Hall, and it was an object of some criticism for almost everyone because it was not a very merry Christmas and it was almost ironic to have it there because the atmosphere just was not conducive to celebrating the holidays.

I would say three-quarters of the Great Hall was an open space with benches and tables where everybody set up headquarters and kept their bags and attaché cases and other belongings and stayed in the same place every day. The other portion was actually the visiting area, and that was just fenced off by a barrier, and we were allowed to go beyond the barrier and sit with the visitors. But that was the only partition. Visitors came every day in the afternoon. Most of the people were just marking time, not knowing what would happen to them.

We knew one family who came to visit us. In fact, they were very helpful in expediting our departure from Ellis Island. They retained a lawyer for us and also a clergyman, a Catholic priest, who was very helpful, and I think they were able to go to the various offices that required certification, such as the Yugoslav consulate in New York attesting to the fact that indeed we had been Yugoslavs and that my father was a prominent industrialist.

The person we knew in New York was the doctor who actually brought me to life. He was from Vienna and became quite prominent in New York, Bernard Achner. He had a wife and daughter and I remember the frequent visits on their part, and then we became close friends for many years thereafter. . . .

One day, we were told my brother's papers were in order. The reapplication was accepted. There were a number of Ellis Island administrators and employees who circulated among the detainees from time to time, telling them the status of their situation or what was being done and if there was any change. And it was one of these individuals who came and told my parents that finally the papers were in order; we could begin packing to leave. This was a day or two before Christmas, and it was the biggest Christmas present we could have wanted. My parents were absolutely elated because until that point, we didn't know if we would be deported somewhere or if we would remain on Ellis Island for many months.

I remember for days just before that looking through the huge windows from the Great Hall—not just at the New York skyline but also the Statue of Liberty, which was facing the other way. She was showing us her back as if sending us a message. So finally we were on the ferry back to New York, and we could see the face of the Statue of Liberty, and things brightened up. By the time we reached Manhattan, our friends were at the dock. This was the doctor and his wife, and they took us to the Hotel Franconia on West Seventy-Second Street, and we had a suite and two bedrooms, I believe, and a little kitchenette, which was something new in hotels as far as we were concerned. We had never seen a hotel where you could do your own cooking. But this wasn't the only new thing we would encounter. I remember the first night we went to Times Square, and my father took us to a cafeteria and I'd never seen so much food—the trays weren't big enough to hold everything. We had a marvelous dinner, and afterward we went to the Astor Theater and saw *The Great Dictator* with Charlie Chaplin. How timely, right? That was a marvelous introduction, really, because a film like that could not have been seen in Europe at that time. And seeing the spoof on Hitler made us aware that finally we were in the land of freedom. . . .

My parents adapted well here. They began taking intensive English lessons, and my father decreed that from now on we were not to speak any other language but English. And that was quite funny because their English was not as good as my brother's and mine. We often had to say things twice and in different ways in order to be understood, but as soon as we tried saying something in another language they understood—Yugoslav, Czech, German—they quickly shushed us and said, "Only English!" So that was the order of the day, and that remained the order from then on. They really wanted to project being American absolutely.

My father quickly looked at various business opportunities. He was fortunate in that he was able to get money out of Yugoslavia before the war and invested it in a small textile enterprise in Connecticut and later also in Massachusetts. And those became very active businesses, particularly once America got into the war because he was producing a number of materials needed by the armed forces, so he did quite well.

We never saw my grandmother again—my mother's mother. She stayed in Czechoslovakia. We received word sometime during the war, I think it was 1942 or 1943, that she had died after an operation. My aunt, my mother's sister, and her daughter and husband perished in concentration camps, and my uncle and aunt and cousin in Zagreb also perished in concentration camps.

We went back to Yugoslavia for the first time in 1985, some forty-five years after we left. After this trip, I wrote a book about my visit called *Maribor Remembered*, which was published in 1987, and there is a possibility they may make it into a movie. But they all say that, don't they?

I guess I'm in America.

ANIELA SZELIGA
BORN JULY 29, 1919
EMIGRATED FROM POLAND VIA GERMANY, 1949, AGE 29
PASSAGE VIA THE *GENERAL HARRY TAYLOR*

She came from Letownia, a small, predominantly Catholic farming village east of Krakow near the Ukrainian border. She was nineteen years old when late the night of February 7, 1939, Nazi troops stormed her village and abducted her and thousands like her back to Germany to serve as forced labor on work farms to help feed the soldiers of the mounting German war machine. She was liberated by the English in 1945 and spent another four years in an Allied Forces military installation, where she met her husband and gave birth to her daughter, before coming to America with refugee status, eventually settling in upstate New York.

The town was really just a lot of farms, and we worked on a farm. We also made extra money making baskets. All different kinds. They say "Made in Poland" on the bottom. They sent them all over the world. I remember even to Japan. America and Japan were the best customers for us. And we were busy. Almost everybody in town made baskets. There was no factory. Everybody made them in their own home. We had a big room, and my father, my brothers, my sisters, and I all did it. Most of them were made of the wicker—wicker baskets. They were wholesale. We made about a dollar or so per basket. At that time that was big money.

I lived there about twenty years. I grew up in this town. There were about five hundred houses, farms, and they had straw roofs. Our house had about three or four rooms. We had no running water, and there was an outhouse, but we were happy because we didn't know any different. You have enough to eat and are well dressed, and it wasn't really too bad.

The house was made of logs, heavy logs. The house was just one floor. It was heated by a brick stove in one corner. We'd make a fire and then cooked on the top of some kind of iron, not stone, and we baked bread there, too. We got grain from the farm. Whatever we had, we raised ourselves. We would just buy salt and sugar and things like that, but not anything else. We had everything. To store potatoes, we dug big holes in the ground because in winter it was below zero, awful cold, and we covered the potatoes with straw and dirt and then dug out the potatoes as we needed them. They were really nice and crisp. That's how we kept things. And we had a storage room where we kept the grain and milled it to flour. That was a hard job. I was a young girl. Part of it was because there was very little meat. We would butcher one pig, a big one, before Christmas, smoke it, put some salt like salt pork, and that's what we had.

The summers were hot. I remember when I was about seven years old I watched cows and horses in a pasture on a rope. I had about two or three cows and one little calf. And they were so lovely I just hugged them. We would go to school and then come home and work in the field. There were other small children, ages seven, eight; we went in the field to get food for the cows. I mean, like, we'd go in between potatoes and wheat and dig the wheat for the cows. That was really hard work, honest to God.

My clothes were nothing to be proud of, believe me. At least I was lucky: I had shoes. But most children, only wintertime you went to school with the shoes on because it was cold, and when you came home, you had to put the shoes away and just walk barefoot because you had to save the shoes for the whole season. The shoes, most of them were custom made from a cobbler in town.

We went to school like eight o'clock in the morning for half a day, five hours, and so we didn't learn much, you know. There was no high school where I grew up. I had just a sixth-grade education. The school was four rooms. I lived almost across the street, so I walked to the school. But some lived six, seven miles, and they walked even in winter, through the snow, through the fields, to the school. It was just that way.

I had one teacher. And she was a mean one. She was strict.

If you did something they [the teachers] didn't like, they got out a big stick and they punished you [gestures with her hand] and sometimes you'd get it over here [gestures to her back], especially the boys.

We made different kinds of dolls and played hopscotch, different things. We had lots of friends growing up, especially in my home; we were well off compared to others. My best friend, she was very poor, and in her family there were seven children. The mother and father died very young, so the oldest brother took care of them. Many times I stole bread from my home and gave it to her to give to the sisters because I felt sorry for them. They didn't have shoes; they couldn't go to school. That was poverty! But even the old people, they were poor, too. They were undernourished. They had no meat. Maybe they had some bread, some potatoes, but most of the time they were hungry. When I look back now, I think to myself, "My God, what some of these people went through!"

So my mother, she had a big heart, she was a very good woman, and she felt sorry for them. So on Saturday or Sunday morning, she gave me cheese or butter or eggs or flour and milk to bring to the poor people to help them survive. The old, the *babushki* [women who wear head scarves], they said, "Oh, God bless you, child, and may God give you luck in your life, and your mother, too, because she's such a good woman."

Our town was about 99 percent Catholic, and every Sunday we had to go to church. There were no excuses. We did have friends, neighbors, who were Jewish. And they were really friendly with us, but they were so strict about Kosher and what they wouldn't eat. But I was brought up that you had to go to church no matter what. In wintertime some people didn't go because they didn't have shoes. But summertime, all the older women, they went barefoot. They walked about six, seven miles to church, and High Mass lasted about three hours. And there was no pew for anybody, just a cold cement floor, and we had to stand or kneel, very few pews. There were choirs and an organ. This was a big church. It was the only church in town.

My mother married twice to two brothers. During World War I, my mother's first husband was hanged over by the church by about eight men because they thought he was queer, but he wasn't. They hanged him near the church. I have two half-sisters from him.

My mother later married his brother. I was the first child of the second husband. And my father, I'm going to tell you the truth—I don't even want to talk about it with my granddaughter. He was a very strict and mean man. He didn't respect us at all. But my mother, she was an angel.

Fig. 32. Asian immigrants arriving in 1940 at Angel Island—called the "Ellis Island of the West"—in California's San Francisco Bay. Now a national historic landmark and state park, Angel Island processed more than one million Asian immigrants, primarily Chinese, between 1910 and 1940. This photo was taken shortly before the facility closed for good. Photograph used by permission of the National Archives.

Her name was Mary. She was from the next town over. She was a nice-looking woman when she was younger, but after my father, she was worn out. She had a tough life. She lost all her teeth, and there was no way to get [new] teeth, but she was an angel. She wouldn't hurt anybody. She was friendly, talked to everybody, respected everybody, and she was a very good mother. She gave us things which she couldn't have, because we were young, and she said, "You girls, you need it, you take it."

There were five children in the family: two half-sisters from the first husband, and then from the second husband, my father, I was the oldest, and then I had a brother—he was younger—and then the youngest was the sister. But between us children there were no differences.

My grandparents had died except for my father's mother; she lived with us. She died when she was about seventy-eight years old. She wasn't sick. She just lay down and died. She watched us when we were small children, and she was very good with us. She had big pockets in her skirts, and she always had something in them for us. And she said, "When you're good, you're going to get something." So she'd get things for us.

My father took care of the field with the horses and plows, heavy job. But the women, they did much more than the men. They worked in the field, came home, took care of the livestock like milking the cows and feeding every animal, and then cooked. I don't know how they did it. Believe me, they worked about twenty hours a day, summertime anyway.

I peeled potatoes; that was one of my jobs. We had a great big pot to cook potatoes, so I peeled them. And I got the vegetables ready, too. When I got older I worked from morning till night, and then I made the baskets. And then my father, he went to the city with the baskets to sell them, but he didn't bring back much money.

I knew about America because my uncles wrote to my grandmother. And they sent dollars once in a while. One dollar was worth nine or ten zloty, so you could buy an awful lot. One uncle was in New York and one in Massachusetts. But then when my grandmother died, they stopped writing. To me, growing up, America was like paradise.

There was a tavern in town, but the women, they didn't drink, they didn't smoke. They just worked the fields, made baskets, bore babies. But the men, they went to the bar and they got drunk, and they got nasty, mean, and beat up the women, the wives, and children. Oh, God, believe me. It was an awfully hard life.

My father was in World War I in Russia and he said how they almost froze to death, and how he prayed to God there would never be another war again. Well, when World War II came, I remembered his words. I was twenty years old. Everything was shut down, and the people were afraid because the Germans came with tanks and bombs, and the people didn't know where to go.

It was all so sudden. I remember it was February 7, 1939, when the

Germans came and the war started. They dragged thousands of young people away, just picked them up. They dragged us to Germany to work on farms there, but you're a slave, because you don't know if you're going to be alive the next day or not; they might pick you up and put you in a concentration camp and kill you for nothing.

When they first came, they came right away with bombs and bombed part of the town, and many people were killed. After that, there was chaos because they had police soldiers in the fields, and the Germans, they came with the big tanks. They were bad. I can't even describe how bad they were. And then they took the people to Germany, boarding us on trains. They took me on February 7. We stopped in Krakow. I remember it was a high school, and we stayed there, and we slept on the floor for about four or five days, maybe more, and then we came to Germany. It was February 14 when we got to a farm there, and they were waiting for us.

The next day soldiers woke me up. I didn't understand German, but it didn't take me a long time to learn—especially when you're young, especially when you're with them all the time. They [the Nazis] showed me that I'm going to milk cows, clean them, clean the barn, everything. And I said, "Oh, God, I can't." But they forced me. So summertime was really bad. We got up about three o'clock in the morning, and they would knock on the wall of the barn, and we went out to the field—there were eleven of us, all women—and we got food for the cows, came back, fed them, milked them, cleaned the barn, had something to eat, coffee and bread, and back to the field, worked until noon, brief rest, then back on the farm, cleaned the barn again, milked the cows, and we had dinner. I mean, I couldn't say that I was really hungry. I tell myself, "God punished me."

We did have bread in Germany, thank God. And then we finished up and were ready to go on the field and work till about eleven o'clock at night. I was the strongest one, or the foolish one, because I got the men's job: we cut with a [gestures] scythe all day. I don't know how we did it. And then the next day, two o'clock in the morning, the knock on the wall came to get us up.

The Germans didn't take my mother or my father. They didn't get my sisters because they were hiding. They later told me they dug a hole under a barn, but the Germans destroyed it, so they had to keep digging. So every night they slept under the ground because the Germans would come at night and look for people to take away. So she said, "Maybe you're lucky that you went over there. At least you slept in bed." And we did, for over five years. I went to Germany, and my brother went to a farm in Bavaria.

There was no heat where we slept. When you got up in the morning, you had ice on your featherbed because there was no heat. The bed was awful cold. During winter there was this much [*gestures vertically with her arms*] snow on the windows. And the German soldiers and farmers, they had special hot bottles they kept on the stove that they put in the bed before they went to sleep so they got some warmth. But we didn't have any, and you couldn't get any. They wanted work out of us, so they kept us alive. I mean, they fed us. We couldn't eat what we wanted, but at least you've got enough bread.

So we worked on this farm for over five years, and there was a farmer who had seven sons in the war. He was a friendly person, though, because the German people are cold, even to their own. But one son came back from the war briefly, and we asked him, "What's going to happen?" He said, "I shouldn't say this, but we [the Germans] are going to lose the war, and if we do, you'll never get out of this barn alive." That's what he told us. He also said, "If somebody finds out that I told you, I'll be hanged, and so will you," because they were hanging people.

We grew things on the farm for the German troops. They were very strict with the food. But we found a way to hide pigs so we had meat to eat. We wore wooden shoes. Wintertime there wasn't much work on the farm, so they sent us to the forest to cut wood by hand with a big saw, but it was below zero. We brought some food to eat, but the food was frozen. Still, we ate it because we were hungry. And we came back, and there was no heat whatsoever, nowhere except the barn, so we were lucky to come in the barn and warm up a little bit.

There were no Jewish women there. No Jews. Where I was working, there was eleven of us women, different nationalities, POWs: French, Serbian, Greek, Polish, Crimean, Byelorussian. We heard that there were Jews somewhere, but there was some kind of cover-up that there were not.

I remember near the end of the war somebody had a shortwave radio, and they said, "They're losing, they're losing, they're going to lose." It was 1945, and the English came late one night with so many airplanes, the next morning you couldn't even see the sun. And the noise! The earth was shaking! Day and night they bombarded the Germans: boom, boom, boom, boom, boom, boom. I remember it was April 27, 1945, when they came from the sky. . . .

The German people were scared. They knew this was the end. We were happy that we were going to be free. The airplanes were flying very low, so when Germans were not there, we just waved to the English so that they knew that we were there. But when the Germans were there we couldn't do it. We had to lie down on the ground. Then the big tanks came in, and it was the first time in my life I saw a Negro. He was in one of the tanks. He was a big guy with big hands.

We were free! Some of the soldiers spoke Polish, German, but most spoke English, and they said we didn't have to work anymore, that we're going to be free, and they're going to evacuate us. They told us not to work in the barn, but the cows were making noise because they were hungry. They had to be milked. And we did, for the sake of the cows, you know.

The German farmer who owned the farm we worked on, he and his wife were worried for their sons. They were really afraid that something was going to happen to them because they didn't come back from the war. I felt sorry for the ordinary German people because they were Catholics, too. They were afraid. It wasn't easy for them either. They were free too now, but they still suffered as we did. They were afraid a bomb was going to come overhead and kill them.

When the farm was liberated, everybody was so happy. They hugged and shouted, "We are free! We are free! We're going to go home! We're free!" We were there until June, and they took us by truck to the military barracks. We were there for about four years. But after we found out the Communists were in Poland, we said, "We don't want to go home."

The Russians we knew, just regular people, had told us how bad it was under the Communists. But at Yalta, Roosevelt, Stalin, and Churchill made a deal that when the war was over the Russians got Poland. It was impossible in Poland until 1979, when I went back. But my father and my parents were already dead.

I was married in 1945 in September in Germany. His name was Jacob. My first husband. Once a month they [Allied Forces] allowed us to go to church. Not the regular church, but a chapel beside a hospital. That's where I met him. He was Polish, too. Then Genny, our daughter, was born at the military installation in November 1946. . . .

We had to have a sponsor to come to America. My husband had family that lived in Carnegie, Pennsylvania. My husband's uncle. They were our sponsor. But the uncle died suddenly, and we didn't want to be a burden, so we were transferred to my husband's distant cousin on a farm in Richfield Springs, New York.

We took a boat from Bremenhaven, Germany, the *General Harry Taylor*. It was a nice boat; especially because I had a baby, they gave us the officer's cabin. So we were lucky. But the men had to stay with the privates and soldiers upstairs. My first time on a boat, and it was a big boat. From Bremerhaven we stopped in Cherbourg [France], then New York. The ride lasted about ten days. We arrived at one o'clock in the morning at the Statue of Liberty. By eight o'clock they started to process us. We came with very little.

But we felt very safe and very happy to be in America. We had heard so much—that America is good and free, with opportunities for the people who care, who work and save. Some people thought dollars grow on trees. But I knew that you have to work and you have to save, otherwise you'll be poor again.

After inspection on Ellis Island they told us where to go because the sponsors were there to meet us. And they served us donuts [*laughs*] and different things to eat. We were there all day until seven o'clock at night, and then a mini-boat took us to the train station [in New Jersey], and they put us on the train and told the conductor to keep an eye on us because we didn't understand English. We each wore a tag. And then we took the train to Utica, New York. We arrived at twelve o'clock at night, and a farmer was there waiting for us and brought us to the farm [in Richfield Springs].

We slept in an attic, which wasn't my American Dream. Believe me, I cried all night like a baby. Somehow I was shocked. I expected America to be different. It was hot, and that May it was awfully hot—so much so the farmer even sprayed water over the roof to cool it down so we could sleep. At the same time we were grateful that they were good enough to bring us over here. They gave us milk, and things like that, and a roof over our head.

We stayed from May till the following February. Then we moved to Herkimer, New York, and we worked in a furniture factory. There were many Polish people there. My husband was a finisher and I was an assembler. So I put furniture together with a hammer and electric drill and hand drill. I was happy just to make some money. When I got my first check, I said, "Oh, I kiss him, I'm going to put it in a frame." But I couldn't, because I needed money.

In the factory, American people worked there. We were not welcome. You could feel it. They didn't say much, but we were not welcome. Some people, they were already jealous of you, or something. I really don't know. They were not our own people.

When we worked, we got a babysitter for our daughter. She was four years old when we started to work. Then she went to school, which was right there, so there weren't any problems.

I should speak better English. I didn't go to school because I couldn't, because you've got to work, you know? In the home we spoke Polish all the time so that Genny would learn it.

For me, being in America the freedom was the thing: that you can go to church, you can speak, you can write, you can talk. . . . In Poland, people from the cities didn't respect ordinary people from the country, even the priests. Our priest thought he was the Almighty. I found it's not like that over here; you can go to your priest, shake hands, talk freely like I talk to you or to anyone. But in Poland you couldn't, and it was a free Poland when I grew up. But there's freedom—and then there's real freedom. . . .

Several years ago, I went back to Poland to visit for about a month, and when it was time to leave, my sister said to me, "Aren't you sad to go back to America?" I said, "No, I'm not sad. I know I was born here, brought up here, but America is my country now, my adopted country. America is first and Poland is second because America is my bread and butter now and I am happy. I don't complain. I just say, 'God bless America!'"

PART 2

AMERICA'S NEW
IMMIGRANTS

1954–2010

Chapter 7

1950s

This decade saw America make great strides to restore itself as a haven for immigrants. The Refugee Relief Act of 1953, like the Displaced Persons Act of 1948, allowed many refugees, displaced by the war and unable to enter the United States under regular immigration procedures, to be admitted. With the start of the Cold War, Congress passed the Hungarian Refugee Act of 1956 and the Refugee-Escapee Act of 1957, offering a new home to the "huddled masses" seeking freedom, opportunity, and escape from tyranny. The drawback to America's open heart and outstretched arms was public concern that America's postwar policies were too open and let in Communists, subversives, and organized crime figures along with legitimate refugees, which only fueled the paranoia of McCarthyism, characterized by heightened fears of Communist influence on American institutions and espionage by Soviet agents.

KEY HISTORIC EVENTS

★ 1950: The Korean War starts; the Internal Security Act bars admission to any foreigner who is Communist or who might engage in activities "prejudicial to the public interest, or would endanger the welfare or safety of the United States."

★ 1952: The Immigration and Naturalization Act makes the quota system even more rigid and repressive, except for a token quota granted to those from the Asia-Pacific region.

★ 1953: The Refugee Relief Act rescues more than two hundred thousand immigrants who live in Communist countries in

Eastern Europe, including granting visas to more than five thousand Hungarians after the 1956 Hungarian Revolution.

★1954: Ellis Island closes its doors, a symbol of the ending of mass migration; the federal government declares the island "surplus property."

★1959: Fidel Castro becomes dictator in Cuba, his army rolling victoriously into Havana, shortly after which he declares, "Power does not interest me, and I will not take it." Emigration from Cuba spikes.

MIGRATION FLOWS

Total legal US immigration in 1950s: 2.5 million

Top ten emigration countries in this decade: Germany (576,905), Canada and Newfoundland (353,169), Mexico (273,847), United Kingdom (195,709), Italy (184,576), Austria (81,354), Cuba (73,221), France (50,113), Ireland (47,189), Netherlands (46,703)

(See appendix for the complete list of countries.)

FAMOUS IMMIGRANTS

Immigrants who came to America in this decade, and who would later become famous, include:

George Voskovec, Czechoslovakia, 1950, actor
Zbigniew Brzezinski, Poland, 1951, political scientist/statesman
C. L. R. James, Trinidad, 1952, historian
Ted Koppel, England, 1953, broadcast journalist
Patrick Macnee, England, 1954, actor (*The Avengers*)
Elie Wiesel, Romania, 1955, writer/Holocaust survivor
William Shatner, Canada, 1956, actor

Andrew Grove, Hungary, 1957, chairman/CEO of Intel

Rita M. Rodriguez, Cuba, 1957, international financier

Gene Simmons, Israel, 1957, rock bassist (KISS)

Derek Walcott, Saint Lucia, 1958, poet/playwright

Kevork S. Hovnanian, Iraq, 1958, real estate entrepreneur

Benoît Mandelbrot, Poland, 1958, mathematician

Itzhak Perlman, Israel, 1958, violinist

Elisabeth Kübler-Ross, Switzerland, 1958, psychiatrist
  (*On Death and Dying*)

Fred Hayman, Switzerland, 1959, Beverly Hills retailer

Gloria Estefan, Cuba, 1959, singer

Jacques Pépin, France, 1959, chef

AVA RADO-HARTE
BORN FEBRUARY 1, 1941
EMIGRATED FROM HUNGARY, 1956, AGE 15
PASSAGE VIA US MILITARY AIRCRAFT

From an affluent Jewish family, hers is a dramatic story of a mother and daughter and their flight to freedom from Russian Communism during the Hungarian Revolution in 1956. Today, she lives in Miami Beach and serves as the executive director for the Center for Emerging Art, a nonprofit arts organization. Divorced, she has a daughter who lives in Croton-on-Hudson, New York; a son who lives in Forest Hills in Queens; and four grandchildren. "Am I happy?" Her voice cracks with tears. "I am happy. Well, I'm crying now, but I'm happy."

I was born the day Germany bombed England. I emigrated from Budapest, Hungary, in 1956. I was fifteen years old. We came to the United States by plane. It was a military aircraft, part of the US Air Force that was bringing Hungarian refugees to the United States. We escaped from Budapest to Vienna, Austria. Then we got the notice that we were coming to the United States, and we went from Vienna to Munich and were put on an air force plane to Camp Kilmer, which was an air force base in New Jersey. That's where they were processing the Hungarian refugees.

I lived with my mother. I came from an affluent Jewish family, but everything had to go during Communism. With Communism, you're not allowed to be affluent. My mother didn't have to do anything, work, I mean, until 1954, when the Communist government was cracking down on all the Hungarians and if you didn't have a job you were put away somewhere. You had to have a job. So she got a job as an administrator. The Russians confiscated our home. The Russians took everything. Even when we moved into Budapest, it was into a smaller apartment. The Russians divided the apartment into two—because it was too big for a mother and daughter.

The Hungarian Revolution started October 23, 1956, against the Russian Communist occupation and the government. I was in my second year of high school, and me and my friends were gathered near this

Fig. 33. Ava Rado-Harte. Photograph used by permission of Robert D. Jenkins.

famous statue on the banks of the Danube River when suddenly university students and Hungarian revolutionaries took over a nearby radio station, which was about two or three blocks from where I lived.

Then that night and the following day, the Russians came in with tanks and all the military, and there was a lot of fighting and Molotov cocktails. Many people were shot dead on the street. I remember I wasn't allowed to go out until four or five days later. My mother didn't let me go out. And then my girlfriend and I were talking. It was always a dream, a fantasy, to come to America because my mother had sisters in America and my grandfather used to travel back and forth to America in the early

1900s because he was importing and exporting paprika and spices before I was even born. He brought one daughter to America in the 1920s and another daughter came to America in the early '30s, so for me it was always a fantasy to come to America.

My mother's sister used to send all these beautiful clothes and packages filled with things. To me America was the land of fantasy, the land of wealth. One of my mother's sisters lived in New Jersey. They had a 120-acre farm. The other sister lived in Miami Beach, and they had apartment buildings and orange groves. So I told my girlfriend, "Let's escape, let's go to America," and like a good little girl I went home and I told my mother that my girlfriend and I are going to escape and go to America, and one thing led to the other, and my mother wouldn't hear of it. Not that way. She wanted to come, too! She had always wanted to come to America, ever since World War II, when we had to live in a ghetto.

So my mother, my uncles, and cousins arranged for a guide to help us escape. We took a train to a border city near the Austrian border, where we checked into a hotel under the guise that we were going to a pig roast in a nearby town. That night when the train stopped in the town, Russian guards interrogated us, and we said we were going to the pig roast. We checked into the hotel, and after midnight, the Russians came again. They knocked on the hotel room door and wanted to know who we were, what we were doing in the city, and again we told them the same story: we were going to the pig roast.

The following day, we actually did go to the pig roast. It was at the home of a family who had arranged everything for us, and we met the guide there who was hired to take us across the Austrian border. We had to take another small train to a small village on the border, and when we were sitting on that small train, a Hungarian peasant woman with a black dress and black scarves was looking at my mother and me, and she said, "They're walking to their deaths."

Apparently some people were shot in the forest the night before. Of course, my mother's face went white, but nobody said anything. We just sat there, and then when we got off the train, the Russian guards were there again with questions, so our guide had us go to the back of the train and then under the train in the dark to nearby houses and gardens. We were hiding and walking in the dark through gardens and gates until we got to this forest on the border. We were still in Hungary. The Russians set flares to catch the escapees because Hungary was occupied, a Communist country at the time, and the Russians were looking for Hungarians trying to get out. Each time a flare went up, we hit the ground so they wouldn't see us, and the only thing we had was the clothes on our back, and my mother was carrying a man's attaché case which had watches and vodka in it in case we got caught—the Russians always wanted watches and vodka. We were walking a long time through the forest, hitting the ground each time a flare went up. It was me, my mother, her boyfriend, my father's cousin and his wife, and two little kids—I think they were eight and ten years old. I was already a big girl. I was fifteen years old.

My father had died in Siberia. He was in the Hungarian army, and then suddenly Jews were not allowed in the Hungarian army, and all the Jews were carted off to the eastern front and put into labor camps by the Germans. This was 1943–44. And that eastern camp was captured by the Russians, and it didn't matter to them whether they were Hungarians or Jews or Germans—a prisoner was a prisoner—and all the prisoners were taken to Siberia and so my father was in Siberia until 1948, when they had an agreement to let the prisoners go, but he had died. His best friend came back and brought my father's ring to my mother and told us that he was dead.

Back to the forest. So we walked a long time at night in the forest. One time we got lost, and it took a long while for our guide to find our way again. He finally took us to the first place that had a light on when we crossed the border. It was a tavern. I don't remember the name of the town, but there was a tavern, and my uncle took off his wedding band and he gave it to somebody to give us money so he could make a phone call and could call another relative who was living in Vienna, and he made the phone call to Vienna, and the Austrians put us up in a church basement that was set up for refugees.

The Russians could not touch us in Austria; they were not allowed.

Austria was a free country. So once we crossed into Austria we were safe. However, the guide who took us across was arrested. Everybody knew that Hungarians were taking people and smuggling them across the border as escapees for money.

My mother's sister and brother escaped a month after we did, and they were arrested while trying to escape. They went back to Budapest and had to appear in front of a judge, and it wasn't until the second attempt a couple of months later that they were able to get to Austria.

My uncle's cousin from Vienna, who had been the director of the Vienna Opera House, came and met us with two very official, big cars—Rolls Royce, or a Bentley or something—and he put us up for a couple of days at his country home until he was able to find us lodging at a hotel in Vienna. Once we were in the hotel, my mother was able to find the agency that was processing the Hungarian refugees, and we went there and the quota was still open, and considering that my mother had two sisters in America, we were put on the top of the list. I think we stayed at the hotel for about a week to get the paperwork processed, and then they took us to something like a holding pen before they put the people on the plane.

So we were in these military-like barracks for about two or three weeks. Each day, people were waiting for their names to be called to get on the bus that was taking the refugees to Munich because they were flying the refugees out of Munich to America. Some people, of course, were processed to go to Israel. Some people went to Canada. Some people went by boat. It was December 24, Christmas Eve, when our names were called, and it was one of the most beautiful trips.

We got on this bus that took us from Vienna to Salzburg to Munich, and we drove through the mountains and the beautiful snow and saw the Christmas decorations, and literally when we got to Munich airport—I'm going to start crying in a second now that I remember—they played the American and Hungarian national anthems as we were getting on the airplane to come to America. It was very, very emotional. The flight took twenty-six hours. We had to stop in Iceland, and we flew into Newark, New Jersey, I think. I just remember wanting to be the first one off the plane, and I was!

We were taken to Camp Kilmer, an air force camp. We were put in marine barracks. We had them call my mother's sister, my Aunt Alice. She and her son came the next day and picked us up and took us to their farm, and I was put into tenth grade in Freehold High School in New Jersey. I understood English because as a young girl I had to learn English and piano. So I knew how to play piano, and I was learning English all along from an English lady who came and taught me when we lived in Budapest. So I understood some words. I was the first Hungarian refugee at my school, so my picture was in the local newspaper with a caption, something like: "The first Hungarian refugee, Ava Rado, in the tenth grade at Freehold High School. . . ."

We stayed in New Jersey for a month, and my mother, may she rest in peace, decided that we were going to go to Miami Beach to her other sister, which we did. I was put in Miami Beach High School in the tenth grade. I went there for half a semester. We stayed with my aunt for about a month, until my mother—she just didn't know what to do. She didn't want to marry the boyfriend. So what she did was, my aunt knew a friend, and this friend was the mother of a very wealthy husband and wife. They had a winter home on Sunset Island, a very affluent island near Miami; his regular home was in Pittsburgh, and his summer home was in Canada. He was the head of a large trucking company. And the grandmother lived with them, and she said, "Why don't you and your daughter come live with us? You can help me cook" and help their daughter and the husband, who just ran his business, and he played golf. . . .

So we moved to Sunset Island, I went to Miami Beach High, and then came April and we went on his private plane and he flew us all up to Pittsburgh. I went to high school in Pittsburgh, lived with them, and then my mother said, "I can't do this," so we got our own apartment, and since my mother was a good cook, she wound up making Hungarian strudel for Weinstein's Deli in Pittsburgh. While all this was going on, her sister and her brother made it to Austria, but by that time, the quota to the United States was filled. So my aunt and uncle and cousins lived in a camp in Austria provided for the Hungarian refugees for two years before they were finally able to come to America with a visa in 1959 to New York.

So my mother and I moved to New York. My mother knew how to sew, and she had a friend who said, "I can take you into Bloomingdale's, and you can do some alterations." She said, "Yes, sure, I can do it." So she went, she did that for a while, and needless to say, she was really good at it and she wound up becoming the designer assistant to Pierre Cardin and Olivier [Gagnere], and that's how she wound up. She died in 1997.

I went back to Budapest in 1973. I was thirty-two years old, recently divorced, with a son and a daughter, and I said to my girlfriend, "I'm here in America seventeen years, but I want to go back." And she said, "Well, why don't you? I'll watch the kids." That was December 1. By December 3, I had my airline ticket and a passport ready to go, and I didn't even think about applying for an entry visa. For all I knew at that time I could have been turned back. So I got to the airport in Budapest and I said, "I'm here! I'm Ava Rado!" And I came to visit my grandmother, actually my step-grandmother. My real grandmother died in 1943. My grandfather remarried, so I had a step-grandmother. And it was a big emotional moment to knock on her door: "Here I am!" Of course, I called my cousin, my mother's other sister's daughter who stayed there, and she was in a very good position there because her stepfather was the head of the Hungarian auto factory and the biggest Communist and they traveled in diplomatic cars and all that—so I called her and said, "I'm here! Come pick me up!" And she came and she picked me up. In 1973 it still looked like it did in 1956, with many of the buildings still burned out from the revolution. I remember it was very gray, very dim. It was still under Communism, and that was weird for me because after seventeen years of living in freedom in America, I now had to report at the police station as to where I was staying, how much money I brought with me, what I'm spending my money on, etc. That was really weird!

I'll tell you one other thing. I love my life. My life is beautiful. I love where I am. However, I tell you if I didn't have children and grandchildren, I don't know where I'd be living. I say that because that's just a fact. I could live in the mountains with friends. I could live in Russia. I could live in any part of the world. So why am I in Miami Beach? Because I'm still stuck in Miami Beach. That's why I'm in Miami Beach. I had a house in upstate New York, and I just sold that because when I bought the house ten years ago, I bought the house with the fantasy and the dream that my kids would be coming over on Friday nights for dinner and I'm going to have wonderful weekends with the grandchildren and have great Sunday brunches, but the reality is this is America, where families are nuclear families. The parents and grandparents are really not in the picture, not like it was in Europe.

And one of the things that I really miss are the family dinners that we used to have on the farm in Budapest or even at my aunt's house in Miami or at my mother's house when we lived in New York—when all the aunts and uncles and cousins came—and those days are long gone. The new generations don't value this.

So what I have learned is, this is what we have. This is what is. And this is what we have to love. And it's a sad thing to say, but unless I say that . . . [*pauses*], I can't go through life not accepting and not loving what I'm doing and where I am. I have to accept it, and I have to love it.

Am I happy? [*Her voice cracks with tears.*] I am happy. Well, I'm crying now, but I'm happy. I'm fiddling with jewelry, actually.

STEVE KESCHL
BORN AUGUST 20, 1926
EMIGRATED FROM AUSTRIA, 1957, AGE 30
PASSAGE VIA BOAT FROM BREMERHAVEN, GERMANY

He is the longest serving doorman in New York City history. A member of Local 32BJ of the Service Employees International Union, he has been the doorman at 460 East 79 Street in Manhattan for more than fifty consecutive years! The twenty-story apartment building was completed in June 1960, and Steve, then thirty-three, came on as the doorman before the first tenant moved in, and he has been there ever since. Now eighty-three, he is friendly, good-natured, always smiling. He speaks in a thick Austrian accent—his words come out in a short, sweet, staccato. "For thirty-eight years I work six days a week straight," he said. "But they cut me back. I only work five days a week. I'm off Saturdays and Sundays now."

I was born in a straw house, my father's house, in a village called Szent-péterfa, right on the Austrian border but on the Hungarian side. It used to be Austria, and then it fell back to Hungary. So I see myself as more Austrian than Hungarian. My parents and grandparents were Austrian. My name is Austrian, everything is Austrian.

However, my parents met and married here in America, in Northampton, Pennsylvania. They came here when they were teenagers— I don't know what year, before the 1920s. I don't know if they were American citizens. They found each other here; then they made some money and went back home in 1926 to buy land in Szentpéterfa. A rich man was selling his land. I was born that year, 1926.

Within a short time, they returned to America and left me with a nanny, a very good nanny. She took care of me. I never can forget her. A nice lady, and she had her own kids—but she loved me the best. She was Hungarian. We were five together. We were four boys and one girl; they've all since died.

My parents worked, saved, and after five years in America, in 1931 came back home again, this time to build a house on the land they had bought earlier. They had a farm, and we worked the land. They came back with my two brothers: my older brother, Joe, and my younger brother, Frankie. They were born in America. I was the only one who was born in Europe. . . .

Fig. 34. Steve Keschl, in front of 460 East Seventy-Ninth Street, the apartment building where he has worked as a doorman for more than fifty consecutive years. He holds the honor of being the longest-serving doorman in New York City history. Photograph by the author.

I came to this country because there was the Hungarian Revolution in 1956. Before I came to America, I said to Frankie, "Come with me to Vienna and let's register, and we can go to America together." Joe had already come here. And you know what Frankie told me? He said, "If you want to go to America, you can go to America, but I'm not going." Because he loved the farm. He had gotten a house and everything from my father's first cousin when his son died in the war [World War II]. So Frankie stayed. He had a farm, a stable full of animals, and his animals were everything to him. He loved animals and the land. Six acres around the house. He said, "If you want to go you can go, but I'm not going."

When I came to America, I wrote Frankie a letter. We were writing all the time. I said, "It's a good thing you did not listen to me and come here because everything here is so strange," and also, he was not one, like me, to help himself. [*He laughs.*] I don't think he would have been happy here. Because he loved the farm. He was a farmer.

We lived close to the Austrian border. I had heard this one left, that one left. I knew Frankie wasn't coming. So I don't say nothing to nobody. I just went in the house. I had nothing with me. Nothing at all, and I went to the border. To the Austrian border—like from here to across the street. And I went there, and I spoke German, and I said to the Austrian soldier, "What will happen to me if I cross over and I stay?" And he said, "You're here already! You don't have to go back. Don't worry; you'll be taken care of."

So I crossed the border to Austria in '56, and a lot of people knew me there, and I knew this village there very well. And then I heard you had to go to Vienna to register; America would take only so many refugees. There was a quota. I went to Vienna right away by myself—this was New Year's Eve 1956. Then they put us on a train to Bremerhaven, Germany, then a boat to New Jersey, and I came to America.

My older brother, Joe, was already living here in the Bronx. He came to the boat and picked me up. I hadn't seen him in more than twenty years. I didn't know if I would even recognize him, but I did. The boat landed in New Jersey someplace because I remember he came to pick me up there. I don't think it was Ellis Island, though. I was thirty years old when I came to America.

So Joe picked me up on a Saturday, and he said, "You have to rest up a little bit." And I said, "No, I don't want to rest up——I've been resting enough. I want to work."

So on Monday I went to look for a job, and I found one at Horn & Hardart restaurant [the first food service automats in New York City and Philadelphia] on East Fifty-Fifth Street in Manhattan.

The manager knew Joe, so Joe introduced me: "This is my brother. He just came to America and he'd like a job. He'd like to work."

The manager said, "He can start tomorrow."

So two days in America and I start to work!

I was at the restaurant for three years, and then I heard about this brand new building that was going up soon at 460 East Seventy-Ninth Street, and the super of the building said he wanted to see me. He was German. He was also the super of the building next door at 440 East Seventy-Ninth Street. So he managed both, and he told me about the doorman job, and I said to him, "Well, I don't want to quit my job. I have to make sure it's steady."

And he said to me in heavy German, "You do what I tell you to do and you're going to be fine." [*He laughs.*] And that was over fifty years ago! People started to move in in June 1956. I got my green card and citizenship early on.

I stayed here all these years because I like my job, and each time somebody didn't show up, they said, "Steve, don't go home. We need you!" I would stay and work sixteen hours a day. I was always available. How do I do it? You have to love people. Then people love you. I've gone through seven supers; I had no problem with them. [*He laughs.*] Also, I'm always on time. I don't think I was ever late in all these years. [*He laughs.*] I'll keep doing this as long as I'm healthy. Part of it is I cannot stay home. I love to be between the people. So this is my home. I like to go from home to home. I have two homes. One time I was going to work, and I told my wife, "I am going home now." [*He laughs.*]

There's still a few tenants who live in the building from when I started. Most of them did not move out; they simply died. I had a good relationship with everybody, particularly the old-timers. I found my wife here also. The people who introduced us still live here. These people took an apartment when the building opened, and my wife came with them— she was a nanny for their little boy. So they told me about her. A friend said she's Irish. I say, "Oh, no!" Because Irish like to drink!

Turned out she was German. We were married a year later. Her name is Elizabeth. We had one son. He's in electronics. He lives in Long Island. He's married. I have four grandchildren. I don't see them too often. They don't come too often. . . .

Elizabeth and I live in Pelham Bay in the Bronx. I was here in America five years and I bought my house. I have a nice garden. Everybody was jealous! My older brother Joe was jealous. Five years in America and he buys himself a house! I bought it from the previous owner. I asked, "Why do you sell your house?" He said, "Because my wife cannot walk up the stairs." They were an older couple. I said, "I love your house—I'd like to buy it." You know what he says? "You don't have to go to the bank to get a mortgage. The house is all paid off—we'll give you the mortgage!" He said, "If you love this house and you're only in this country five years, you don't have to go to the bank." I told him how much we could put down, because my wife had a little saved, I had a little saved, and that's how we bought the house. And I will stay in that house as long as I live.

. . . My typical day to work, I take the subway straight. I live near the subway. I take the six train, the local, that's my regular train, no bus—but by the time I go home, the local is an express and then I walk home. I never take no buses, no nothing, and from Lexington Avenue, I walk a few blocks to here. When I get home, Elizabeth has dinner ready. My dinner is always ready. She cooks everyday something else usually.

She knows I love soup and cake. That's my secret to a long life: soup and cake! I used to bake, too. I still bake every so often. I used to bring it here to the building; people tasted it. Everybody knows my apple pie. They had a party for me. They say, "Are you going to bring something?" They gave me a few times party, you know? In the building. This last time in May [2010], they celebrated my fiftieth anniversary! And they didn't want me to bake. The party was for me, they said. They will bring the apple pie and they said, "It was good, but yours is the best!"

My favorite soup is chicken soup. Chicken soup I like. My favorite cake is any cake—but especially apple pie. Elizabeth knows how to bake very well. She makes cakes. In German we call it "torte," and the big cakes she bakes, too. If we have parties, she makes cookies and everything she makes. Those are my two favorite things: soup and cake, and it has to be every day. When I went to doctor once, he said, "What kind of medication you take?" I was about forty-nine or fifty years old. I say, "Yes, I take medication. Homemade soup and cake! This is my medication. . . ."

I went back to my village three times in my life. The first time was in the early '70s, when my parents were still alive. I went with my wife and my son. He was three years old. My wife's family is also German, so we went to Germany and then to Austria and then to my village on the Hungarian side. It was so nice to see the people. I still recognized them, and they recognized me.

The second time I went home because my father was going to die soon, so I saw him before he died. My older brother Joe is still alive. He's ninety. He's in Florida now.

The third time I went when my younger brother Frankie was sick, and you know what happened? In a few days I was going to come back to America; he said to me, "Are you counting your days to go back?" [*Serious look, quiet voice.*] He was counting his days to die! [*Choked up.*] I was going to the airport, and I said to him, "I'm going to leave now—I'm going to Vienna to the airport," and then Frankie, he just closed his eyes and he died. [*He cries.*] Just like that. He was seventy-six. The same morning when I was leaving he died. The same morning! He just closed his eyes. Like that.

We were very close. I was his big brother. We grew up together in our village. My parents came from America and brought him back home. So he was born in America but raised in Austria with me. I didn't see him too much because when I came here he stayed in our village. But we were always writing and everything.

I tried, but I could not change my papers at the last minute to stay for the funeral. I had to come back because my time was up on the visa. I said goodbye to him, but I never got to bury him. [*He cries hard.*] I wanted to stay, but I could not change my papers. [*Long pause; then he gathers himself.*] But at least I saw him before he closed his eyes.

JACQUES PÉPIN

BORN DECEMBER 18, 1935
EMIGRATED FROM FRANCE, 1959, AGE 23
PASSAGE VIA THE *ASCANIA*

With a suitcase in each hand, he immigrated to this country in 1959, having been the personal chef of General Charles de Gaulle at the "French White House," and holds the distinction of having turned down a similar position at the Kennedy White House when being "the chef" was at the bottom of the social scale. After two days in America, he found work at New York's famed Le Pavillon restaurant and spent ten years at the Howard Johnson Company. In 1974, he was injured in a car accident and doctors said he would likely not live, much less walk again. Jacques beat the odds and went on to become an internationally recognized French chef, television culinary pioneer, and author of more than thirty cookbooks who, along with close friend and legend Julia Child, paved the way for the success now enjoyed by so many of today's television and celebrity chefs. The recipient of numerous awards, he is among an elite group that has received the Chevalier de L'Ordre des Arts et des Lettres and the Chevalier de L'Ordre du Mérite Agricole, two of the highest honors bestowed by the French government. A master teacher, he has imparted his extraordinary knowledge and experience to students for more than two decades at Boston University and the French Culinary Institute in New York, where he is dean of special programs. A devoted husband and father, he has been married for more than forty years to his lovely wife, Gloria, whom he met when he was a ski instructor and she was his student. "I recently celebrated over fifty years in America," he said. "I came here and loved it, and I never wanted to leave."

I was born in Bourg-en-Bresse, a small town about forty miles northeast of Lyon in France in an area very well known for the chicken, the chicken of Bresse, considered the best chicken in France: blue leg, white plumage and the red cock—so the red, white, and blue colors of the French flag.

I was practically born into the restaurant business. My father was a cabinetmaker by trade, but my mother opened her own restaurant, though she was never professionally trained, and my aunt had a restaurant, a second cousin had a restaurant, another aunt had a restaurant. I'm the first male to go into that business in the family, but often in America people think of the chef in French cuisine as purely male. Now it's true that in the Michelin Guide, most of the twenty-one or twenty-two three-star restaurants in France are [led by] male [chefs], but there are like 138,000 restaurants in France. So most of it is still cooked by women, believe me!

I grew up during World War II. At that time we didn't have any television, we barely had radio, there were no magazines—so we had kind of blinders on. As a result, you do what your parents do. So for me it was either being a cabinetmaker like my father or getting into the restaurant business like my mother, and I was excited about the restaurant business. All the excitement, the people, the noise, I loved it, so I went into that business. I never would have thought in my head I could become a doctor or a lawyer or one of those things; you didn't really stray from your family's business, or go outside the character domain of your family, and so you had kind of blinders at the time. Life was much easier than it is for young people now because, in a way, life was decided for you.

My mom had a very simple type of family restaurant. I remember my brother and I, before going to school in the morning, around seven thirty, we'd go to the market, which was a mile long beside a river. The market opened at three o'clock in the morning and finished at eleven o'clock in

Fig. 35. Chef Jacques Pépin in his private kitchen, in a separate building from the main house, at his home in Connecticut. Photograph used by permission of Melissa K. Coan.

the morning. So my older brother and I, we'd go with my mother with a big bag, and my mother would walk to the market and buy on the way back, trying to get a better price—"Your case of cauliflower won't be good tomorrow. I'll buy it from you for half price"—and that's what she did because every day she had to go to the market and do that. I remember in 1959 at the restaurant it cost one dollar for the price of a meal, or five francs, and that included three or four choices for first course, then main course, a choice of vegetable, a choice of dessert. So you take a dish of each of those to create a menu, you had a carafe of wine with it, you have the bread, you have the service, tax included. One dollar, you know!

So to be able to do it for that, you didn't waste anything at all. Everything was used. And that kind of approach is reflected in my own cooking. I am very miserly in the kitchen, maybe because of that. Certainly we were used to saving money. We waste so much food here [in America], you know? When I go to a restaurant, I first go to the garbage to see what it is, and I'm amazed!

As I say, I grew up during the war. I remember my father disappearing to go into the Resistance. One time the Germans came to our house, and he jumped through the window and disappeared for like two or three years. He would appear occasionally and bring us food, sardines or something, because he had a wife and three kids.

We lived near the bridge of Lyon, the big bridge next to the railroad station—so it was an official point, a targeted area, and the bombardment started with the Italians throwing a bomb on the station there, and it blew out part of our house. Well, my father was gone in the Resistance. My mother was working in the restaurant with my grandmother. Fortunately we were all in the garden that day, so no one was touched, and we stayed with a cousin while the house was repaired. Remember, there was no telephone at that time, so my father would reappear, and all of a sudden he had come back to the house and we were not there, so he tried looking for us at some cousins' house.

We got blown up three times. The second time it was the Americans, who blew out the railroad as well as the same side of the house the Germans blew out, but we were not in the house either. The third bombing was when the Germans left France at the end of '45—they blew out the

Bridge of Lyon, which blew out part of the house—so three times we were blown up, but three times we were not there, so we were lucky. But my father—it's probably why he had a heart condition—came back three times to find part of his house demolished. [*He laughs.*] Certainly I remember the Americans as well, running after the American tank, which was my first experience with chocolate and chewing gum which got thrown out of the tank by the GIs. I had had chocolate before the war, but I was too small to remember it.

For primary school education, you had to go to school until age fourteen to pass, and I was in that class when I was twelve, so I was way ahead in class and my brother was too. My brother became an engineer.

For me, I asked for a dispensation and took all of the exams when I was barely thirteen and went into apprenticeship as a chef because this is what I wanted to do. It's not because I couldn't study in school. I was doing quite well. But I knew from the beginning this was what I wanted to do.

At that time, my mother had a restaurant where she lived, in a suburb about seven, eight miles south of Lyon, and I left home when I was thirteen and returned to Bourg-en-Bresse, where I was born, and went into apprenticeship at Le Grand Hotel de l'Europe, which was considered the best hotel there. The chef there had actually gone to school with my mother, so she knew him, and so he took me in as an apprentice. There were four apprentices, and it was a three-year apprenticeship where you work seven days a week with no days off. You start at seven or eight o'clock in the morning and work until about ten at night, and at the end of the month you had four days off, so if there were four weeks in a month, I could take my clothes, my chef jacket, hat, pants, my apron, my towel, the sheet off my bed, everything back to my mother for her to wash and then bring them back. I would go back and forth to Lyon once a month.

When I finished my apprenticeship, I went to work for the season, a summer job, at L'Hôtel d'Albion, a lakeside spa town in the Alps. It was a big hotel where you worked four months of the season, seven days a week, no stop because this is the season. I came back to work in Lyon at a restaurant for a couple of weeks before going to Bellegarde, which is a town close to Geneva, a small town where I became the executive chef for the winter at L'Hôtel Restaurant de la Paix, which was something, considering I was not quite seventeen. In truth, though, except for the dishwasher, I was alone in the kitchen. The son-in-law of the owner who was the "real" chef spent most of his time in the nearby ski resort of Chamonix, plus the winter was pretty slow in sleepy Bellegarde, so the owner of the hotel took me on as the chef. I was there for about five or six months during the winter, returned to Lyon to work for awhile at a local landmark restaurant, and then I went to Paris. I was seventeen.

I had never been to Paris, but I told my mother I had a job which I didn't have, so I took the train. When I got there, I went to La Société des Cuisiniers de Paris, meaning "Society of the Chefs of Paris," sort of like an employment center for chefs, and you can go there in the morning and you give your name to become a member. Then you're classified as second or first company, or *chef de partie* [also known as a "station chef" or "line cook"], or whatever your position, your age, where you've worked, and then they get you a job for the day. You work a job maybe three days, four days—sometimes a month or more—so there was always a job. In the morning, for example, you have a restaurant, a brasserie, and the chef doesn't come, or something happened, the restaurant calls La Société. I don't know why a place like this does not exist in New York, which has something like eighteen thousand restaurants, because it would be very useful.

So I worked in a lot of restaurants before working at the Hôtel Plaza Athénée on the Champs-Élysées. I pretty much worked there the longest time of any place that I worked. I worked at the Plaza Athénée for over six years. I usually worked on my day off, and very often during vacation time I went to La Société again to make extra money, so I probably worked in over two hundred restaurants in Paris on my days off.

In 1956, I was called into military duty. Usually they sent you to the army or sometimes to the air force, less so the navy, except for cooks—La Société had an arrangement with the navy to provide them cooks. In France, if you work on a destroyer, for example, you will have a petty officer to go with you to the market. You will have only so much money per day, so they want a professional who knows how to budget, buy, and it's not like the whole navy eats the same thing—they eat whatever the chef cooks that day, maybe something special like lobster for Christmas or the fourteenth of July [Bastille Day], so you really have to save your money. I was sent in the navy to boot camp in southwest France, and it was during the Algerian War, and then I went to do marine training. I was in good shape, so I was sent for military training, and I was supposed to go to Algeria in the marines, but I could not be sent at that point because my brother was there at the same time, so I ended up not going.

I was sent back to Paris to the admiral's mess in the center of Paris because I had worked at the Plaza Athénée [and] Maxim's. Then I had a friend from Lyon who I met there, and he was the chef of the secretary-treasurer, but he had never worked in Paris, and he said, "I would appreciate it if you would come and help," because he was making dinner for the secretary of state and other people, and he said, "I'm not really that good in classical cuisine," and I said, "Fine." I had a room in town, so I was kind of free. And I started doing dinners for them at the Treasury, and then my friend was released from the army, so they asked me to stay on. The government was going through many rapid changes at the time. The prime minister then had all the power in France. The president of the republic was like the Queen of England—he didn't have any power before General Charles de Gaulle changed the constitution from the Fourth to the Fifth Republic, so with all the changes I ended up as "First Chef" of the prime minster at L'Hôtel Matignon, which was, and still is, the residence of the French prime minster. Then the government changed again, and it was at that time that de Gaulle came back to power, so I was there and stayed on with de Gaulle.

I admired him. To start with, de Gaulle was like six foot five. He was thin and tall, and he was practically blind, so he'd always look at you this way [sideways], so he appeared even more important, even though he couldn't see anything. [*He chuckles.*] His wife was very small. During the time I was with de Gaulle, I served heads of state like [President Dwight] Eisenhower, [President Josip Broz] Tito, [Prime Minister Harold] MacMillan, so as the chef it was a great experience. But it was a totally different world then than it is now because at that time the chef would be in a hole somewhere. You would never be called to get kudos or complimented or applauded or whatever. That did not exist, period. Never once. They didn't even know who was in the kitchen!

I saw General de Gaulle twice a week to do the menu for the week and especially for the Sunday meal after church when they held a dinner—the children, grandchildren, and so forth—but at that time, the president just went through the kitchen, said hello, and that's about it. You never had any kudos or compliments or anything like this. There was no publicity of any kind, so certainly that was one of the reasons that I didn't go to the White House later on: because I had no inkling of the possibility of publicity and the promotional value of this because it didn't exist. A cook by definition at that time was in a black hole somewhere, and that was it. I was used to being invisible. . . . You work with a young chef [now] and they want to find their dish; they want to create and find what they want to say. When I was in the kitchen, the idea was to work in a great house like the Plaza Athénée or Maxim's in Paris and to try to do it exactly the way it was always done in that house. So that the lobster soufflé, for example, at the Plaza Athénée—which was pretty famous— well, any one of the sixty cooks in the kitchen could have done it and not known the one who had done it. So the idea was to identify yourself with that, rather than now [when] it's the opposite; to detach yourself from that and be different or peculiar or whatever, which is another training altogether. [*He laughs at the irony.*]

By 1959, I wanted to come to America. Everyone wanted to come to America! And at that time there was more of a difference than there is now. I figured I would go, work for a couple of years, learn the language, and come back. I wasn't married. I could literally do whatever I wanted, and although my mother would have liked me to work in her restaurant and stay in France, I also had a friend at the Plaza Athénée who knew a pastry chef who worked in Chicago somewhere that led me to someone named Ernest Lutringhauser, a guy from Alsace with a restaurant in New York called La Toque Blanche, or "The White Hat." He came on vacation every year to Paris, so I corresponded with him, and we met and he said, "Yes, absolutely, I can sponsor you if you want to work in the States." At that time it was pretty easy because according to the law in the United States there was a quota. They accepted only so many immigrants from different countries every year, and the quota for France was never filled, as opposed to, say, Italy, where almost a third of the population immigrated in the 1930s and there was a huge waiting list going back eight, ten years before you could come to the United States with an immigrant visa, but France? No.

I went to see someone in the de Gaulle cabinet who said, "Go see Mr. Wood at the American Embassy. I'm going to give him a call and give him this letter." Well, Mr. Wood happened to be the vice consul at the American consulate.

I had my green card in three months! It was the spring of 1959. I waited, I think it was ten days after the six-month limit that I had to leave because I wasn't ready to leave that fast!

I came on a student boat. Actually, my parents took me to Le Havre and I took the *Ascania*, which was an old converted luxury boat that was bringing home something like twelve hundred American students who were studying in Russia and all over Europe. It took thirteen days to come to Quebec, and everyone was singing and playing guitar late into the night, and it was the end of the fifties. . . .

From Quebec, I took the train to Montreal, and from Montreal, I took the train to Grand Central Station in New York. I arrived with my two suitcases [*laughs*] and went straight to that man who had sponsored me. He put me up at a YMCA for two weeks until I found a room. In the meantime, he introduced me around. With the background I had, there was no problem finding a job. I came here on the tenth of September 1959, and a couple of days later I was working at Le Pavillon, which was the best restaurant in the country at the time, and a week later I was enrolled at Columbia University.

I went to Columbia to learn English for foreign students. I took an entrance examination, and I did fairly well, considering that I had been studying in Paris for like six months at a private school before I came here, and considering that I had no ear at that point. I couldn't understand anything people were saying. So I ended up in an intermediate class for English, and then I went on to another class and then another class for about two years until I got to what they call "English for Freshmen."

I spent twelve years as a student at Columbia. I went from 1959, two or three years of English for foreign students, and eventually went into the regular college. At that time, there was no formal culinary degree. Didn't exist. I got a BA in 1970 and then went on to graduate school. I got my master's in '72 in eighteenth-century French literature, and I was working on a PhD, and I had finished the requirements for that, and I wrote my dissertation proposal, but they rejected what I wanted to write about. I had thought about quitting the kitchen and becoming a teacher, a university professor, because I loved literature, so I thought, why not combine the two? And I proposed a doctoral dissertation on the history of French food within the context of civilization and literature starting with the playwrights and poets of the sixteenth century, and they said, "Are you crazy? Food? This is too trivial for academic study. . . ." So it was at that point I had enough. I said, "Fine."

It's interesting because this is what I teach now at BU [Boston University]. We're offering a master's of liberal arts with a concentration in gastronomy, and this is the class that I have given for several years now. Ironically, two weeks ago, I gave the commencement address at Columbia for graduation, and the president of the university, a friend of mine, introduced me and said, "Considering that Jacques was refused to write his dissertation here because of his subject, which would really be appreciated like now. . . ." So it's true: things have changed. It's another world.

My mother loved it here. Each time she came here she absolutely loved it, and she had her green card even though she wasn't living here. She'd come for three months, sometimes teach a couple of classes here, and each time she had to go back, she had to do a tax assessment. Even with a green card you have to pay your taxes before you leave the country. So each time she would come, it was like a nightmare for her to fill out those papers. She hasn't been here in the last few years. My mother is still alive. I spoke with her yesterday, actually. She was ninety-five a few weeks ago [in 2010].

Le Pavillon was a great restaurant, but for me, with the training I had in France, I didn't think it was that great, frankly. I thought it was good, but I had not worked in any other restaurant here, so I could not really make a comparison. In the spring of 1960, Pierre Franey, who was the executive chef there, had some problems with the owner, Henri Soulé, and it turned out that we all left.

A patron of Le Pavillon was Howard Johnson, the man who created the company, and he told Pierre, "You're going to work for me one day."

So eventually he asked Pierre to go work with him. Pierre had been in this country a long time because he came for the World's Fair in 1939, so he had been here more than twenty years. It was a time when Kennedy clan used to come to Le Pavillon. It was usually led by Joseph P. Kennedy, the father, and then of course everyone else; he was the man running the show. And at that point they came in spring 1960 to discuss the campaign or whatever, and they were always seated at La Royale, which was the best table and most visible one in the restaurant, and at that time a photographer snuck in and started shooting pictures of them. Martin Decré was the maître d of the restaurant, who the Kennedys knew well because they came there almost every week, and Joseph Kennedy said, "Martin, get that guy out of here!"

Soulé was at another table and overheard. Soulé was like Napoleon there. [*He laughs.*] "Decré! You will do no such thing!" Soulé said. Every head in the restaurant turned. "It's only Soulé who decides who stays or who doesn't stay at Le Pavillon," or something to that effect, some disparaging remark. He said it like, "Who do you think you are? You think you are already in the White House?"

The Kennedy clan left and never returned to Le Pavillon.

So at that point it also happened that the brother of Martin Decré, Fred Decré, was with Robert Meyzin, the general manager of La Côte Basque, which belonged to Soulé too. The two of them left to open Le Caravelle, so that was a big blow to Soulé. Roger Fessaguet, who was the sous chef at Le Pavillon, also left Pavillon to become the executive chef at Le Caravelle. Roger asked me to go with him there, and the whole Kennedy clan moved to Le Caravelle.

So a couple of months after that, Joseph P. Kennedy spoke to Robert Meyzin, now the owner of Le Caravelle, and said they needed a chef at the White House. So Roger Fessaguet, who was the executive chef, called me and said, "You should go there. I gave them your name, and they are looking and they are very interested."

Meanwhile, Pierre Franey asked me to join him at Howard Johnson's; he needed an assistant. He made an appealing offer, and I said, "I don't know." Pierre didn't tell me the White House would be a great thing for me, so it didn't really push me to go there, and for me, as I said before, because of the experience that I had in France, having been chef of the "French White House"—where I had never been in a newspaper, television didn't exist [for up-and-coming chefs], it had no bearing on my life. So I said, "I am starting at Howard Johnson's," which was another world altogether, and I was at Columbia so I really didn't want to go to Washington, DC, and so I said no to the Kennedy job. They called me again a month later. They said they had looked at a couple of other people, and I said no again. With twenty-twenty hindsight you realize the possibility for publicity, but at that time I was totally unaware of it. Also, with Pierre, there was no limit to what we could do. Howard Johnson said we had to approve the food, so we started cutting down the dehydrated onion and put fresh onion, replacing margarine with butter, and started doing things like beef burgundy or whatever, and I started doing five pounds in the kitchen, and then I'd do fifty pounds, and in the kettle outside, two hundred pounds, and eventually three thousand pounds at a time. I worked with two chemists, and that's when I started learning about the chemistry of food about bacteria and quality control and so forth.

During that time, I was going to Columbia, so it was great. I worked at Howard Johnson's from seven o'clock in the morning to three in the afternoon in Queens Village near Jamaica, and then I went to college. I stayed with Pierre Franey for ten years, and then I left to open a restaurant on Fifth Avenue called La Potagerie with a group of investors. And I would not have been able to do that if I hadn't had the training at Howard Johnson's and was doing large production type of things. And then eventually, as a consultant, I set up the commissary at the World Trade Center with Joe Baum [who owned celebrated New York restaurants such as the Four Seasons, the Brasserie, and the Rainbow Room], and again, I would not have been able to do that if I hadn't had the training at Howard Johnson's. Even after, I was a consultant for the Russian Tea Room, the same way too. Howard Johnson's was a long American apprenticeship, but quite valuable for me. . . .

I met Julia Child in 1960 when I was at Le Pavillon. Craig Claiborne came, and he had just started at the *New York Times* as a food critic. He came to do a piece on Pierre Franey, and I met Craig, and we became good friends right away. I lived on Fiftieth Street. Craig lived on Fifty-Third Street, and he introduced me to Helen McCully, who was the food editor at *House Beautiful*, and she was very feisty and very well known in this country at that time, and she had never been married, never had kids, so she kind of became my surrogate mother: "Don't wear this, don't do that, do this, do that," fixing me up with all the girls in the office [*laughs*], and through Helen I met James Beard, and then in the spring of 1960, Helen told me, "You know, I want you to look at a manuscript." She showed me a manuscript for a cookbook, and she said, "The author is a woman from California, and she's coming to New York next week. She's a big woman and has a terrible voice. She's going to come, so let's cook for her." And that was Julia, but no one knew Julia because she had never done a book, so she'd never done television and was totally unknown. But what I want to say [is] within six to eight months after I was here in America, I knew the trinity of cooking, which was James Beard, Craig Claiborne, and Julia Child. So the food world at that time was quite small, extremely small, as opposed to today—it's another world altogether. And certainly the status of the chef, which, at that time, was considered uninspired and very low on the social scale, but now we are genius! [*He laughs heartily.*]

It has changed a great deal. In my early days, any good mother would have wanted her child to marry a lawyer or a doctor or an architect, but not a cook! But now, as I said, WOW! We are genius, you know? [*He laughs.*]

So I knew Julia because of Helen, and I started doing articles for *House Beautiful*, and then eventually I was asked to do a book, *La Technique: An Illustrated Guide to the Fundamental Techniques of Cooking*. I had finished at Columbia. I decided not to do my PhD. I didn't know at that time whether I was going to move into academia. Like many of us who are artisans, we have a bit of a complex about not having much of an education. Well, at that time at least, the study I did at Columbia prevented me from having a complex about not having an education. I could see that even at Howard Johnson's. They had college kids who graduated from Cornell [University's school for hotel and restaurant management], and Pierre Franey would be a little bit intimidated by them because they were college graduates, when they knew absolutely nothing about the food world and when Pierre was a much brighter person. But they couldn't do that with me because I had graduated from Columbia and they had absolutely no knowledge of food whatsoever, so it did change my view of many things, and I don't think that I could have done what I did in life if I hadn't studied at Columbia.

In 1974, I had a very bad car accident. I had fourteen fractures. I broke my back, my two hips, my leg, my pelvis. I wasn't supposed to live; I wasn't supposed to walk. So that was certainly a catalyst to start pushing me in the direction of writing about food, and coincidentally, at the time cookware shops with little cooking schools attached to them started opening up all over the country. When I went to the West Coast, I would go to a school for three weeks in San Francisco and another week in Los Angeles and another week in Eureka, California, and then they'd say, "We booked you for next year," so I had a schedule like that for forty weeks a year, selling books all over the country and doing cooking classes and all that. I was the first. I was there when it started.

So that led to appearances on television, a morning show here and there, and I had already started with Julia on PBS in '62 or '63 after she did her book *Mastering the Art of French Cooking* and she said, "I don't want to do it anymore. You should do it." So I saw some people at WNET in New York, WGBH in Boston, and they wanted to do it. They had to raise money, and I did a couple of shows, and one thing led to another. And eventually I did a series in Jacksonville, Florida, in '82 in conjunction with a book, and eventually I started doing them at KQED in San Francisco and have to this day. A series is thirteen shows. Each time we do a double series, or twenty-six shows, which is about 130, 140 recipes, so that's what makes a book. That's why I have so many books: because I do a series with each one. I think we've done something like thirteen series of twenty-six shows for KQED since 1989, I believe. My daughter Claudine and I have also done a bunch of shows together, and we're still doing them.

I hooked up with KQED in San Francisco because they asked me there, and because they raised the money. I'm part of the rostrum there, and that's it. They've always raised the money for me. I mean, if you look at Lidia Bastianich or Ming Tsai or Mario Batali or most of the chefs who are on television now, they are all executive producers of their own shows, but they have to raise the money or get involved in it, and I have never done that. If I had to, I wouldn't know where to start! So they [producers at KQED] raise the money for me, and I don't need to be executive producer because I'm the one who decides on the content of the show anyway. I do the recipes. No one can decide for me what I'm doing. So I am, in a sense, the executive producer, except that I don't have to raise the money, which—if I had to raise it, I would probably never do television again! Why? Because it's another world and I'm not good at that, calling people.

In addition to this, I never went to the Food Channel Network or others, although they asked me several times, because they wanted me to go with them, but they wanted me NOT to be with PBS at the same time, which I didn't like. And Julia and I were very happy with PBS because we don't have to kowtow to the sponsor or endorse any product. In fact, I don't have the right to endorse any product, so that makes it much easier—so I can focus just on being a chef.

What happened was Julia lived in Cambridge in Boston, and she bought a house there in 1949, I believe, so by the time I started teaching at BU, which was in '82, each time I would call and see Julia. I would have breakfast at her house or lunch, or we'd go out for dinner at night because she was very good friends with the person in charge of the BU program. So we decided to do a class together at BU, and almost from the beginning, the two of us were onstage doing demonstrations and it was great fun. And at some point I said, "I think we should do a special for PBS," so we did a thing at BU called "Cooking in Concert," which was three hours of us cooking on stage with a big audience, maybe five hundred people, which they taped as an hour-and-a-half special for PBS. This was the summer of 1982, and it ended up being one of the most watched cooking shows on television ever. Remember, the Food Channel Network didn't exist yet, so this was great. We continued doing classes together and doing more appearances together, and we said, "Let's do another one." So two years later we did another "Cooking in Concert" special for PBS, and that was the catalyst or the genesis for the shows with Julia in the midnineties. Julia was around eighty-five at the time.

I was always friends with her, ever since we met in 1960. I mean, we argued all the time [*laughs*], but we were really good friends. People don't realize. They say, "Were you impressed when you met Julia?" Well, no.

When I met Julia she'd never done a show; she hadn't done anything. I remember the first time we met at Helen McCully's, we actually spoke French. Her French was better than her English. She had just arrived from Paris. She had been working there for five years. She went to Le Cordon Bleu. She knew all those chefs in Paris, and she already joked that we started cooking together because she came to Paris in 1949 and I was in apprenticeship in 1949—of course, I was only thirteen years old. In the movie *Julie & Julia*, the part that related to Paris was really truly the way it was and the way I remember it because it was the same time when I was in apprenticeship that she was in apprenticeship. That's why that show took place from 1949 to 1960, when she did *Mastering the Art of French Cooking*. . . .

I am celebrating more than fifty years here. One of the reasons I stayed in America is because I thought the people were so nice—the easiness of life here, as opposed to Europe and the class system there, which was much more strict. People who come to this country come to get a better life, a better economic life, a better job, or because of political reasons or racial reasons or whatever, which was not my case at all. I had a very good job in Paris. I had family. So I didn't come here for a particular social or economic reason. I came here just to see. I loved it, so I stayed.

But America is different than it used to be. At that time, people would tell you how great you were; there was a humility. Now? It's "We are the greatest, we are the best, we are the strongest, and if you're not the greatest, not the best, oh my God, you're not American!" People have become so macho in this country! That did not exist before. People were not macho like that, and I don't know why it turned.

The face of America is quite different, too. I mean the social or the ethnic face of America is different than it was fifty years ago. If I were to advise someone about coming here, I would say the first duty is to learn the language! I came here and I learned the language! I didn't come here to speak Spanish or French or another language. That's kind of ridiculous. The language here is English and I intend to speak English, you know? And if you are here, whether you come from South America or any other place in the world, you should speak English! You don't come here to speak Russian—although people would not because there are not that many Russians or that many French or whatever. But if there *are* that many Spanish or that many Chinese, and [they] are in a certain enclave area of the country, you still have to speak English.

I would never move back to France because I'm much more American than French now. When I go there now I feel like I'm in another country, in a way. I feel kind of claustrophobic in Europe. I mean, the scale is different and the mentality is different. After fifty years here, I've become totally American. It would be difficult for me to live there. Contrary to many of my friends, it took them quite a number of years to decide if they were going to stay in this country and retire in France. For me, I have never had that hesitation. I came here and loved it and never wanted to leave. . . .

My greatest pleasure now is cooking with friends. Cooking for the family. It all amounts to this, you know? Enjoying life is this. Like yesterday. Some friends came. We played boules [a game played with metal balls popular in France and Italy] for two hours. We drank five bottles of wine, and we cooked dinner together, and I did that the day before yesterday, too. I did lobster, corn, coleslaw. They did a book a few years ago which was about our last meal, and they asked fifty chefs what their last meal would be, and I said if you have extraordinary bread and extraordinary butter, it's hard to beat bread and butter. [*He laughs.*]

I don't know if there is one thing in particular I'm more proud of. I can't really think of any big disappointment. I did more or less what I wanted to do, you know? [*He pauses.*] Life has been good. I have done many things. I have been very lucky in many ways. Certainly, I feel lucky to do what I was able to do—so many books and TV shows. I have done more than I ever dreamed I would do. I love to paint; I even have some of my paintings in a museum. I'm very proud [*more softly*] of our life together, Gloria and I. We've been married so many years, more than forty years, since 1966, so that's a long time. And my daughter Claudine, I'm proud of her. She can get me crazy; she studied at BU for her BA, and then went for a master's in political science, and then dropped the whole thing and married a chef and gives some cooking classes. They have a child [*pauses, smiles*], so I'm a grandpa. That's good, too!

Fig. 36. In the wake of Fidel Castro's rise to power, Cubans who managed to escape are processed as refugees at an American Red Cross installation in Port Everglades, Florida, May 24, 1963. Photograph used by permission of the Statue of Liberty National Monument (National Park Service).

Chapter 8

1960s

The 1960s were a historic decade for immigration, as America's current system of legal immigration dates back to that time. In 1965, Congress amended immigration law by supplanting the national origins quota system with a preference system designed to reunite immigrant families and attract skilled workers. This change in national policy meant that the majority of applicants for immigration visas were now coming from Asia, Mexico, and Central and South America, rather than from Europe. It marked a radical break with previous immigration policy and has led to profound demographic changes in America. But that's not how the law was viewed when it was passed at the height of the civil rights movement, during a period when the ideals of freedom, democracy, and equality had captured the nation.

KEY HISTORIC EVENTS

★1960: Cuban refugees paroled into the United States.

★1962: Special permission granted for admission of Hong Kong refugees.

★1963: President Kennedy urges Congress to pass new legislation eliminating the national origins quota system.

★1965: President Johnson signs into law the Immigration and Nationality Act or Hart-Celler Act, a historic immigration bill because it abolishes the restrictive national origins quota system, which established country-by-country quotas that discriminated against southern Europeans and Asians. The new measure provides for admission on the basis of skills and family reunification.

★1966: The Cuban Adjustment Act provides permanent residence for Cubans admitted into the United States after January 1, 1959.

★1969: President Nixon signs a bill amending the Immigration and Nationality Act by removing its prohibition against acquiring citizenship within sixty days prior to a general election.

MIGRATION FLOWS

Total legal US immigration in 1960s: 3.22 million

Top ten emigration countries in this decade: Mexico (441,824), Canada and Newfoundland (433,128), United Kingdom (220,213), Germany (209,616), Cuba (202,030), Italy (200,111), Dominican Republic (83,552), Greece (74,173), Philippines (70,660), Portugal (70,568)

(See appendix for the complete list of countries.)

FAMOUS IMMIGRANTS

Immigrants who came to America in this decade, and who would later become famous, include:

Yo-Yo Ma, France, 1960, concert cellist
Carlos Santana, Mexico, 1960, rock guitarist
David Byrne, Scotland, 1960, musician (Talking Heads)
Seiji Ozawa, Japan, 1960, conductor
Plácido Domingo, Spain via Mexico, 1961, tenor/conductor
Andy Garcia, Cuba, 1961, actor
Zubin Mehta, India, 1961, conductor
Oscar de la Renta, Dominican Republic, 1963, fashion designer
José Canseco, Cuba, 1964, baseball player

David Ho, Taiwan, 1964, AIDS research pioneer
Peter Jennings, Canada, 1964, broadcast journalist
John Cleese, England, 1965, actor/comedian
Wayne Wang, Hong Kong, 1966, film director
Neil Young, Canada, 1967, singer-songwriter
Eddie Van Halen, Netherlands, 1967, electric guitarist
Leonard Cohen, Canada, 1967, singer-songwriter
Arnold Schwarzenegger, Austria, 1968, actor/politician
Deepak Chopra, India, 1968, self-help guru
Emilio Estefan, Cuba via Spain, 1968, music producer
Daisy Fuentes, Cuba, 1969, model
Dave Matthews, South Africa, 1969, singer-songwriter

Fig. 37. Actor Andy Garcia (*The Godfather Part III, Havana, Ocean's Eleven* series) emigrated from Havana, Cuba, with his family in 1961, when he was five years old. They arrived in Miami. Photograph used by permission of Greg Gorman.

IRIS GOMEZ
BORN JULY 28, 1955
EMIGRATED FROM COLOMBIA, 1960, AGE 5

She emigrated from Cartagena, Colombia, when she was five years old and grew up in New York and Miami. Out of five siblings, she is the only member of her family to go to college. Today she is a nationally recognized public-interest immigration lawyer in Boston, an expert on immigrants' rights who has frequently lectured on the subject. An accomplished writer, she is the author of two poetry collections and the recipient of a prestigious national poetry prize from the University of California, and she recently published her first novel, Try to Remember, *which draws on her personal experiences growing up as a Latina in Miami and her experiences as an immigration lawyer. "There's nothing more rewarding than feeling like you're able to earn a livelihood by helping others who are in more difficult circumstances than yourself," she said. "I really believe that's the greatest way to have meaning—to feel that when I leave this world, I will have hopefully done something to have made it a little bit better for others."*

I was born in Cartagena, Colombia, right on the Caribbean coast, one of the most beautiful cities in the world. I lived there until I was five years old, and my extended family continues to live there. I was just back recently, and I brought my kids and my husband, and it's much developed now in the sense that the old colonial buildings, its heritage really, were all cleaned up, repainted, and propped up so that they would endure. But it's still preserved—its beautiful colonial character, and the balconies and the narrow streets with beautiful poetic names and the walls that go around the city. The Spanish built many of the forts in a similar way as in Cartagena, a very similar style of architecture.

We came to America in 1960. We came by plane. My father had come the year before and gotten a job in the New York City area. And so when we first arrived, he and an uncle were already working, so we emigrated the following year and made our way through several different housing arrangements until we finally got an apartment in Queens. My father worked in factories that probably no longer exist.

Unfortunately, when it came to learning English, I had to sink or swim when we first arrived in New York. I went to school, and I'll never forget the first days, just sitting there and not understanding anything that was going on except for people's gestures. Sometimes I think maybe

Fig. 38. Iris Gomez. Photograph used by permission of Susan Wilson.

it made me a better writer because it caused me to have to listen very acutely to what people were trying to convey, and I think that sort of helps you to be a good depicter of how people communicate.

Both my parents, particularly my father, really wanted the children to have a better life, and he struggled because he was one of eleven brothers and sisters and he lost his father at a young age. And so no one had a higher education or even the opportunity for that, and he really wanted that for his kids, and he really believed in the American Dream and saved up the money to bring his family here. At that time, there were three children, and my parents had two more when we got to the United States, but that was their hope: that we would live out the American Dream by getting a college education and doing better for ourselves than they had been able to do with working-class employment.

We were fortunate in that we were able to buy a house. We later moved to Miami, where a lot of our extended family had settled, and that was a time when the south Florida real estate market was much more affordable, so that people who worked in factories and were single bread-winners could actually accomplish that.

I was the oldest, so I was able to go to college. I went to Michigan State and eventually to law school and to graduate school. But my siblings ended up not going to college. My older brother went into the service and held ordinary employment jobs in Miami. Another brother died when I was twenty-one. My next younger brother became a UPS worker and committed suicide. I was already away in law school in Boston at the time, so I wasn't privy to all the details of what was happening in his life. He was still living at home. It was a real tragedy and a heartbreak for my mother, as you could imagine. My father had already died by then, so it was very sad and hard on her.

We went to Florida in '67, and for me it was a really wonderful experience in some ways because the growth of the Cuban community was just taking off down there and I felt a real home in my relationships with friends in my neighborhood, which was increasingly becoming a place where Cubans, as they got settled, got the support they needed as refugees to then buy houses, so our neighborhood in southwest Miami became very Hispanic. I found a sense of community in that culture even though we were Colombian, but I felt very grateful to have peers who were living like me in an American society, but also had families where Old World culture, traditions, and customs were very much a part of our consciousness.

I pursued writing; I just didn't pursue it as a career. I have always written since I was a young girl. I had a great interest in poetry; I just loved to write. I was always very good in my English classes. I edited my high school newspaper, and then in college I took courses in the writing program even as I was earning what was called a Community Services degree because I knew I wanted to have a job working with low-income communities. Then in law school I went to Boston University School of Law. I took courses in the graduate writing program in poetry while I was in law school just for the joy of it, so I've always kept my hand in it as a labor of love.

The great thing about my novel is that I was able to tell two important stories. One is the immigrant experience and coming-of-age experience of a Latina in a culture that is very strong in family values and in honoring your family and being true to them, but also there's a part of a society that expects young women to become independent and autonomous. How does a girl from a traditional culture navigate that without betraying either herself or her family?

Miami came from its roots in the old South. It was a quiet and sleepy town. There was always some degree of diversity, certainly in the African-American community that had been there a long time. There was, for example, the Bahamian culture that rose up in the Coconut Grove area, but in general, the city had some racial diversity but it had not been developed that much. The drainage of the Everglades was a process that took time and eventually freed up the land in south Florida so that as migration was occurring from both the north and the Cuban exodus, there was land available to be developed. So as that process escalated, Miami grew up really fast and became very international, very cosmopolitan. So I thought it was a really beautiful setting for the coming-of-age, multicultural experience such as that of Gabriela, the protagonist in my novel: a person who is forced to grow up quickly in circumstances that involve not just her own family but a larger society that itself is changing. So for me that was an interesting way of telling people about how Miami changed because nowadays people go down there and no one would even imagine that Miami was once this sort of sleepy place with canals and newly finished sidewalks that is now just so shiny and large and the gateway to commerce with Latin America, and just completely different.

For me, I had a very positive experience growing up in Miami. There were not that many Colombians. Now the Colombian community in Miami has just flourished. It's an enormous population down there. The Central Americans also grew in large numbers between the time of the Cuban diaspora to today, but when I was there I felt a lot of affinity. Now it could be that the part of Colombia where I'm from, Cartagena, is a coastal area that shares many similarities with other Caribbean cities in Cuba, Puerto Rico, the Dominican Republic, so perhaps I was drawn and felt immediately at home with the food and the music and their way of speaking Spanish. Everything resonated with me, so I think I had a very wonderful Latinization process in that respect. I did not feel a sense of competition—which perhaps did exist, but it wasn't my experience.

The other story I wanted to tell in the novel, which draws on this other part of my life, is my career as an immigration attorney. I wanted to tell about the unique reality of lawful immigrants, people with green cards, who are allowed to be here and are not the undocumented people we hear about so much in the press. Yet they are subjected to many of the same rules that apply only to immigrants, so that they can lose their green cards easier than a US citizen who would never lose their right to be in the States. I felt that story was very much a part of my professional experience and has really broken my heart time and time again. I wanted to tell that story so that one could reflect on the morality of that kind of double standard and how it affects the immigrant's sense of whether or not he or she is included as an equal member of society.

In some respects, the culture is very welcoming, in the sense that we have this very noble tradition here of being what the Statue of Liberty embodies: a place where people can find refuge. And in Massachusetts, I also feel we have a really wonderful tradition in that respect. For instance, Senator [Edward] Kennedy was behind the [1980] US Refugee Act, which I am so proud of—that we were able to enact a law that really eliminated barriers, so that people would not be persecuted and they'd actually be able to get legal protection here. So I think on the one hand, that is a wonderful tradition, but I do believe that many of the laws have gone too far, such as those that involve the commission of crimes by immigrants who are lawfully here. And so, for example, in the novel, the father is losing his mind and he doesn't understand what's happening to him and his experience is very unpredictable, and so his conduct is also unpredictable. So when he gets into trouble with the law and potentially hurts someone, it raises the question: Should he be punished beyond whatever the ordinary criminal consequences are with exile? Loss of legal status? Loss of his home in the United States? To my mind, I think that's too harsh a penalty and it interferes with the ability of immigrants to have faith that they really are as welcome as the Statue of Liberty and the cultural message suggest. So it creates a sense that there's a double standard.

The organization I work for is a legal services institution—legal policy work, litigation, training, education materials—all aimed at bettering the lives of low-income people. And then my focus is on low-income immigrants in our state [Massachusetts]. So I will do all kinds of things, ranging from training public and government officials about the different kinds of immigration statuses and documents, to suing the government or an entity that is violating the rights of immigrants, to trying to persuade the government that a particular policy or interpretation that hurts low-income immigrants ought to be reconsidered or adapted or changed. So, for example, the Haitian earthquake victims were given temporary protected status. We are involved in efforts to make sure that the information about the details of that status is distributed to people in the Haitian community, including the clergy. So this is my way of giving back. There's nothing more rewarding than feeling like you're able to earn a livelihood by helping others who are in more difficult circumstances than yourself. I really believe that's the greatest way to have meaning—to feel that when I leave this world, I will have hopefully done something to have made it a little bit better for others.

As for the Arizona controversy, as a matter of law, I think that the litigation that has been filed by all the national groups against the law will ultimately prevail because the states are not supposed to be in the business of regulating immigration. But on a deeper level, I think it's very tragic because what it means is it sends a message—not just to undocumented people or, in this case, undocumented Latinos—that immigrants aren't welcome in Arizona, and that's very inhospitable and sad, and it can only hurt Arizona.

There are two key aspects to this. One is the mythology that immigrants are committing crimes, which is not borne out. Pretty much if you read any study, go to the American Immigration Council or online and find recent data specific to Arizona, which shows that immigrants actually commit lower levels of crime than the native born, and that immigrant crime rates go up the longer their time here in America because this is where they learned it. [*She laughs at the irony.*]

So protection against crime is not a valid, rational justification for it. As far as the federal government's abdication of its duty to act, I agree that the federal government should be enacting legislation to rationalize our immigration law system, which has been broken for a long time. The right way for the state to address that is to pass other kinds of resolutions, perhaps encouraging Congress to use its clout to influence its own leadership to act on immigration reforms rather than simply enact the laws themselves. And that would be an equally valid and democratic response that would be legal, and Arizona would not be shooting itself in the foot.

I have found that most immigrants want to work and make their own way, even though there is a public perception that they wish to take advantage of public benefits. That's counter to my own experience. My experience, from young people to old people, is that they want to work and need a legal avenue for doing so and getting work permission. I've recently been working a great deal with the students, the young people—we call them the "DREAMERS." They're part of the movement to reform not only the entire immigration system but create a pathway for children who came here as undocumented kids brought here by their parents, perhaps as infants, and they have grown up here with essentially all the same aspirations as kids who are native born, but they get to a point in their lives where they can't get to college or can't get jobs because, lo and behold, they don't have legal documentation. It's called the DREAM Act, and it's pending in Congress.

It's a very promising piece of legislation that, if enacted, would allow young people who have lived here for a certain number of years, and who are planning to go into the service or to college, to access instate tuition in the state where they live and a path to obtain legal status. I'm on the board of directors for NILC [National Immigration Law Center], but I've had organizational clients who are involved in championing that legislation, so I have a lot to do with it and supporting them. And it's been very interesting: as I've been going around reading from my book or talking about it, some of these students have come to my readings and then talked to me afterward about their life experiences. . . .

Anything that would be legislated by Congress would have to be a compromise of all the different interests in this area from all sides. But some of the elements that I think would rationalize the immigration laws so that they make more sense for the future are some sort of a legalization program for the people who have been here working hard, contributing to our society, paying taxes—who want the same thing we all want, which is security [and] to be able to bring our kids up right. And secondly, the numerical limitations on bringing relatives to the United States are just completely unrealistic. You shouldn't have waiting lists for a sibling to be reunited with his or her lawful relatives. The numbers are not logical anymore. They don't really fit with today's realities and the global nature of our society. And thirdly, this whole issue of fairness and proportion in how we treat people once they're here, like the one I've written about in my novel, about subjecting people to loss of their green cards many years later for very small crimes that, if committed by a citizen, would not incur such a harsh penalty.

I feel very blessed and lucky that my life has given me a lot of opportunity, and I'm thankful to both my parents for the sacrifices they made. I sometimes wonder what would have happened if I stayed in Cartagena. I have this cousin there who is my age, and she is a lawyer as well, but she was also a beauty queen a few years ago, and I was in Cartagena in January and she had taken a leave from her job to work in the mayor's office. It was amazing because as we talked about all the high-power issues of women who try to do too much, both personally and professionally, and we were both reflecting on how we would be the same wherever we were because we're trying to do more with our time than we could. So she's sort of my parallel half of me who went on to live there.

I first went back to Cartagena in college. It was really wonderful. Most of the older generation that was there on my father's side has died. All the Gomezes are deceased, but back then, there were more of them and a huge extended family. To even go to my grandparents' home the first time, I brought home [from there] a beautiful picture they hung in their house of my mother when she was maybe fifteen or sixteen in its original frame, and they gave it to me to bring back, and it was a really touching chance to be with them before they died.

I became a citizen as an adult, after 1996. I had to take the test, and I went to the American Red Cross in Boston, and there I was sitting with people who would ordinarily be my clients [*laughs at the irony*] and I was so embarrassed to get up. I didn't want anyone to feel bad, so I just made myself sit there until enough of the people in the group left before I took mine because I was embarrassed. A graduate from law school, a practicing attorney, working in immigration law, sitting in a room taking the test with everyone else—bizarre. And the sad thing is some of these folks around me had taken the test before and failed, and they're trying so hard, but adult learning is very different from learning as a kid.

How would I advise immigrants thinking of coming here? I've worked with a lot of persecution victims: people who have been tortured, held in detention for prolonged periods of time in clandestine jails. I've worked with people from Africa, Central America, all over the world, and for them, it's not really a choice. I think it's a question of survival. The human spirit has an instinct for survival that is beautiful and noble, and whatever people have to do in that situation to get out of their country to come here, I think they have to pursue it. I have a lot of sympathy for people who come here with false documents because it was the only way they could get out of that kind of situation, so for them it would be arrogant for me to even pretend to give someone in those circumstances any advice about how to do it.

But as far as wanting to come here to have a better life, I just salute them for their desire to do better for themselves and their children, and the main thing is to continue—even after they come here—to help those who are not in as good a situation and who are still adapting and try to give back some of what they've gotten.

It has not helped that we've been in a sustained period of economic difficulty. I've been touched by layoffs, and everybody in my community has been touched by layoffs. There have been very wide-ranging dramatic economic consequences over the last few years. And pro-immigrant and anti-immigrant attitudes fluctuate with the economy. So certainly that's affected the "promise" of the American Dream versus what's ultimately delivered. But to me, the deeper way that we've changed is that at the beginning of this nation's history, there were the people who first settled here, who were one group, and then the new groups gradually made their way in, so there was still a "They are they, and we are us" [mentality]—but today, increasingly, and not just in terms of immigrants but in terms of the descendants of slaves, we have a much more racially mixed population, so much more racial intermarriage when at one time there was prohibition on racial intermarriage, so now it's like, "We have met them, and they are us." [*She laughs.*] So I think that over time, perhaps the biggest transformation is that what an immigrant is is almost a myth because now we've mixed in our families and in our blood all these immigrant communities, and so it's harder and harder to separate out one from another.

The "promise" is also affected by the back-and-forth of the other economies. I mean, we have this joke in Massachusetts: For a long time we had a lot of undocumented Brazilians in Massachusetts, and for some reason each community and ethnic group sort of carves out their own niche, whether they're taxi drivers or restaurant workers, but the Brazilians, for some reason, ended up largely in these cleaning companies, and they were very good entrepreneurs, but then the Brazilian economy began to turn around and get better while our economy was going down the tubes. So the joke was, "We're all losing our cleaning ladies." [*She laughs.*] So it's a much more global world, and as things get better in one place, the outflow and the inflow get reversed.

ANDRÉ SOLTNER
BORN NOVEMBER 20, 1932
EMIGRATED FROM FRANCE, 1961, AGE 28

He grew up in a small Alsatian town on the French-German border. He came to America from Paris in 1961, recruited as a young chef for a new upscale French restaurant in New York, which he would later own. That restaurant turned out to be New York's legendary Lutèce, a four-star restaurant that in its day was the benchmark against which other restaurants were compared. It opened in 1961, and he operated it for more than thirty years. Julia Child once called Lutèce the best restaurant in the United States. Old guest books read like a "Who's Who in America." Chef André cooked for them all, from regular folk to presidents and everyone in between. A chef's chef, he is the quintessential classically trained French chef, revered by his peers and the recipient of innumerable awards, including the prestigious Meilleurs Ouvriers de France, Officier du Mérite National, the Chevalier de L'Ordre du Mérite Agricole, the James Beard Foundation Lifetime Achievement Award, and the Légion d'Honneur, the highest decoration in France. The coauthor of The Lutèce Cookbook, *he has served for more than twenty years as Délegué Général of the Master Chefs of France and more than fifteen years as the dean of classic studies for the French Culinary Institute in New York. A devoted husband, he has been married since 1962 to his wife, Simone, whom he met in Paris at a restaurant where she was a waitress and he was the chef. They never had children, but they worked together to create culinary magic of their own. "In Europe, we think America is the land of opportunity, and it is, but it doesn't come by itself," he said in his thick Alsatian-German accent. "It's not free. The freedom's not free. You have to work for it. If somebody asked me if they should come, I would tell them if you're serious, if you're disciplined, and if you're willing to work—you don't fail."*

I was born in Alsace in a little town called Thann. It was a nice little town near the mountains, the Vosges, eastern France, about seven thousand people. I grew up there until the age of fourteen. School stopped at that age, and then you had to decide what you were going to do, and my first choice was to be a cabinetmaker because my father was a cabinetmaker. I also had an older brother who was a cabinetmaker, and my mother was completely against having two sons in the same business. I said it doesn't matter because I also loved to cook. I used to watch my mother cook and how she did tarts. There were no other chefs in the family, but my mom was a very good chef-housewife. She was an amateur chef. She inspired me and gave me the love for cooking.

In those days, to be a chef you had to do an apprenticeship. So I did an apprenticeship at the Hôtel du Parc in Mulhouse, which is about twenty miles from Thann, and I spent three years there in apprenticeship. We worked long hours, twelve- to fifteen-hour days there, six days a week, sometimes seven days a week, and were paid very little. My first year I made about six hundred francs, which was a little over a dollar a month, plus room and board, and the second year it was about two dollars and the third year about three dollars a month. And like most apprenticeships at that time, it was very tough—brutal, even.

For example, next to where I did my apprenticeship was a restaurant called Le Paon D'or, and the chef there punched the apprentice, knocked him out, threw him in a garbage can, and put the lid on! [*He laughs.*] The parents of the apprentice later took the chef to court, and the chef was banned from Alsace for ten years! Ironically, I later hired that apprentice when I was a chef in Paris at Chez Hansi. And the banned chef? I bumped into him years later in New York. I was walking home, and at Second Avenue and Fifty-Fourth Street, there was a French restaurant, and the back door of the kitchen was open, and being a chef, if we see a kitchen we look in, so I look in, and who do I see but him. I said, "What are you doing here?" and he said, "André, what are you doing here?"

Where I worked, they put you pretty far from the head chef. His name was Rene Simon. He was my first chef, and he was tough, too. One time he slapped an apprentice, who fell back on a pile of coal—in those days we cooked on coal stoves—and he grabbed him by the shirt, dragged him across the kitchen floor, opened the door, and threw him out. The next day, seven a.m.—that's when we started work—the boy was there, he was at work, because we admired the chef. He was a very good chef. And believe it or not, he was a nice man, too, but he was a disciplinarian, and so to be an apprentice, sometimes it was brutal. We worked sometimes from seven a.m. to two a.m. the next morning without sitting down. He was very tough, but I loved him. [*He laughs.*] I was fourteen and a half when I started. I did three years under Rene Simon, and he was my mentor. He taught me what I know about cooking, and he also gave me the love for cooking. He's really the chef I admire the most in my whole career because he was very talented.

Fig. 39. André Soltner in front of Lutèce, the legendary New York restaurant located at 249 East Fiftieth Street, in 1980. Photograph used by permission of the Soltner family.

After my apprenticeship, I took a certification exam all young chefs had to take to become a professional cook in France, and from there on, like most other chefs, I went from one city to another and from one restaurant to another. I started in Mulhouse and from there went to work at the Hotel Royale in Deauville, big hotel, maybe twenty-five cooks; the Palace Hotel in Pontresina, Switzerland; and the Hotel Acker in Wildhaus, Switzerland, near Zurich. I came back to France for my military service. I was drafted into the Alpine troops in the French Alps. I didn't tell them I was a cook; otherwise they would have put me in the kitchen, and I love to ski. I was always a skier. Then, after a few months, I was sent to Tunisia, to North Africa, because of the troubles between Tunisia and Algeria and France. In the Alpine troops, we were in the mountains in Tunisia. We were there for nine months until I was released in April 1955.

My idea then was to go to Paris. For a young chef, Paris was it because there were lots of jobs, many restaurants. I began working at Chez Hansi, an Alsatian restaurant, as the "round man." The restaurant was open every day, six days a week, so I changed posts and replaced the cook who had the day off. I was chef de partie, which means you take care of one part of the kitchen. So one day I might do sauces, another day vegetables [and so on], so I had the full experience there. After a few years I became sous chef, and a few years later, I became head chef. At the end of my time there, I had fourteen chefs and two pastry chefs working under me.

I was there for six years, but if you stay in the one place too long that's not good, and then I had an opportunity to come to this country. I played Ping-Pong® in a chef's club. My pastry chef and another pastry chef, we played together. And the other pastry chef had been to America and worked at Idlewild Airport [now Kennedy Airport] as a chef for a man in the airline catering business. His name was André Surmain, who planned to open a restaurant, a very high-class restaurant, in New York, and he was looking for a young chef. This pastry chef told Surmain about me.

So Surmain flew to Paris and had dinner at the restaurant where I was working. After dinner, he asked for me and told me about his plans for Lutèce [the name comes from "Lutetia," the ancient name of Paris] and said, "Are you interested in coming to America?"

At first I was a little surprised. He promised me a lot of things and convinced me to come. But I was already a little brainwashed because when I was a child my grandfather came here earlier. He came to America, one of two boys and two girls. They came through Ellis Island around 1900. He was a baker. The two boys were bakers. They came to New York and then went west to Nevada and California. So he told me all the time about Nevada and California, and so finally I said to Mr. Surmain, "OK, let's try it. I am willing to come." So I went to the American consulate in Paris, and I left two hours later *with* the green card; people don't believe me anymore because now to get a green card is so difficult, but in '61 the quota for France was never full, so it was easy.

A few months later, I came to New York. I was thinking I would come for a year or two, learn English, and go back. That was my plan. I really wanted to see how people lived here. It was not for the money because my salary in Paris was the same that he offered me in New York: ninety-five dollars a month. But, you know, I was single, I was just twenty-eight, and he said if things worked out he would make me a partner, and I thought, OK, let's see. What did I have to lose? I had met my wife, Simone, by then. She was a waitress at Chez Hansi, and I was dating her, but I came here single. I said, "OK, if I like it there I will come back for her. Then maybe we will get married and she will join me." And that's eventually what we did. She came about a year and a half after me.

So I flew to New York, and at first you feel a little lost if you don't know anybody. But the next day I started my job, and we opened the restaurant at 249 East Fiftieth Street. Most of the employees were French, so I got along very quickly. And right away, I must say I liked it because the people who came in, American people, they were different than the clients in France. In France they could be a little snobby, you know, but here I noticed right away a big difference in the relationship with the customers, and I liked it very much.

My biggest problem was I didn't speak English, but I am Alsatian so I spoke both languages, French and German, so it helped me a lot, especially for the food buying because many suppliers spoke German. So I had a little difficulty with the language at first, but I didn't have time to go to school, so I just picked it up as I went along.

We opened Lutèce in 1961, with Surmain as the owner and me as the chef. But it was not well known then, and the big problem was that Surmain charged high prices right away. We were very expensive. We were the most expensive restaurant in New York, maybe the most expensive in the United States at that time, and that hurt us very much, and we didn't do much business. And then little by little we did better, but after a year and a half I felt it wasn't quite working out as I had hoped. We just had different philosophies, and he also had promised many things, so I said to Surmain, my boss, "Look, this is not really going as I hoped. It's time for me to go back," and he said, "No, no, no, André. You cannot go now! The restaurant is doing better, much better now than a year ago. If you stay, I will take you as a partner."

I said, "You told me that in Paris two years ago and that never happened." He said, "No, I mean it. You stay and we go into partnership."

He sold me 30 percent of the restaurant. We were partners until 1972, when he decided to go back to Europe and I bought his shares. Our partnership did not go too well. It did OK, but he didn't work hard. And I believe in working hard and always being there, and he was away all the time. He sailed to Europe, and he had a farm in Majorca, Spain. So I said, "Yes, I have 30 percent but I'm doing all the work." My wife worked the front of the restaurant—taking reservations, greeting customers—while I worked the back, and we decided it wasn't fair and decided to leave, but Surmain said, "No, no, no. I'm fed up with this business. I'm burned out! I don't want it anymore. I leave!"

I said, "OK, but if you leave, you leave." So we drew up papers. It took about nine months to find a way, you know? Because I didn't have the money to buy his shares, and then we found a way to do it, and he left and I bought him out in 1972.

When he left I thought I could do it because I was in the kitchen; I was not in the dining room. I was the chef, but I was a little scared and shy. This was a huge thing for me and I thought I could do it, but after two or three months my accountant came. He came every two weeks, and he said, "Look, André, it doesn't look good. You don't have enough cash flow. You have to pay staff. You have to pay the suppliers and everything. If you don't bring money in, the company will go under. You cannot survive."

I said, "What do I do?"

"You have to look for money."

This was the beginning of 1973. It was wintertime. I put a coat on over my chef's jacket and went to Bankers Trust on Fifty-Second Street and Third Avenue. I went to the teller, and the teller asked, "How can I help you?"

I said, "I need money." He was smiling a little bit and said, "Go to the gentleman over there in the office and talk to him."

So I did. I told him, "I have a restaurant and I don't have the necessary capital," and he said, "How much do you need?" Well, I was a cook, you know? I was not a businessman. I said, "I don't know. I think it was $40,000." [*He smiles.*] Remember, $40,000 in 1972 was a lot of money. He made me fill out a few papers, but he did not ask me much. In France, they would have asked me everything, including when my grandfather was born [*laughs*] and the last time I went to the dentist. So he made a few calculations, drew up a few papers, and I signed everything and left the bank with $40,000 on the spot. They put it in my account. Just like that. Today when I think back, it's just unbelievable, you know? And I never saw the banker again.

Soon after, Malcolm Forbes—he was a customer, and I always took to him a little bit, and one day he came in and said to me, "André, I heard André Surmain left?" I said, "Yes." He said, "André, if you need money— whatever you need, you tell me, I'll give it to you." He didn't say "I'll lend it to you," he said, "I give it to you! And if one day you can pay me back, you pay me back," but I never took him up on his offer because in the meantime the bank gave me this $40,000. When Malcolm Forbes passed away, his son Steve called me about two or three months later. Steve was also a customer. He said, "André, you're in my father's will." [*He laughs.*] As a gesture, I guess, Malcolm Forbes put $1,000 in his will for me!

Around this time, I became a citizen, but in my mind I was already a citizen. When I came here, I felt good right away. I already had a green card, so I didn't think going for my citizenship was important. But my lawyer said, "Look, André, you're not a citizen. You have a liquor license; if, God forbid, something should happen, you could lose your license. You should be a citizen." But who really pushed me was then governor of New

York Hugh Carey. He came to eat many times—his office was on the same block as Lutèce—and he said something once to me, and I said I wasn't a citizen yet, and he said, "You're not a citizen? I'll sponsor you." So I called my lawyer and said I wanted to be a citizen, and I went downtown to take the test for citizenship like everybody else. . . .

Before Surmain left, we never did one hundred covers. He always said, "If we make one hundred covers I'll pay for the champagne," but we never did it. After he left, we changed the ambience of the restaurant. He was a little snobbish, you know. He snubbed the customer a little bit if he didn't like the way they looked or dressed, and we changed that and made it more comfortable. We quickly went to 120 covers. We were still expensive, but we were in the same price range as a few other French restaurants in New York—Le Cirque, Le Caravelle, Le Cygne, Le Grenouille. We cooked traditional French cuisine, and I would go from table to table and personally greet the customers, make them feel welcome, and if I had good relationship with a customer, I always had one or two Alsatian dishes that were off-menu, like my potato tart. When I grew up my mother did what's called *tarte aux pommes de terre* or potato pie that I loved. It's my favorite dish, and it's very simple to make. It's hard-boiled eggs, potatoes, and bacon done in a pastry—very inexpensive to make, so I could not put it on the menu and justify charging thirty dollars for lunch.

We were rated four stars in the *New York Times*, and that gives you a big push. We once were in *Playboy*. We were rated the number-one restaurant in America. And for two years after that people came from all over—from Kalamazoo, you name it.

If there was one customer, President Nixon was one of the great guys for us. He was so gracious. Always so nice. He stopped in the kitchen; he talked baseball or football with my guys. He would come with a large party, and I would say, "Mr. President, what would you like?" And he would say, "Just order for me like you usually do." And there was once an article in *Newsweek* about Nixon, and they were talking about dining, and Nixon was quoted as saying, "Our main favorite is Lutéce because we like owner André Soltner so much—and now and then we go to Le Cirque." When this article came out, it was a huge thing for us [*makes grand gesture*]. We refused people. Unbelievable! That was a real boon!

I helped bring Alsatian wine here to America because I used to serve it at Lutéce, and to thank me, the town in Alsace where I was born put this memorial in the vineyard. There was a ceremony with the mayor and a senator to thank me, and I thought, what could I do for them? And then I had an idea. President Nixon liked Alsatian wine very much, and I thought if he could say something about how much he likes this wine. . . . So one day he came, party of eight. I said to Nixon, "You know, Mr. President, the wine you like, it would be nice if you could give me a few words," and he said, "No problem, no problem."

Then I said, "Should I call your secretary to tell her?"

He looked at me and said, "You think I'm going to forget?" [*He laughs.*] I said, "No, no." What a smart guy he was! He gave me a letter about how much he liked the wine, and at this ceremony with the mayor and the senator, I gave them the letter from President Nixon. They have it now at the town hall there. . . .

To run a successful restaurant, you must be serious and you must be present. I was always at the restaurant. If I wasn't there, I would not open the restaurant, and that's it—you cannot cut corners. Same is true with the customers. They look for value. They know you will make some money, and they understand that, but they want value. If you say "fresh" to a customer, you have to be serious, and if it's not 100 percent fresh, don't serve it.

We rarely had staff meetings. I asked from my dining room staff that they were clean, welcoming to customers, not snobbish French [*smiles*]— that was a big one—and to stay serious. My kitchen staff was serious, no drinking, clean, and on time. We had discipline, you know? I incorporated many of the things I learned from Rene Simon. His rule was if you start at seven a.m., then it's seven a.m., not five after seven. I had the same rules. And I respected my staff very much and expected that they respect me the same. There were forty-two staff. That's a lot, and that's why a restaurant has to be profitable.

Today you have Jean-Georges Vongerichten, Daniel Boulud, Thomas Keller—it's completely different now because the business is different. You see these guys and they have four, five, six restaurants—they're real businesspeople. I had one restaurant, and I never considered myself a businessman. I considered myself a craftsman, a cook. But they came along because it was a different time. They became businessmen. They are still chefs—they are good chefs; otherwise they would not be where they are—but to be in the business now you need backers, investors. To open a restaurant in Hong Kong or Las Vegas for me, at my time, it was not so. I had offers, but it was not my time.

I once had Japanese people approach me. It was the beginning of going bigger, and they came to me about opening Lutèce in Japan, and I said, "I'm not interested." They said, "André, you owe us the courtesy to listen to us." I said, "OK," but in my heart I was always a chef, a cook, you know? So we had a meeting in an office, a big building, and there were five, six guys there, and they said, "We would like to open seven Lutèces in Japan." And I said, "I'm not interested. I have a restaurant." They said, "Keep your restaurant." I said, "What do you want from me exactly?" They said, "We want you to be in Japan three months a year . . . ." This was around 1990, and they said, "But the rest of time you can stay with your Lutèce in New York—it's yours, not ours, and that's basically our deal."

I said, "Let me think about it," and I came home and told Simone because my wife was always with me in business, and I said to myself, "What will I do in Japan for three months?" I was thinking maybe I meet a Japanese girl and I wind up getting divorced. I called them back and said, "Forget it."

We decided to sell the restaurant in 1994 because it's a very tough walk, you know? We started to get a little tired, especially for my wife; she was very much involved. And the owner of Ark Restaurants came once for dinner, and he told me that he might be interested in buying Lutèce—and Ark was a big company; they had something like thirty restaurants—and asked me if I would sell. And I said, "Well, everything is for sale," and I was sixty-three years old then, and I said to my wife, "What do you think?" We knew we had to stop one day.

Ark bought the restaurant, not the building. I still own the building. I gave Ark a fifteen-year lease, but after nine years, they couldn't make it go and closed in 2004. They couldn't make it, I think, because it was a very personal restaurant. It was Lutèce, but it was André Soltner. It was not personal anymore. People think with a restaurant you make millions, but to make money in a restaurant is not an easy thing. You have to be there. You have to watch it and control it, and they didn't have that. So they didn't make money. A restaurant has to be profitable. If you don't make money, you go under, and it's not the money you put in your pocket, but to pay your suppliers right away and keep your staff. You can tell them, "You're part of the family," but that works for six months, so they also have to find their advantage, so you have to pay them a little more and things like that. To make money in a restaurant, you have to be there, and you have to watch *everything*. . . .

And whatever happens, be humble. If somebody is successful and they get a big head, it disappoints me very much. You know, André Surmain, we are still friends—he'll be ninety soon—but he was a bit of a snob, so when I wanted to bring him down to reality, I always said, "André, we are soup merchants, don't forget that. We are not ambassadors. We make soup, and we sell soup." And that's very important, especially now, in an era where chefs are very recognized and they are suddenly stars, celebrities, but it should not go to your head. Stay humble!

And be serious, and when I say serious, I mean disciplined and not to think that you come to America and America is waiting for you. America is not waiting for you. Put that in your head. You have to earn it—otherwise you don't make it—and it's not easy. In Europe, we think America is the land of opportunity, and it is, but it doesn't come by itself. It's not free. The freedom's not free. You have to work for it. If somebody asked me if they should come, I would tell them if you're serious, if you're disciplined, and if you're willing to work—you don't fail.

In Europe, when you say you are an immigrant, it means you are maybe a little lower than all the others and I don't want to be nice to you, but I must say that here you don't have that feeling. If you don't speak English the way you should, nobody looks at you. Everybody thinks it is normal, and that's really what I like the most here. You don't have any complex to be an immigrant. In France, I remember the Italians or Spanish people, they were accepted too, but they were a little not the same level, really. But here it isn't so, and that is really the nice part here. I really feel at home here, I really do.

In the past, we went back to France normally every two years, and for many years now we've had a house in the Catskills, which I like very much because the Catskills looks a little like Vosges, from where I come, the same type of mountains. So we have a house there at Hunter Mountain, and there are at least ten other chefs who also have houses. So on Sundays we cook and eat together. Restaurant people are like circus people because we are in a business where we have a little odder hours than others. We try out our new recipes and things like that. We do our own cider, and we ski. We have our annual chef's ski race that we've been doing for more than thirty years. . . . But these days my wife and I go on a lot of cruises. I go as the guest chef. We go once a year; some years two or three times. Recently we went on a cruise and the son of Nikita Khrushchev was the guest speaker for politics, Sergei Khrushchev. I was for cooking. He was for politics. We've gone on over thirty-four cruises. . . .

My fondest memory is that I'm happily married almost fifty years now and that we're still together. We had success, but it didn't go to our heads. No children, though. That's my disappointment. *C'est la vie.* You know, you cannot change some things.

EMILIO ESTEFAN
BORN MARCH 4, 1953
EMIGRATED FROM CUBA VIA SPAIN, 1968, AGE 15

He came from an affluent Cuban family. When he was fourteen years old he went with his father from Cuba to Spain, leaving behind his older brother and his mother, who stayed to look after her father, and spent eighteen months in Spain before coming to Miami alone to live with his aunt and uncle. He went on to become the producer/husband of singer Gloria Estefan, one of the top-selling artists of all time, with more than one hundred million albums sold and seven Grammy Awards to her credit. She emigrated from Cuba with her mother when she was two years old and settled in Miami, where she and Emilio later met. Today, Emilio is a nineteen-time Grammy Award–winning producer, songwriter, and founder of Estefan Enterprises, which encompasses everything from music publishing, television, film production, and artist management to hotels, restaurants, and real estate. "I would advise others to have respect for a country that gives you an opportunity," he said. "It doesn't matter where you come from; we all cry for this country."

I was born in Cuba in a town called Santiago de Cuba, which is all the way on the other side of the island from Havana. When I was a kid, Castro took power, and the whole thing I remember in the house was conversations about being in a Communist country because they were taking everything away, and that made the whole difference for me. I mean, even when I was ten years old I heard my mom and my dad talking through the doors. My mom was crying, saying if I was going to stay in a Communist country, what will happen when I reach military age, which was fifteen, and I was eleven years old then, and I remember that I cried all night.

In the morning I told my mom, "I have to leave Cuba."

And she said, "Well, how are you going to leave Cuba? We'll probably never see you again."

Then when I was fourteen, I said, "I want to leave with my dad." Because he was talking of leaving.

She said, "Well, you know something, I'm gonna let you do it because I feel [*pauses*] don't do it for me, do it for you. I think it's a great thing that you'll be able to live and realize the American Dream and live in a free country."

Fig. 40. Gloria and Emilio Estefan. Photograph used by permission of Estefan Enterprises.

So I made the decision to leave when I was eleven years old, but I left when I was fourteen.

The life there when I was a kid—it was a country that was converted to a Communist country, so people lived in fear. They were arresting a lot of people. I remember when Castro changed the money into Cuban dollars. I never met Castro, although he used to live really close to my house. He went to the same school as me when he was a kid. The same school in Santiago. He was born in Santiago de Cuba.

I remember one day they [Castro's men] came to my house, and they went to my mom and my dad's room, and he used to have a safe inside the room. They took him to open the safe, and he got nervous, and they took the [whole] family to the patio with machine guns. They thought that we were hiding something, that my father was hiding dollars, especially dollars, because they were looking for dollars. Then they used some dynamite and blew the whole safe—and to me all those elements are what convinced me to make the decision to leave Cuba. And not only me—I didn't want the rest of my family to live in a country like that.

My father used to own a factory, a clothing factory. We were not really millionaires, but we were well off. And my father was a poker player, a professional poker player. He won the lottery twenty-seven times in his life! He was a very lucky guy. And he was always up and down; sometimes he was filthy with money, and sometimes he was totally broke. He played at the hotels. He used to play at all the casinos in Cuba. I mean, he loved to play. Sort of like [in] the movie *Havana*. My mom took care of the home, took care of us. I had one older brother.

To me, the decision to come to America was not about money. I always looked at the United States as a place that represented freedom, that you have the right to free expression, have the right to any dream. But to me, more than anything else as a kid, I was afraid to live in a Communist country, and I saw what my mom and my dad were going through and my whole family.

When we used to have dinner or lunch, we had to talk quietly because they were afraid somebody was listening to them. So my whole motivation was really fear—fear that I should live in a country where I am afraid to talk or have my opinion. I saw everything that was happening with my family, and then my aunt was arrested because her son escaped to an embassy when he was around twenty-one. They came the next day to her house and said that she probably knew that he was escaping from Cuba. And she said, "I didn't know that."

She really didn't know! They put her in jail for almost fifteen years just to punish her. Fifteen years in jail! She served the time, then she came to Miami, and then she died. I mean, it was amazing. And so being a kid and seeing all these elements and the pain that I saw with my family, I said, "I have to leave." Even though it was the hardest decision I made in my whole life because I realized I may never see my mom or my brother again for the rest of my life.

The day I left, I remember when it was time to say good-bye to my grandfather and the rest of my family, I knew I was never going to see them again. But at the same time I remember going to the airport and holding my mom and my brother and then getting onto the plane to go to Spain. We went to Spain because that was the only way out. At the time, there was no direct flight to the States. And my mom was of Spanish descent, so they gave us a visa to Spain.

I cried all the way from Cuba to Spain. My dad and I flew to Madrid.

We got to Madrid at night, and when we got out of the plane and we started walking, I remember feeling cold and how the cold weather was so different for me. I remember it was late at night at the airport and the airport was empty. But I saw two priests at the end of a corridor, and I was crying, and my dad told me, "Everything will be OK. Just take your time. Things will get better for the family."

We were almost homeless in Spain. When we came they helped us, but we had to go and eat in a church because we didn't have enough money to eat in a restaurant or to buy food. My father couldn't take any money out of the country. When you leave Cuba, you're not allowed to take anything—not even one penny. You can take just what you're wearing and that's it. So some relatives and friends in Miami sent us money to help us, and my dad and I found a small apartment. We had left behind my older brother and mom and her father, my grandfather.

The idea was that my dad and I were going to go to the United States and bring my mother and my brother later. My mother said, "I don't want to leave until my father passes away," because her father was still alive. He was too old. He didn't want to leave home, leave Cuba. Later on, after we got to Miami, I told her, "Listen, you did what you have to do, but my dad and me—we need you here." It was a hard decision because my older brother was at the military age, so he couldn't leave.

We were in Spain for eighteen months before I got a student visa to come to the United States. My father was not able to come with me right away, so I went alone. My aunt in Miami sent money for my ticket. The plan was for me to go ahead, get to America, and then petition for my father because as a child, a minor, you were given priority to be reunited with the parent. I think we also had refugee status, although we never collected money or anything. I flew to New York and then took a connecting flight to Miami, and I called my uncle and said, "Here I am!" I was fifteen years old by then. My uncle came to pick me up at the airport, and we went to see my aunt and the rest of the family.

At that time, my aunt and uncle had fourteen kids in their house, and all of military age, because when we lived in Cuba, if you were fifteen years old you were not allowed to leave the country. So every family would try to get their kids out before they were fifteen and make sure they were safe. I was so happy to see them. My dad and I lived with my aunt and uncle for many years in Miami, and then after my grandfather died in Cuba, my mom came through Mexico to the States.

In Miami, I remember we used to go to Freedom Tower [a historic 1925 landmark building that serves as a memorial to Cuban immigration to America] to collect food because they gave out food once a month, oatmeal and cheese and many different things for the Cuban refugees. . . .

I went to school in Miami, but I needed to work. My goal was to get money to bring my family here to America. So I went to school, and I went and applied at Bacardi [Rum]. I knew the family. I grew up with the Bacardi family in Cuba. We went to the same school. And they said, "You're a minor, so you have to get a special permit." So I asked for a special permit, and I worked at Bacardi as an office boy.

I also convinced my uncle to get me an accordion because I wanted to make money. It was the only instrument I knew how to play. So we went and got an accordion for $177. We got home, and my aunt told me, "What are you doing? We don't have money to pay even rent. How are you going to pay for this accordion?"

I said, "Don't worry. I'm going to play, and I'm going to make money with this." So I went and played with this guy who used to play the violin, and we would play for tips in a restaurant. It was a really old-time famous Italian restaurant in Biscayne. Sometimes we collected five dollars, ten dollars, fifty dollars; it all depended on the crowds that night. After school, I used to change in the car, and I used to go and play the accordion for tips.

One day the Bacardi family was having a party and they needed a band, and I knew all the songs from Cuba on the accordion, so I brought a percussionist and a bass player and we played all the Cuban songs. We were a big hit. So they used to call me and say, "Come and play at the party," so I used to go and play the accordion, and that's how the whole Miami Sound Machine got started.

I met Gloria when she was rehearsing in church as part of a group, and I went and listened to them, and I saw Gloria and I said hello. It was a nice group. And then like three months later, I was playing at a wedding and Gloria passed by, and I said, "Oh, you're the one who was singing [in church]. Please come and sing a song with us." And I heard the sound, the Latin music, and I thought this would be a great sound for performance.

So she came to the party and I asked her to perform at the wedding. And she came and I loved the whole sound, and I said, "This is really great! We should do something together. If you want to perform, we can do it this weekend." And she came with her grandmother, her mother, and her sister. Gloria was very young at the time. She was only about seventeen, eighteen years old. She was studying psychology at the University of Miami. She sang at church, but not professionally; she was just a kid.

Gloria and I had a lot in common. We were both born in Cuba. We loved music, family, and both of us when we were young were separated for extended periods of time from loved ones. For me it was my mother; for her it was her father. He was a motorcycle policeman. He once was a motorcycle escort for the wife of Batista [Cuba's president, Fulgencio Batista], before Castro. Her mother was a kindergarten teacher, and they lived a comfortable life in Havana. But when Castro came to power [January 1959], Gloria's parents decided to leave the country until things quieted down. Gloria was two years old at the time. Her mother flew into exile in Miami with Gloria. Castro had not yet closed all the flights from Cuba to the United States. Her father joined them a month later. They had very little money, spoke almost no English, and settled into a Cuban neighborhood near the Orange Bowl [now Sun Life Stadium] in Miami [Gardens]. Then her father went off to train for a secret mission, which was the failed Bay of Pigs invasion [April 1961], and was taken prisoner by Castro's forces. He was in a Cuban jail with hundreds of others for nearly two years. Gloria was too young to understand what was going on, but if she asked, her mother would say, "He's away working on a farm. . . ."

As a singer, what I saw in Gloria was something that was different. She was bilingual. She spoke English, Spanish, and French fluently. I loved her voice and the way she sang, and I said, "Listen, I would love to bring you into the group." I wanted to call it Miami Sound because I felt it was the sound coming out of Miami at the time that fused American and Cuban music in a unique blend. And then that started the whole Miami Sound Machine in 1976, and we recorded the first album, and it became huge. It was number one almost all over the world.

I went back to Cuba when my brother's wife died. This was about thirty years ago, 1980. She committed suicide and left him stuck there with the two kids. And Castro at the time was allowing anybody to leave, and you could bring your family to the States and get a boat and bring them back and the States approved that, so I went in a boat. I never went in a boat before, so I got lost.

When I got to Cuba, they told me my boat was too small. So I called my brother and said, "Listen, I'm in Cuba but I'm not allowed to take you because the boat that we came in is too small," and he said, "Forget about me—don't even care about me no more," and he hung up the phone. And I got really worried, and I knew this was the only chance to get him out of Cuba. So I went back to the States, and I had a good friend in Costa Rica who knew somebody who was close to the president, and they helped me. It took a lot of work, but we got visas for him and his kids to go to Costa Rica, and the Cuban government finally let him go. They gave him a hard time. And then he got to Costa Rica and applied to the US consulate and he came to the States.

I would advise others to have respect for a country that gives you an opportunity. It doesn't matter where you come from; we all cry for this country. We feel that we belong in a way, even though we were not born in this country. We feel that we have an honor, that we're welcome, that we're realizing the American Dream. In this country you can have opinions, different opinions, and anything can come true. At the same time, like I always tell people, to become an immigrant or a citizen of a country, you always have to have respect for the country, and that's what me and Gloria have felt all our lives. We never take our citizenship for granted. We appreciate what we have. We always want to give back to the country.

Chapter 9

1970s

Immigration in this decade was heavily influenced by the Vietnam War. The US withdrawal from South Vietnam in 1975 and the subsequent Communist takeover of South Vietnam, Cambodia, and Laos triggered a new wave of refugees, many of whom spent years in Asian refugee camps waiting to get into the United States. The number of legal immigrants had now steadily increased for three straight decades: from 2.5 million in the 1950s, to 3.22 million in the 1960s, to 4.25 million in the 1970s.

KEY HISTORIC EVENTS

★1972: US State Department issues guidelines dealing with requests for asylum.

★1974: US Supreme Court upholds INS rules permitting Canadians and Mexicans to commute freely into the United States to perform daily or seasonal work.

★1975: The Ford administration's budget to Congress asks for an increase in spending to curb illegal immigration. US Supreme Court rules that the Border Patrol cannot stop a car and question its occupants about their immigration status because of Mexican ancestry; thus, "profiling" is not legally permitted.

★1977: Justice Department approves entry of more than five thousand Soviet Jewish immigrants.

★1978: Hundreds of Haitian refugees enter the United States after the Bahamian government orders them to leave or face deportation.

★1979: Justice Department has the INS enforce a statutory ban on admitting homosexual aliens.

MIGRATION FLOWS

Total legal US immigration in 1970s: 4.25 million

Top ten emigration countries in this decade: Mexico (621,218), Philippines (337,726), Cuba (256,497), Korea (241,192), Canada and Newfoundland (179,267), Italy (150,031), India (147,997), Dominican Republic (139,249), United Kingdom (133,218), Jamaica (130,226)

(See appendix for the complete list of countries.)

FAMOUS IMMIGRANTS

Immigrants who came to America in this decade, and who would later become famous, include:

John Lennon, England, 1971, Beatle
Colin Firth, England, 1971, actor
Isabella Rossellini, Italy, 1971, actress
Jon Secada, Cuba, 1971, singer-songwriter
James Cameron, Canada, 1971, film producer/director
Rudolf Nureyev, Soviet Union, 1972, dancer
Wolfgang Puck, Austria, 1973, chef
Alex Trebek, Canada, 1973, game show host
Patrick Ewing, Jamaica, 1973, basketball player
Mikhail Baryshnikov, Latvia, 1974, dancer
Sir Anthony Hopkins, Wales, 1974, actor
Dan Aykroyd, Canada, 1975, actor/comedian
Martina Navratilova, Czechoslovakia, 1975, tennis champion
Iman Abdulmajid ("Iman"), Somalia, 1975, model
Agostino "Dino" De Laurentiis, Italy, 1976, film director

Jerry Yang, Taiwan, 1978, cofounder of Yahoo!
Joaquin Phoenix, Puerto Rico, 1978, actor
Michael J. Fox, Canada, 1979, actor
Ang Lee, Taiwan, 1979, film producer
Sergey Brin, Soviet Union, 1979, cofounder of Google

STELLA DUSHATS
BORN MARCH 14, 1937
EMIGRATED FROM RUSSIA, 1977, AGE 40

She is from St. Petersburg, Russia, where she was a teacher and her husband was an accomplished and well-known architect. Anti-Semitism drove them, along with their sixteen-year-old daughter, to America to start over in search of a better life. They settled in San Jose, California. She became a bookkeeper. He got an entry-level job at a San Francisco architectural firm and worked his way up from there. She is the first cousin of famous Ellis Island immigrant Isabel Belarsky, who immigrated to America through Ellis Island in 1930 when she was ten years old and was interviewed in my previous book, Ellis Island Interviews: In Their Own Words. *Isabel is the daughter of Sidor Belarsky, the famed Yiddish singer and conductor, whose music was featured in the Coen Brothers movie* A Serious Man. *Sidor and Stella's mother were brother and sister. "We knew if we work hard we will get everything," Stella said in her thick Russian accent. "But in Russia it didn't matter. You could work hard and get nothing, and if you were Jewish, you got less than nothing. You felt like a second-class citizen."*

We came to America by plane from St. Petersburg to Vienna, Austria. We stayed there for a week and then flew to Rome. We stayed there for nearly four months, and then on April 13, 1977, we flew from Rome to New York and then to San Jose, California. The Jewish Federation of San Jose took responsibility for us.

We left Russia because of problems with being Jewish at that time. It was very difficult to live there and to build any future for my daughter. A lot of Russian Jews emigrated at that time. People would point at you as a Jew. And my daughter, for example, she was the only Jewish girl in her classroom, and everyone would taunt her and point at her: "You are Jew! You are killer!" They said Jews in Israel are killers because they killed the people to keep their land. And she would come home crying, and the teachers were watching that and doing nothing. For example, for me, I was a teacher; I had to be there and listen to what the students had been saying and talking about, and there was not much I could do. My daughter, Galina, was sixteen when we left Russia.

Fig. 41. Stella Dushats (right) with her first cousin, Isabel Belarsky (left), in front of the Metropolitan Museum of Art in New York in the late seventies. Photograph used by permission of the Dushats family.

I was a teacher in chemistry and biology in high school. I was married. My husband passed away three and a half years ago after forty-seven years of marriage. He passed away the day after our forty-seventh wedding anniversary. We married on December 25, and he passed away on December 26. He was an architect. He was involved in the reconstruction of the main part of St. Petersburg. We had already built our careers because we finished university and had been working. But we didn't know what would happen with our daughter because only 3 percent of young Jewish people could go to university. And the whole situation with Jewish people in Russia was you never knew what could happen. In the street, you could be abused because you are Jew; you could be told in your face, "You are dirty Jew." All the time we were told and reminded that we are Jews and that in Israel they are killers and you are part of these people, that kind of stuff. Nobody tortured us, but you could be beaten on the street and it wouldn't be by the government, but by regular people. Even now, people said when Stalin passed away [1953], it was exactly the time when all the Jewish people from all the cities were supposed to be transferred somewhere—who knows where? All the trains were ready to take all the Jewish people together to transfer to Siberia or somewhere east. There are a lot of books which are now available to the public to read about what Stalin's plan was. . . .

Our life in Russia was a hardworking life. Put it this way: I was a teacher and my husband worked many hours each day. We didn't starve. You know, we are educated people. We like theater, we like music, but moneywise, we didn't make so much. We didn't travel because it wasn't allowed for us to travel to different countries. But we did go in summertime to the countryside sometimes and traveled to the Baltic countries, which were close to us, north of St. Petersburg.

I had some friends who were in America, and they gave information about us to the Jewish Federation. There were a lot of Jewish organizations in communities in different states and different cities that had been taking care of Jews, such as the one headquartered in New York called the Hebrew Immigrant Aid Society [HIAS]. They had actually been taking care of us, and there was an office in Rome that had been helping us, and they distributed immigrants to different states and different cities, and that's how we came to San Jose.

We flew to New York, into JFK, and stayed overnight in a hotel before we continued on to San Jose. My cousin Isabel and her mom, Clarunia, found out from HIAS where we were staying, and they met us there at this little hotel in New York. We were sitting there in the lobby crying and talking the whole night, and the next morning we flew to San Jose. At that point, Sidor, Isabel's father, had passed away two years earlier, so Isabel and Clarunia were living together in Brighton Beach, Brooklyn, and I guess we could have gone there. But they [HIAS] told us it would be much better if we go to California—more opportunity, especially for Galina's education because college in California was free. They said it would be better to build our life in California, and they were right because we were very happy here. They said it was too crowded in

Brooklyn, that in San Jose, there weren't so many immigrants, so we could have more attention, more help for our first few months than we would in Brooklyn. We also had a friend who came to San Jose a year before us, and HIAS had an office here.

Fig. 42. Isabel Belarsky with her father, Sidor, the famous Yiddish singer and conductor, in 1947. Photograph used by permission of the Belarsky family.

It wasn't the same process as the people who came through Ellis Island. This was organized before we left—an organized immigration process. We had a visa just to get here, and then as soon as we came, HIAS had wonderful volunteers here. I'm still friends with them. And they took care of us, and they took us to the office to get permission for work. It was not a green card. We would not get our green cards for another couple of years, but we still had the permission to live here and to work here.

We lived in an apartment. HIAS took care of everything. They paid the rent on the apartment. But I remember being very scared because we didn't know English. We didn't have anyone here. Sometimes when the telephone rang we were scared to pick it up because we didn't understand English. I learned a little bit back in Russia many years ago, but our English was very limited. For example, when my husband had to make a speech the first morning at his new job, he said, "Thank you, us, that we came to you." [*She laughs.*] So I took English classes. There were forty-five people in a class, but [it was] only two hours a week.

My daughter didn't know any English. She started English at school. She went to high school in tenth grade. Then she went to summer camp for three months, and she picked up enough English to go to eleventh grade, and the next year she finished and got her high school diploma.

I went to bookkeeping classes. My husband had gone through the newspaper, and he said most job ads were for bookkeepers. I started working in San Jose at the British-American Club as a bookkeeper. My husband got a job in San Francisco in some architectural office. He went to San Francisco every single day in the morning, taking the bus, taking the train, and then working there, but of course it was very helpful because drawings are drawings so he could look at any drawing and understand what's going on.

After work, almost every day, he would take English classes. In Russia they used the metric system, but not here. So the owner of the company here said at his first interview, "You first have to learn about inches and feet." Imagine, this was a man who was a big person in Russia, and so many people knew him because he was very knowledgeable about the old buildings in downtown St. Petersburg. He was accomplished there. He had worked many years already. He went to technical college, and after college he was in Russian army for three years because in Russia you must go into the army. So with his first job here he was like a beginner. He was treated like he was just starting out again. Because it was a different system, different buildings, different measurements, so it was a very difficult time for us. When we first came here, and I would say I'm from Russia, most Americans then knew only Siberia and vodka. I said, what about Tchaikovsky? What about the Bolshoi Ballet? Do you know anything besides Siberia and vodka?

We didn't have friends. We were very limited moneywise; he made just $3.75 per hour, and I made $2.50 per hour. We had a grownup daughter. We weren't hungry. We had enough food, but it was hard to go through such a transformation. Morally we were very down, but at the same time we were free! We felt like if we worked hard we could accomplish a lot. And that's how we started—day and night, sleep a few hours a day, but the main thing [was] our daughter did go to school and that was our main happiness, you know?

She graduated high school and then went to West Valley Community College. At the same time, she worked, and then she got married quite young. She was in her early twenties when she married a Jewish boy who also came from Russia, but after that she did go to San Jose State University, and he went there too and graduated, and that was our happiness and we could forget about all the difficult times. And, again, as I'm saying, it wasn't the same like people who went through Ellis Island, where nobody helped them—you know they just got there and that's it. But emotionally I would say it was an absolutely different atmosphere for us than Russia because we were free and we could do whatever we want. We knew if we worked hard we will get everything. But in Russia it didn't matter. You could work hard and get nothing, and if you were Jewish, you got less than nothing. You felt like a second-class citizen.

The first time when I went back to Russia with my husband was in '79. All my relatives came to talk to us, and we said, "You have to immigrate right away," and actually the same year all my cousins from my mother's side, Isabel's aunt and all our cousins and children, they are all here now in San Jose, except for two cousins who are in Israel. We have no relatives anymore in Russia.

My husband went on to work for the city of Palo Alto for twenty-two years, and he did very well and was well known and respected in his field. I have a swimming pool. When my husband used to come home from work, the first thing he did was go for a swim. He loved to swim. . . . [*She pauses.*] Then three and a half years ago, I lost my husband. He had cancer. He never knew he had cancer, and he passed away in four days. [*She pauses again, more upbeat.*] But I have my two granddaughters. I have a beautiful house, and my daughter has a house, and my daughter paid for her children to go to private school and then to private university, and my daughter and her husband both work very hard, and I still work.

In America, if you work hard and you want something, you will get it. I am so happy we came here.

ARIANE DAGUIN
BORN MARCH 12, 1958
EMIGRATED FROM FRANCE, 1977, AGE 19

She comes from an affluent family of restaurateurs in the Gascony region of France. By the time she was nineteen, strained family relations led her to America to make her mark. She considered journalism and studied political science but eventually returned to what she knew best: the food business. In 1985, with a partner, she started a company from scratch. It was a gourmet wholesale food company called D'Artagnan, named after the charismatic Gascony nobleman popularized by Alexandre Dumas in the novel The Three Musketeers. *Today she has 123 employees and twenty-nine trucks, and she grossed more than $50 million in annual sales in 2009. She built a network of more than 250 farmers in ten states and abroad that supplies more than three thousand restaurants across the country, including virtually all the three- and four-star restaurants in New York, and is credited with being the first to make foie gras in America. She is the author of the book* D'Artagnan in New York, *which was recently published in France to rave reviews and recounts her travails in successfully building her business. "We started with $15,000," she said. "The day we opened the door officially, we had thirty-five dollars left in the bank account."*

I come from Gascony in the southwest of France. I left to come to America for a bunch of reasons. I come from a family of restaurateurs. In my family everybody's in the food business. When they're not in the food business, they are in the farming business, or hunting or fishing. So ever since I was very little, all I learned about was food. In Gascony, everybody lives for food. So I wanted to see if there was something else in life. Also, my father owned a hotel/restaurant in Auch, the capital of Gascony, which got two Michelin stars. He's retired now, but he was a big figure in gastronomy and nouvelle cuisine. He invented how to cook the migrate, the breast of duck, and he was a big personality. I was the oldest child. My brother is a year younger and my little sister is seven years younger, and in the family it was never said, but it was clear that I was not going to take over the hotel area—that my brother was. He was groomed for it, but I wanted to show what I was worth. I was proud . . . so that's why I came here.

Fig. 43. Ariane Daguin, in her New Jersey office at D'Artagnan, proudly displays the certificate of US citizenship she received in May 2010. Photograph used by permission of Cengiz Ozdemir.

I like to write. So I thought maybe I would become a journalist. But I took political science at the university in Toulouse, and then one thing led to another, and I came to America and got a job as an au pair in Connecticut. I was accepted at Barnard College in political science, dropped out, and then worked as an employee at the Three Little Pigs, which was a charcuterie, a little store on Thirteenth Street in Manhattan. So I went right back into food. Why? I ran out of money. My parents and I were not really speaking at the time when I left to come here.

I would never have gone back to France because I didn't want to come back with nothing. I wanted to show that I could do something with my life. I really wanted to show that I could do something without my father's influence because I saw all the girls whose fathers were the same level as my father. They would end up in a public relations agency presenting champagne or something, and I would hear people say, "Oh, she's there because of her father," and I really didn't want that. I wanted to show that I could do it on my own. I wanted to impress my parents—my father, in particular—and I was mad. I was the oldest, and I could have taken over the hotel.

But now I'm so glad that I didn't. I'm so glad that it turned out this way. I am totally thankful. Because I came here and I had to fight, and I ended up doing something that I love, starting a company that is my second baby and living a life that I really, really enjoy.

For five years, I worked at the Three Little Pigs. It's a retail store, but right away I said, "Instead of selling a slice of pâté to the housewife, we should make the whole pâté and sell it wholesale to Balducci's around the corner and all those specialty stores and gourmet shops," and my bosses at the time, two French guys, said OK.

So I brought in a friend of mine I had met at Columbia University at the International House. His name was George [Faison]. He was in the dormitory there, and he was a Texan—everybody else was a foreigner; I guess they still think Texans are foreigners—and he was a young American who would come with us Europeans once a month. We would spend all of our money at a good restaurant, and he was the only American doing that with us. So we became friends, and he was finishing his MBA, and so he was ready for life and liked to live. And so I'm with those guys [at the Three Little Pigs] for a year now and we want to expand and do wholesale, and I said, "George, we need you," and he joined us because the two owners were really overwhelmed. I was pretty good at selling, quality control, the new products; I was in charge of that, all the logistics and the finance. But the owners didn't have much of an education in France. They knew how to cook and they made pâtés, but soon it became bigger than them, you know?

I stuck with them for five years, and one day two guys arrived with foie gras in their hands. This was 1979, and I couldn't believe it: "What do you mean, foie gras?" I thought it was not allowed in America. They said, "What do you mean? There is no law against this." They were Israeli and they came with American partners, and they had started a farm here for making foie gras up in Monticello, New York, and they wanted to see how they could sell the stuff commercially. Their forte was the processing and the slaughterhouse and the breeding and all that stuff, so I absolutely wanted to be a part of this. For me, it was historical. The first foie gras in America!

I started the negotiations. Then one day, my bosses and I went up to the farm in Monticello, and on the way up they talked with each other about it really for the first time. They knew where I stood on this. And along the way, during the two-and-a-half-hour drive, they became more and more against signing the exclusivity agreement.

I was so pissed off and sad, beyond belief! I had worked on this for three months to convince those farmers that we would be the only ones carrying their product, and what we would do with the rest of the duck— the breast, the legs, etc.—because the foie gras, the liver, was the most valuable, but you can't throw away the rest; this is where the money is, where you make it or not, you know?

But the father there who owned the farm threw us out, and that was that. They found an excuse not to sign. They insinuated that there was something fishy, and the father got really upset and said, "You're in my office—get out!" [*She laughs.*] And my two bosses were saying, "You know, it's a good thing we didn't go into this," because they had built a good business. They didn't need to take any risks. They had six pâtés; life was good. When one was on vacation and came back the other one went, and so everything was cool. So they didn't want to risk it.

It was on the way back in the van when I knew I was going to start my own company. And I talked with my friend George, and after more than a couple of lunches with margaritas, I convinced him and he said, "OK, let's do it!"

Meanwhile, by the time I convinced him, we had already started looking for a place and put together a business plan where it wouldn't be only foie gras, because we couldn't survive. We needed game and poultry and good food for restaurants. By the time we did that, the farmers in Monticello had panicked already and started selling to butchers and meat wholesalers in Manhattan. So we had to convince them that they needed one more, which they really didn't, but they went for it. We had to pay COD. George resigned from the Three Little Pigs. I stayed. On Sundays I would take the van, go to the farm in Monticello, check the foie gras, and choose them. During the week we would sell them, organize everything, and then after three weeks, I also resigned and we started D'Artagnan!

We started at the beginning of '85, and it went truly well for several years. It was very hard every day. And every day for the first three years, either George or I would come and say, "OK, I'm not coming tomorrow. I leave you the company; it's too hard, too much," and every day, one of us would say, "One more day, just one more day." The company was located in Newark, New Jersey, because it's close to the airport, near Manhattan, good highways in the northeast corridor from Boston to Washington, DC, for shipping. We started with $15,000. The day we opened the door officially, we had thirty-five dollars left in the bank account. Because we had to pay three months' rent, we had to find a truck. The truck was a lease we took over from a guy who wanted to do some orange juice thing that didn't work out—it had to be a refrigerated truck—but we needed a logo to paint on the truck.

We discovered the logo at a bistro in Greenwich Village and the bartender overheard us. We were deciding the name of the company, and I said, "D'Artagnan, it has to be D'Artagnan," and then the bartender overheard and said, "You know, in my native country in Russia, I'm a graphic designer." So we explained the company and it's going to be called D'Artagnan, named after the musketeer, and in two seconds on a cocktail napkin he drew the logo that we still have today! We took our last $2,000 to paint the logo on the truck. At the time I was living in Fort Greene, Brooklyn, which was not as civilized as today, and I parked the truck. The next morning, there was graffiti all over it. I cried on the sidewalk. . . .

George and I eventually had a big breakdown. He tried to buy me out. . . . We had a clause between us. It's called a "shotgun clause." We were partners fifty-fifty, so we had to take out life insurance—one partner on the other partner—that if something happens to one partner and they die, the other partner has life insurance for half the value of the company. In that way, the company doesn't suffer the loss of one of the partners.

The shotgun clause also said that if one day one partner doesn't agree with the other, they have the right to put an offer on the table—any offer—and the other one cannot say no. The value is set by the first partner, and the second cannot go lower or higher—the value is already set. It's either, "Yeah, I take it" [sell you my half at that price], or "No, it's me" [buy your half at that price]. So George did that to me, [but] as part of the terms he said, "Thirty days." In other words, the terms in his letter were the amount of money and thirty days. But the amount was so enormous, there was no way I could raise it in thirty days. It was impossible.

In the meantime, my daughter and I were supposed to leave on vacation for three weeks to China, and everything was organized with friends of mine. So that weekend I called my daughter, who was at my parents' in Gascony, and I said, "I don't think I'm going to be able to come to China because I have this thing that's happening with George, and I'm sorry." She was fifteen at the time. "Do you still want to go to China?" We were to go with a friend of mine and his boy. They all knew each other, and she said, "Yeah, I want to go to China," and then she realized that I was not going to come, and then she realized what I just said—that I may lose the company—and she said, "But what if I wanted to work at D'Artagnan one day?"

And that's when it hit home. That was the thing that made me want to keep it at any price. Over the years she went to demos with me. We did cooking classes together. We were attached at the hip, you know? And I'm not married, but that touched my heart. Because up until then, I was thinking, "What do I do? It's a lot of money maybe I should just forget it and go back to France, open a little restaurant, and that's it."

But after what she said, I was resolved: "I have to get it! He's not going to do this to me after twenty years of business together. I cannot let that happen. I have to find that money!" I cannot say how much, but it was several million dollars for me to buy him out.

So I knocked on doors and realized in July everybody was on vacation and it was going to be very difficult. And I was at the Fancy Food Show in Manhattan, and I had three bankers who came to visit me at the booth, which was very difficult because George was there. We were both looking at each other. The employees knew something was dead wrong; it was so bad. And one banker, a French banker, said, "I'm going to help you," and he did. He went to France. He called me. I remember it was Bastille Day, and he said, "Yesterday I had a meeting with my guys, and it's a go-ahead!" That was July 14. George had given me the shotgun clause on June 17, so I had to declare my intention on July 17—so I made it by three days, just in time. I remember I was in front of Provence, the French bistro [since closed] in the meatpacking district, and I bought a drink for everybody and nobody knew why. [*She laughs.*]

My father and I made up. When the company started to stand on its own and I started to have good publicity, he became very proud of me, but he never said anything to me. Never! He doesn't talk. Even this year, our twenty-fifth anniversary, we did a big party. I invited two thousand people to Guastavino's, under the Queensboro Bridge. We had a big plane full of Gascony people who came to the party—chefs, rugby players, musicians, friends, family, my parents. We asked everybody to dress in red and white, which are the colors of D'Artagnan but also the colors of Auch, my hometown. And the next day people said, "Wow! Your father was so proud!" And I didn't know. He never told me. Even then, he never said a word.

I got my green card in 1986, and I literally just got my citizenship certificate the other day [June 2010]. I passed the test last month and took the official oath of allegiance. I could have done it a long time ago because I love America, but it was time. Now every time I go to France and come back, Customs cannot look at me like, "If you're not a citizen, why are you here?" Which I can understand.

I love France, of course. And when I went on the book tour in May [2010] in Paris, every journalist at some point asked me one question: "And where are you going to end your days?" But they said it in a way that [meant] I better stay in France because that's what they were expecting to hear. And frankly, every time, I said, "I don't know," which was the truth. I have deep, deep roots with my region of France. I'm not French; I'm Gascon. That's why I named my company after D'Artagnan. He was a hero who really lived in Gascony, was very loyal to his friends, to his family, and, of course, to the king and, especially, the queen. He was a guy who wanted to do things with panache, and that's what I wanted in my company. I wanted to do things with panache. And to this day, I think we've been pretty successful at doing that. Doing it the right way for the beauty of it, not for the "What's in it for me?" It's a totally Gascon way of seeing things, I think. We all think in Gascony that we're descendants of D'Artagnan—the panache, the loyalty, the grand gesture. [*She pauses.*] But I live here. I love it here. So I decided to become a citizen. I decided this is my country now.

PASTOR JIM MACNEE
BORN JULY 2, 1967
EMIGRATED FROM CANADA, 1979, AGE 12

His is an amazing story of faith and recovery. He grew up in the outback of western Ontario, Canada, until age twelve. He emigrated to America when his father accepted a position as pastor at a Baptist church in rural Kentucky. Like his father, he, too, became a pastor. He was twenty-eight, in the prime of his life— newly married, in a new home, having just accepted a new job as pastor of a church, his wife pregnant with their first child—when a fluke car accident revealed he had cancer and had less than a year to live. Against all odds, enduring a remarkable test of faith, he somehow survived the ordeal and eventually returned with his family to his native Canada, a living, walking miracle of a man.

My father was a pastor, so I guess it makes sense that I would become a pastor too. My family is Scots-Irish. Over the centuries, my family historically migrated from Scotland to the west of Ireland, then to Nova Scotia in the Canadian Maritimes, and finally to Ontario, Canada. I grew up in a small rural town in western Ontario. I lived there for the first twelve years of my life. Then my father was offered a job as a pastor at a Baptist church in Kentucky, and we moved there. It was my parents and me. I was an only child.

We moved from Canada to Ashland, Kentucky; it's a small town on the Ohio River near the state lines of Ohio, Kentucky, and West Virginia. It was your typical Midwest river town, where life was slow, family-oriented, with school during the week, church on Sundays, solid American, but very sheltered. There wasn't a lot of crime or violence. It was a nice place to live and raise kids. My father was a pastor at a local Baptist church. My mother was a homemaker.

From an early age, I went to church. I became a believer at age five, was baptized at age six, and by age seventeen, I felt the call from God to go into the ministry. God had been tugging at my heart for some time. I was a youth pastor well into my early twenties. I went to a local college, Marshall University, and graduated with a teaching degree, and then spent one year attending Moody Bible Institute in Chicago, and that changed me. For the first time I saw life through the lens of a large city and not just a small town.

When I went to Chicago, I saw things I'd never seen before. I was a twenty-one-year-old kid, and on Sunday morning I would go with a ministry team to a rest home. I was the preacher. I had a song leader and a couple of others who came along, and every week we had to go to the South Side of Chicago, which was not exactly the best part of town. I saw how great the diversities are and the needs are in urban areas; just the whole cultural dynamic gripped me, and I felt like God was preparing me to have a larger vision than just what I had seen up to that point. I learned two things: awareness—that God wanted me to see things through his eyes, not just through my eyes—and the second thing I learned was preparation, that I needed to really prepare well if I was going to become a successful pastor.

After graduating from Marshall University, I studied for three years at the Southern Baptist Theological Seminary in Louisville, Kentucky, in my quest for preparation. I totally engulfed myself, learning Greek, Hebrew, and then I had all the biblical training.

After that, I was called to pastor at a rural church deep in the heart of Appalachia. They were without a pastor, and I was single at the time, twenty-seven years old. The church had gone through some transition, and so I came in as a young minister trying to revive it.

I met my wife, Sara, there. Of course, you have to remember, as a single pastor a lot of people wanted to fix me up with their daughters or granddaughters. There was a guy in our church who said, "One of these days, someone is going to walk through that back door and you're going to know it's the right person." Sure enough, I was preaching one Sunday and Sara walked in. I had seen her a hundred times, and maybe it was the glow of the light coming through the window that day, but I thought, "That's the person for me."

One year later, I proposed to Sara. Three months later, we were married and awaiting word on an open position for pastor of a Baptist church in northern Kentucky, near Cincinnati. By this time, I had developed a reputation as an excellent pulpit pastor who gave concise, well-organized sermons without looking at his notes. I got the job, and we moved to northern Kentucky and our new home.

It was the fall of 1995, and I was feeling on top of the world. I was a young pastor, newly married to a beautiful brunette. We honeymooned in Florida, and then I started work as pastor of the church. That year just seemed like a lot of firsts for us. Sara and I had our first Thanksgiving together. We had our first Christmas together. As newlyweds, we had also just spent our first Easter together, and by this time Sara was six months pregnant with our first child. Then one ordinary morning in May, everything changed.

I was about to begin my daily routine, which included a visit to a local hospital in Covington, Kentucky, a short distance from downtown Cincinnati, making my rounds offering prayer and solace to those in need. But en route to the hospital, I stopped at a traffic light. Just then, a gasoline tanker traveling approximately forty-five miles per hour failed to brake and slammed into the rear of my car. The impact sent it clear across a main intersection. Fortunately for me, there were no oncoming cars. I had my seatbelt on, and my airbag was deployed, but I didn't feel any pain. It didn't seem like anything was wrong, really, but EMS suggested I go to the hospital for an x-ray.

The doctors didn't like what they saw, so they took additional x-rays, a CT scan, and made an appointment for me to be examined by an oncologist. I suffered no ill effects from the accident. The problem lay elsewhere, it seemed. The doctors told me, "There's a very large mass in your chest," something the size of a softball, that the mass was around my lungs and heart—the whole chest area. It was a large tumor, too large to operate. They did a biopsy from the neck, which revealed it was stage two non-Hodgkin's lymphoma. Cancer. The doctors told me the accident may have saved my life because they said, "If we hadn't found this, you'd probably be gone within a year."

They also said that because of the location and type of cancer that it was, surgery was not an option. I was going to need six to eight months of intensive chemotherapy and radiation treatments, ending sometime around Christmas. The treatments were heavy chemotherapy doses once every three weeks, with radiation treatments one day per week for two months. The doctors said the best-case scenario was that they would somehow shrink the tumor and give me a few more years.

My wife and I were in disbelief. How could this be? Sara really took it hard. This was shocking to her. She was living with me in our new life together. She was pregnant, and now she was faced with the prospect that I may not live and our child may grow up without a father.

I couldn't believe it was happening. I remember being alone in the master bedroom of our home. I just wanted to be by myself. I remember thinking, "This is not the way it's supposed to be," and I cried out to God. I asked him, "Is this really happening?" And then I felt this sense of assurance that swept over my body, saying to me, "This *will* be OK."

The Old Testament speaks about the "still small voice." I felt like God spoke to me through his Holy Spirit, that "this is all in my greater good." He didn't tell me I was going to be healed. He just said, "I am with you." His presence felt so real. I felt him saying to me, "I'm going to get you through this whole process."

So I was probably in denial no more than twenty minutes. I felt drawn to the Bible and particularly Philippians 4:4–7, which I read every day: "Rejoice in the Lord always; again I will say, Rejoice. Let all men know your forbearance. The Lord is at hand. Have no anxiety about anything, but in everything by prayer and supplication with thanksgiving let your requests be made known to God. And the peace of God which transcends all understanding will guard your hearts and your minds in Christ Jesus."

In the following weeks, the disease and the treatment took a real toll on me physically. I lost all my hair. I was pale, gaunt, emaciated looking. I lost much of my energy and strength, and there was a terrible metallic taste in my mouth that never seemed to go away so that food never tasted good. I started to wear hats to protect my bald scalp against sunburn. I was never sick growing up. Just the opposite. I was healthy. Athletic. I didn't smoke or drink. In addition, the irony for me: here I had gone to visit hundreds of people in the hospital over the years—cancer patients, all kinds of patients with serious illness—but I never thought that I would be one of them.

The doctors didn't understand. They said it could be from environmental factors. Genetic factors. I once had an uncle who died of stomach cancer.

There were many questions that I had, but I always found myself going back to the Bible, to scripture, to resolve them. First of all, you have to understand that both believers and nonbelievers can say that it's not God punishing me per se, and that it could be for the greater good of humanity, so to speak; that oftentimes God has cured people, oftentimes he allows us to go through tests and trials to demonstrate his compassion and love, and I really came to the conclusion that if this was God's course for my life, so be it. If I were to pass, and then there was a greater good, then both Sara and I were comfortable in knowing that we had done everything we could and that it was out of our hands because we sought out the best doctors and followed the medical regimen to the T.

In addition, as part of my daily regimen I took walks and read verse. Pray and walk, that's what I did for six months. I felt very reassured that God was going to take care of me, so I really put my faith in him. There were many scripture passages that were therapeutic for me.

But it was Sara who held me together. She did this through her love and refused to let me feel sorry for myself. She has such strength of character. She said things like, "We're going to beat this! We're going to get better!" We developed a strong "we can get through anything" bond. Doctors would fill my body up with chemicals, and I knew I would throw up, but this one particular time, I just couldn't make it to the bathroom of our new house, and I threw up in the kitchen, on the carpet, in the sink, everywhere, and there she was, cleaning up my vomit. It was a very humbling experience.

Then there was the emotional stress of not knowing if my sickness would negatively affect our child in Sara's womb. A sonogram told us it was a boy. Would I be alive to see my son's birth, or even the first few months of his life? But that wasn't all. The doctors told us that due to the chemotherapy, we'd probably never be able to have more children.

In the meantime, I continued to preach every Sunday, as much for my sanity as to reassure the congregation that they were not going to lose their pastor. After all, it had taken the church more than two years to find a new one. I could see the uncertainty every Sunday morning when I preached. I had only been there about seven months. The congregation looked sympathetically toward me: "Here's someone going through pain; let's see if his message matches his faith," but there were doubts and concern. I mean, several people told me, "Until we get the all-clear sign, we still don't think you're going to make it." And they just didn't want to get too close, too emotionally attached. They had just lost a previous pastor, and they were just getting to know us, and then I got sick, and so the attitude of many church members was, "We're going to back off until we know that you're going to be around."

Sometimes I wasn't even aware of how the congregation was behind me because when you go through something like this, you have to walk it alone. I know there were times I absolutely dragged myself to the church for services so as to not to let the church congregation down. I kept them apprised of my medical situation and infused my sermons with the circumstances of my life. One of the phrases I used a lot during this time was, "You can't get bitter—you gotta get better." Meaning you can't get bitter toward God. He has a plan, and it's going to see its course.

We received hundreds of cards and phone calls, and we were on prayer chains across the state of Kentucky. Of course, my mother was at our home almost daily, especially after one of my four-hour treatments, and my condition was showing no improvement. I was about to have my sixth and final chemotherapy session when the doctors informed me that a CT scan revealed that the mass in my chest had *not* shrunk and requested that I undergo additional treatments, and that shocked me.

I didn't expect that. Neither did Sara. She was now in her third trimester, and things looked really bleak. I felt really bleak. And I didn't understand all that was happening. I had faith. I had people praying for me. I had been anointed in the name of God to be healed—so I had all of it.

It felt like our faith was being tested. One day, a woman, a complete stranger, came into my office and said, "I just want to tell you that I heard about your plight and I have bad news: You're not going to make it! God has something else in store for you," and she left like some demonic apparition.

"Who was that?" my secretary asked.

"I don't know," I said. And I never saw her again.

Another time, Sara answered the phone and allowed a salesman to make an appointment, not really knowing what the appointment was for. Turns out it was someone selling plots at the local graveyard. My mother answered the door and she was stunned. She said, "Why are we having this conversation?" She thought Sara and I had made arrangements to buy cemetery plots.

We were feeling low and weary from the stress. We decided to get away for Labor Day weekend to Lake Cumberland in Tennessee. A church member had offered us use of his cabin. So we decided to go there and look at life and hold each other a little tighter. One afternoon, we went to the swimming pool and started talking about what if I don't make it. We talked about the financial aspects of it. Would Sara go back to live with her parents? Or would she stay in Kentucky with an infant? We had to have this conversation. It wasn't something we wanted to have, certainly not in the first year as husband and wife. But there we were having this conversation of what-ifs. I remember some insurance company once itemized the big stresses in life: a move is a big stressor, a new house is a big stressor, an illness, and the birth of a child. I mean, we had all of them going at the same time.

Then, at some point during that weekend, our attitudes became more optimistic, and we said, "Let's go forward and talk about the birth of our son." We were thinking negatively—that maybe things won't go well, maybe I had only a year to live, but our son was still going to be born, so we started channeling our energies positively as to what we could do to make his arrival great, which was only a few weeks away.

Driving back home from Lake Cumberland, I recall feeling what a blessing that weekend had been because it just rekindled our honeymoon all over again. I felt so happy that I had married her. I didn't want that weekend to end—physically, spiritually. Of course, we believed that God was going to take care of us. We were just leaning on him.

The key scripture for me was [Philippians 4:7]: "And the peace of God, which transcends all understanding, will guard your hearts and your minds in Christ Jesus."

I felt like not only was God guarding my heart with that scripture, he was guarding my mind, too, because it was almost like he gave me a covering of protection so that I wouldn't think too far ahead, and in that way stay positive.

But once home, reality set in. It was an emotional low point when the ladies of the church held a baby shower for Sara. We came in that night, and the ladies knew things weren't going well medically, and I think they felt more sorry for us than happy for us, and that they were going to have to find a new pastor again, and that Sara would likely be moving back home, and I'll be in heaven. Gone. This was the bottom.

Then one day, I went to the hospital for a special SPECT scan: a three-hour procedure in which doctors had me drink dye to get a good look at the inside of my body. Everything in a SPECT scan is either green or red. The green is healthy tissue; red is the tumor. The doctor said he would get back to me in a couple of days, but the technician already had the results and let me see them.

I looked at the chart and it looked all green! I was thinking, "Praise God. Thank you, God." I had completed all of my chemotherapy treatments, and it was just miraculous! After the doctor told me the results in person, it was an even greater relief. He couldn't believe it. He was elated! I don't think I heard him say "miracle," but I know he was thinking that. I think it certainly was an act of God, working through those doctors, through those medicines, that he divinely allowed me to heal—not just physically, but emotionally, mentally, spiritually.

I immediately called home. Sara and I both cried. My father wasn't an emotional person, so he didn't like to talk about my illness. It was something we didn't bring up much, but when I was healed, it was like the weight was off his shoulders. He cried. My mother cried. . . .

I reported back to the congregation the joyful news. It was a Sunday service, the first Sunday after Thanksgiving. The congregation of 350 stood on its feet and applauded. Sara beamed. I tried to sum up my feelings that day, which is that God had really guided my heart and my mind. That God can take the bad and turn it into good, that *he's in control!* I was feeling not only hopeful, but that God was going to bring hope and happiness to a lot of people in the congregation who had been there with us and sacrificed and prayed and connected with us through our pain. One man said after the service, "You're the only miracle I know."

Soon after, we were blessed with a healthy seven-pound, four-ounce, brown-haired baby boy!

I remember that day. I just drove around for an hour by myself, listening to my favorite spiritual songs on the car CD player. It was just a beautiful, bright sunny day, and I thought, "I've got my health, I've got my son, I'm going to live! I'm going to enjoy life! I'm so blessed!"

The following year, we were quite surprised when we had our second child, a daughter, and even more surprised two years after that when we had our third child, a son. We were so thrilled to have three healthy children! As far as my health, the doctors say I am cured, the cancer in total remission.

Now I wake up every day thanking God for the blessing and the challenges—because God has allowed us to go through this for a reason, and it's to help others. It's to be an encouragement. I think my surviving cancer was another event to help me become a better pastor. I see it all as a connection. To be a better minister and a better person, and to be able to really minister to people where they are. That's what I want to do. I've learned that even in the darkest valley, God will be with you if you allow him to be.

A few years later, my parents returned to Canada, and Sara and I decided to go as well and keep the family together. Her parents had already passed. And we'd done our work here. It was time to go home. The children were still young. They, of course, were born here, so they're American citizens. So, of course, was Sara. But interestingly enough, my father, mother, and me—none of us ever became citizens. We had our green cards, but that's all.

So we returned to Canada and the life we once knew. It was a simpler life, and that's what we wanted. Fewer people. Less congestion. Less complication. Less drama. More open land. Lakes and streams. Beautiful scenery. Nature. The hand of God everywhere; after all we went through, both for ourselves and our children, this is what we wanted to be near: the hand of God.

That's my story.

Chapter 10

1980s

This decade was highlighted by President Ronald Reagan's 1986 signing into law of the Immigration Reform and Control Act. It was a major new revision of US immigration policy. The law offered amnesty and legal residency to millions of illegal aliens living in the United States. Approximately three million undocumented residents, mostly Mexicans, took advantage of his offer. The law also hoped to curtail future illegal immigration by implementing penalties against employers who hire undocumented workers.

KEY HISTORIC EVENTS

★1980: Refugee Act of 1980 systematizes the refugee process enacted in response to the Cuban refugee crisis and the "boat people" fleeing Vietnam; it grants asylum to politically oppressed refugees. The United States legally admits more than ten million immigrants.

★1984: US Supreme Court narrows a residency deportation provision of the Immigration and Nationality Act by making seven years of continuous physical presence in the United States a precondition for suspension of deportation procedures.

★1986: President Reagan signs into law the Immigration Reform and Control Act, which he hails as "the most comprehensive reform of our immigration laws since 1952."

★1988: More than 1.5 million illegal immigrants jam legalization centers seeking amnesty as part of the nation's
amnesty program; the Redress Act provides $20,000
compensation to survivors of World War II internment
of Japanese citizens and Japanese Americans.

MIGRATION FLOWS

Total legal US immigration in 1980s: 6.25 million

Top ten emigration countries in this decade: Mexico (1,009,586),
Philippines (502,056), Korea (322,708), India (231,649), Dominican
Republic (221,552), Vietnam (200,632), Jamaica (193,874), China
(170,897), Canada and Newfoundland (156,313), United Kingdom
(153,644)

(See appendix for the complete list of countries.)

FAMOUS IMMIGRANTS

Immigrants who came to America in this decade, and who would later
become famous, include:

Elle Macpherson, Australia, 1980, model
Hakeem Olajuwon, Nigeria, 1980, basketball player
Béla Károlyi, Romania, 1981, gymnastics coach (defected)
Pierce Brosnan, Ireland, 1982, actor
Cary Elwes, England, 1982, actor
Midori Got, Japan, 1982, concert violinist
Amy Adams, Italy, 1983, actress (*Julie & Julia*)
Cristeta Comerford, Philippines, 1985, White House executive chef
Liam Neeson, Ireland, 1987, actor
Gabriel Byrne, Ireland, 1987, actor

Dikembe Mutombo, Republic of Congo, 1987, basketball player
Patrick Stewart, England, 1987, actor
Wayne Gretzky, Canada, 1988, hockey player
Mike Myers, Canada, 1988, actor (*Austin Powers*)
Jacques Torres, France, 1988, chocolatier
Salma Hayek, Mexico, 1989, actress
Sammy Sosa, Dominican Republic, 1989, baseball player
Nadia Comăneci, Romania, 1989, Olympic gymnast (defected)
Alexander Mogilny, Russia, 1989, hockey player (defected)
Vlade Divac, Yugoslavia, 1989, basketball player

Fig. 44. Born in the Republic of Congo, Dikembe Mutombo came to the United States in 1987 on an academic scholarship to study medicine at Georgetown University. He went on to play in the NBA for eighteen years. Photograph used by permission of NBA Photos.

JORGE MUNOZ
BORN MARCH 23, 1964
EMIGRATED FROM COLOMBIA, 1980, AGE 16
ENTERED ILLEGALLY AT CALIFORNIA–MEXICO BORDER

He was a teenager when he emigrated illegally through the Mexico–California border with his sister and six other relatives to reunite with his mother in New York. Today he is known as the "Angel of Queens," a school bus driver and devout Christian who donates homemade food to homeless people, feeding the hungry 365 days a year, rain or shine, from the back of his truck under the No. 7 elevated subway station in Jackson Heights, Queens. He started in 2004, serving eight people per night. Hard economic times have put his services much in demand, and now he averages 120 meals per night, 37,000 annually. His homemade meals can translate to 25 pounds of rice, 20 pounds of pasta, 50 pounds of chicken, 150 cups of coffee, and 175 pieces of bread in a single night. For his efforts, he was given the 2009 CNN Hero Award, and in 2010 he was one of thirteen "American heroes" honored by President Obama with a Presidential Citizens Medal. "My mother has always been my inspiration," he said, "and my mother always says, 'If you share, you're OK with God.'

My mother came to America first by herself and left me and my sister in Colombia. My dad died in 1974 in a car accident. My mother was here in New York. She came here and then sent for us. We flew from Colombia to Mexico. It was me, my sister, and six members of my family—my cousins. We were just immigrants looking for freedom. We crossed the border in Mexico to California, and then from California we flew to New York. At that time, it was easy. I don't like to talk about it because I'm afraid I'll say something wrong. I'm afraid because of my sister, my mom is here, and I crossed the border—and a lot of people in this country don't like immigrants who cross the border, I know that. But I'm a citizen now. I became a citizen in 1992, and I got my green card in 1986 when Ronald Reagan passed the immigration reform [law] and we were able to get our papers.

In New York we started a new life. My mom was working. We lived in Woodhaven, Queens and I went to high school to learn English and then I started working part-time jobs. My sister went to community college to study data processing and finished that. I went to trade school to learn about heating and air-conditioning. Up until then I was doing anything I could. I was driving a taxi, delivering newspapers, delivering magazines, delivering groceries. I worked hard because I wanted to pay back my mom for what she did for us. My mom was working in housekeeping, cleaning houses and offices. When my sister came home from college and I came home from my work, we both helped my mom clean the offices. We always did it, us three together. We are there for each other. We are always together.

Fig. 45. Jorge Munoz with his much-deserved award as a CNN Hero. Photograph by the author.

When I finished trade school, I found a job at a hotel in Manhattan, and then I was laid off, so I applied for a commercial driver's license, and then I applied to drive a school bus. I got the job, and one day I was waiting for the kids to come out of school and I saw two people carting a lot of food to the dumpster. I asked them why. The two people were from Colombia, so we talked, and they said they didn't want it, and I asked, "Can I have it?" and they said they would talk to the owner. There was a food processing factory near the school. The owner said, "OK, you can keep it," but he said, "Do not ever say my name or my company name because I could lose my license." He gave me the food, and I brought it home, and I told my mother that we have to find somebody who needs it. We knew a Mexican family with like twenty family members. We gave it to them. Then we got connected to a Puerto Rican family with twenty-five members. Then, like a month later, they didn't need the food anymore because someone in the family found a job.

At the same time, part of Jackson Heights, Queens, had a Colombian neighborhood, so I used to spend a lot of time there, and I started seeing guys in the street walking around, looking for jobs. So one day I lowered my window down and talked to them. They were laborers, so I asked, "What if you don't get a job that day—how do you eat?" and they said, "If we don't have a job, we have nothing to eat." So that's where I got the idea, right there. And it was not just to help fellow countrymen from Colombia, but all kinds of people, immigrants—Mexicans, Haitians, people from Africa, homeless people, regular Americans, black, white. So I tell 'em, "Wait for me here at this corner because I'm going to bring food tomorrow." I had a truck, and the next day I delivered the food. And that's how it started. I had a Jeep Cherokee when I started, and then I got a brand new truck in 2007. It was my dream, and I had a stable job, and I was saving money. . . .

My daily routine, Monday through Friday, I get up around five fifteen in the morning. I start driving the bus around six thirty. I finish my school route by eight, eight thirty a.m. Then I go to the corner with water, muffins. In the winter I go out with hot coffee, deliver donuts. If I don't get donations, I go to places like Costco, BJ's, to get groceries to buy rice, cooking oil. I take home about $630 a week driving a bus. Every week I spend about

$150 on food. I'm back home around noon, rest for half an hour and go back out for my school route. I finish around five and come back home to help prepare the meals with my mom, finish that, put the food in white [foam coolers] onto my truck, go to the corner in Jackson Heights under the No. 7 elevated subway station, and deliver the food between nine thirty and eleven p.m. All kinds of food—stew, chicken, rice, bread, whatever I can get. Then I drive back home and go to sleep around midnight.

I started six years ago, June 2004. The first week my mom and me cooked food for maybe eight people; the second week it jumped to twenty-four because word spread that there's this guy giving out free food. Then, year by year, it increased to thirty-five, then forty-five. I started doing breakfast, too, if I had donations. Then, two years ago, it was 75 meals, and now it jumped to 90, sometimes 140, 160 per night. Last night it was 122. If they get a job during the day, they're not going to wait until nine thirty at night to eat. So now I get volunteers from my church to help us because some months are busier than others. Winters are busier because of cold weather. But if the weather is nice and people get day jobs—cutting grass, removing garbage, things like that—the number goes down a little. Last year, we averaged 120 meals a day, so that's about 37,000 meals per year.

CNN found out about me because of the *New York Times*. A newspaper reporter saw me delivering meals because the reporter used to live in the area, and he said, "What are you doing?" So I explained, and he said, "Can I interview you?" I didn't know the importance of that newspaper. I thought he was going to write a small article, but Thanksgiving Day weekend there was this big article with two pictures. Then, a year later, CNN came in, and I was nominated for the CNN Hero Award. There were nine thousand nominees for 2009. Then that was reduced to thirty. Then ten out of those thirty were chosen to go to Los Angeles to receive the CNN Hero 2009 Award, and I was one of them, and it felt great! I flew out with my mom and my nephew. The other nominees came from different countries. There was one from the Philippines, one from Nepal, one from Iraq, two from Florida, one from Wisconsin. . . . They paid for everything. CNN had the ceremony next door at the Kodak Theatre where the Oscars are, so we stayed at the hotel where the actors stayed. Beautiful hotel! Right by the Hollywood Walk of Fame. There was an award for $100,000. The guy from the Philippines won that. They gave me a trophy and $25,000. My friends, my family were so happy because I was the only Colombian nominee for this award. I even got a letter from the president of Colombia. . . .

I started getting some donations after the *New York Times* article. After the CNN [coverage], I received a good amount for a while, and then it stopped. I still receive donations from people because of the Spanish media. There are a lot of Colombians around here, and they say, "Jorge, here's fifty pounds of rice that's gotten old," or a box of whatever to help me out. There's a couple of Colombian restaurants that will donate chicken. . . .

I don't think I would ever move back to Colombia. The situation there is worse than here—a lot of guerrilla problems. I've established my life here. My mom's here. My sister has a stable job. I've got a stable job. Why would I move? I'd be out of my mind. [*He pauses.*] You know, people think that we are a problem—the immigrants. We are not a problem! There are a lot of problems with everybody, but we are not a problem! [*He pauses again.*] The only thought that crosses my mind is to share. My mother has always been my inspiration, and my mother always says, "If you share, you're OK with God." If you have ten dollars, give five to somebody else. Like me: I have a place to make food, so if I know somebody is hungry on the street, I take a plate and give it to him. I have a strong faith in God. And I believe that the mission I have is because God wants it. I am a Christian. Not Catholic. Not Protestant. A simple Christian. I go to church six days a week. The only day I don't go is Friday. I believe I am doing God's will, fulfilling his mission for me. And sometimes when I feel like I can't go on, I kneel down in my room and I pray to God. I ask him to be healthy and to be strong, and to have the will to keep doing this as long as he wants me to. When God wants me to stop, he will let me know. I feel blessed by him. As of now, we've served over one hundred thousand meals. Where did those hundred thousand meals come from? Only God knows.

DR. MURAT TUZCU
BORN JULY 5, 1953
EMIGRATED FROM TURKEY, 1985, AGE 32

His plan was to come to America, do his physician training, and then return to Turkey to work and live there, but that never happened. He went on to raise a beautiful family and reach the top of his profession, becoming an academic physician and cardiologist at Cleveland Clinic, widely recognized as one of the finest institutions for cardiology and cardiac surgery worldwide. "I'm very happy I came here," he said. ". . . I feel as much a part of this country as I do a part of Turkey. I don't think that I have to choose to be Turkish or an American. I really think that I can be both."

Right before I came to America, my wife and I worked for two years in southeastern Turkey in a small town called Maden, a copper mining town eight miles north of Diyarbakir. We went there in 1983, and in 1985 we left to come to Cleveland, Ohio.

I was born in a city in the southern part of the country north of Antalya, which is on the coast and there are the Taurus Mountains. My mother and father were originally from there. My father was a school administrator; my mother was a schoolteacher. In 1957, they moved to the Asian side of Istanbul. My mother still lives in the house I grew up in. It was a suburb of Istanbul. We were a middle-class family. My father was a very learned man. He read a lot; he had a very broad knowledge of literature, both Turkish and principally French literature; and our house was full of books. For a middle-class family in Turkey, these were not usual things. My senior year of high school I was in American Field Service in United States, a student exchange program that has chapters all over the world. It formed after World War I by the ambulance drivers in the United States Army. That's why they call it "field service": to promote understanding and peace. It's a big organization. They have chapters in every state.

I came [to the United States] in July 1970 and spent a year living with a family in St. Louis, Missouri, in my senior year of high school. It was an eye-opening experience. I was struck by the opportunities for young people and the liberalism and the wealth. It was also the time of the Vietnam War, and I had a brother who was a year older with a low draft number and a brother a year younger, so I suddenly became aware of the issues of the Vietnam War from a very personal standpoint. It was a very tumultuous time. Also, when you're sixteen or seventeen and away from your family and getting along with people you don't know, it gives you some degree of confidence.

Fig. 46. Dr. Murat Tuzcu. Photograph used by permission of the Tuzcu family.

One of the distinct things I remember from my year in St. Louis was being impressed by the public libraries—the availability of books, the willingness of the people to help you, and everything's free of charge. Just to put it in perspective, in 1970 Turkey things were much more limited. There was very little TV, and it took several months for new movies to come to the cinemas. Making an international phone call was very expensive. You wrote letters instead.

I graduated from Parkway Central High School in St. Louis and then spent three weeks traveling around the country with thirty or so other American Field Service kids, so I went back [to Turkey] with a very broad vision, culturally enriched, and my English improved.

Medical school in Turkey was a six-year program. When I went back, I was able to take the exams and get into Istanbul University Medical School. After my second year, I worked as a volunteer in a chest surgery hospital near my home, and I knew right then I was going to work in the cardiology field. In 1968, my father had a heart attack. In my family we didn't have cancer or arthritis; what we dealt with was heart-related problems, so that's one area I was always interested in.

In 1977 I graduated, did a four-year residency in internal medicine, and went into the military. In Turkey it's mandatory. Two years. Then in 1981 a law passed that mandated everybody after graduation from medical school or from residency [would] serve two years in "underserved" areas.

By that time, 1982, I had married my wife, and the following year we both went to the southeast, to Maden, and that was a whole experience by itself. We were assigned to a hospital that was sort of an outpatient clinic. It was an impoverished area. Most of the houses were made of mud brick. This was a place where many houses could not be reached and the trash was collected by donkeys because it was a steep, mountainous area. I remember making house calls in some places that you couldn't even go up by donkey—you had to walk. These were very poor people, most of them completely illiterate. One thing I learned as a physician is that the fundamentals are the same everywhere—that the need of a sick person is the same everywhere, and that the physician's responsibility is to try to heal people when they're at their most vulnerable. Half the job is to heal them; the other half is holding hands and listening to people and encouraging them and giving them some hope.

We stayed for nine months at a small hotel and then moved to a newly constructed apartment, where our first child was born. I had talked to my wife about coming to the United States. I was thirty. My wife was twenty-six. I always wanted to do some training in the United States in heart disease, so I wrote to maybe a hundred medical centers in the United States from that small town. I did not get any response. I just wanted to go for a year in a training program. Then one of my professors from medical school [in Istanbul] knew people in Cleveland. Ultimately, the chief of medicine at the Cleveland Clinic was traveling to Turkey for two days, and after that Kuwait and other places, and [the professor] said, "If you can get a hold of him and spend half an hour to interview you, we'll look into this."

So I traveled by bus from southeastern Turkey to Istanbul. I remember he was staying at a Hilton, so I parked myself in the lobby that day until this Dr. Farmer came. I'll never forget that name. So he came and I called his room. Dr. Farmer later told me that he was impressed with the work I was doing in the southeast, the poor area, my passion about heart disease and so forth, so I think he came back to Cleveland and convinced people that they should give me a chance. They helped me get a visa for physician training that allowed me to stay and train and get paid—but I had an obligation to go back to Turkey after three years here before applying for any kind of permanent status in the United States.

I went to Cleveland in July of 1985. I got a room at the hotel at the Cleveland Clinic for sixty dollars a night, which was like paying half of my salary. Every day I was trying to find a house to rent for us, for my wife and son. In that first week they told me, "Go get your housing," so I got a newspaper, checked the classifieds, and went by taxi looking at places. I certainly did not get much help. They told me they were going to pay me $19,000 a year, but I didn't understand what that meant. If you go to China and they were going to pay you 19,000 in Chinese money, what did that mean exactly? I ended up in a suburb of Cleveland called Shaker Heights. It was a diverse community, and we rented the first floor of a two-story small house.

In the meantime, I struggled to get an understanding of things. The cardiology training program did not have anybody else like me who did his basic training and medicine residency outside the United States. I was coming in at a very high level, and so I don't think they understood that I was coming through a US hospital for the first time at that level. I had never stepped foot in a US hospital before, and so the first few months were stressful. My wife later told me I did not smile during that time. I wasn't beyond my depth; I just didn't know the way. I spoke good English, but I did not know many of the standardized ways of doing things in US hospitals.

My wife's English wasn't as good as mine, but she's a remarkable woman because she adapted and stayed strong, and I have to give credit to her for taking charge of our lives and learning the ways in the United States, forming some friendships, improving her English, taking care of our baby, and everything else because I was working twelve-, fourteen-hour days. I was on call every third or fourth night. We had sold our furniture and car in Turkey, which put $5,000 in our pocket—it was all very stressful because I had to be successful because I didn't want to go back to Turkey after all this and be in a position of failing, but after the first three months I knew my way around.

I was very interested in academics. I knew all the way from the beginning of medical school that I was going to be an academic physician, who not only takes care of patients but does research to advance the field and gets that research published. Our full intention was to go back to Turkey after the three-year program would finish, which I did. I got an extension on the visa, so we spent four years in Cleveland. In 1989, we went back to Turkey. There was nothing available in Istanbul for me, and then Massachusetts General Hospital [MGH] in Boston offered me a job, an academic position with Harvard Medical School. MGH was the Harvard University Medical School hospital, so that was also very attractive to me.

I first went to Boston as a trainee, then stayed on as a junior faculty. By that time we had our second child, a daughter. Also by that time, my visa started to create problems. I could not stay in the United States and work in an unrestricted manner without a proper visa. I had to go back to Turkey. An alternative was to go to an "underserved" area in the United States to get a waiver.

With the guidance of the people at MGH, I took a job in Pittsburgh Veterans Administration Hospital and was there for a year and a half. The intention was then to go back to my old job in Boston, but by then the Cleveland Clinic became a much more academic institution and became prominent in the field of heart disease and cardiology and in 1994 for the first time was rated number one. So in 1992 we came back to Cleveland—by that time I had my green card—and it's been our home ever since. We've lived in the same house, raised our two children here. It's been a wonderful, wonderful time. My son is twenty-five; my daughter is twenty-two. My son graduated from Miami University of Ohio studying philosophy and literature, and my daughter is studying French and English literature at New York University.

I'm very happy I came here. Of course, the job played a very important role in my happiness, but I also think my wife is happy. We were always close, but making a life from scratch in a country that we did not know—just by ourselves with very little support—brought us even closer, and we have a very happy marriage and we're supportive of each other. My job allows me to use my strength to be a leader in the field that I work in and to keep my ties with the cardiology community in Turkey. I am always working with one or more of the young physicians or cardiologists from Turkey. I go back there three or four times a year, almost always related to some educational activity. I see a lot of patients internationally, but predominantly from Turkey, and it allows me to give back. But I feel as much a part of this country as I do a part of Turkey. I don't think that I have to choose to be Turkish or an American. I really think that I can be both.

I think if you come to the United States and say, "I'm part of this country because it is my inalienable right to pursue happiness and liberty and be better and take advantage," this country tells you that you are one of us. Anybody coming here should realize that. You should not live here with a ghetto mentality. You should not live here as a permanent immigrant. You have to be a part of this country—then the opportunities open up. I really think that's very, very important.

JACQUES TORRES
BORN JUNE 14, 1959
EMIGRATED FROM FRANCE, 1988, AGE 28

This high-energy chocolate entrepreneur was born in Algeria and raised in Provence on the Mediterranean coast. At age fifteen, he apprenticed to be a pastry chef. At twenty-six, in 1986, he became the youngest chef to earn the Meilleur Ouvrier de France medal, France's prestigious craftsman award. He immigrated to America in 1988 to become pastry chef at the Ritz-Carlton in Palm Springs, California. He later moved to New York, became pastry chef at Sirio Maccioni's Le Cirque, and eventually left there to start his own chocolate business in a warehouse in Brooklyn with the help of two partners. Today, Jacques Torres Chocolate is a luxury brand with 2009 revenue of more than $10 million, famous for its bestselling boxes of bonbons. He has a bicoastal marriage with his wife, Hasty Torres, who owns and runs Madame Chocolat in Beverly Hills. He's written three cookbooks and hosted television shows on PBS and the Food Network, and he is the dean of pastry arts at the French Culinary Institute in New York. He lives on a boat at Liberty State Park near Ellis Island and feeds wheat bread to his pets, a duck, and Canadian geese that come by his boat. "I am more of an individualist, an entrepreneur, so that's basically why I like it here," he said. "It fits my personality."

I was born in Algeria in North Africa, but at that time it was not an Arabic country; it was a French territory. Then in 1961 it became Arabic. The French who were there left for France. My dad came from Spain and my mom came from France, so I'm a mixture of French [and] Spanish, and raised at a young age in North Africa in an Arabic community with a Spanish background. Then I grew up in the south of France in Bandol, a little town on the Mediterranean between Toulon and Marseilles, so I am basically a pure product of the Mediterranean. My whole ancestry came from here. My father was a carpenter and craftsman, so I grew up learning how to build things. From three years old to twenty-eight, I was in the south of France. I worked there. I did all my classes there. When I was fifteen, I began my apprenticeship at small local pastry shop and became a pastry chef. . . .

Fig. 47. Chocolatier Jacques Torres at the French Culinary Institute in New York, June 2010. Photograph by the author.

I left France for America in 1988. I visited a couple of times before, fell in love. You know a lot of Europeans have this dream about America: The Promise. The Promised Land. The American Dream. Everybody wants to realize the American Dream, and I'm no different from anyone else. Also, there is a very attractive thing here. It's rectangular, it's green and it's called a "dollar." So this dollar thing kind of attracts a lot of people—and, of course, the American Dream, the dollar is part of it, but also not just the dollar. I was successful in France, so for me it was the adventure, the people—I love Americans. I'm a big supporter of America, sometimes more than the Americans I know. So I became an American because I embrace this country. I love it. I love the American way. And now that's about twenty-two years that I'm here.

I came through in 1988. I came here for a job at the Ritz-Carlton Hotel in Palm Springs, California. They hired me with a one-and-a-half year visa called an exchange student visa. At that time it was easier to get than now. And once I got here, I bought a motorcycle. I was twenty-eight. I was a roommate with three ladies [*smiles*] in Palm Springs. They had a big house, a swimming pool—for me this was *wow*! America, you know?

During one of my first nights there a coworker took me to a bar called Pink Ladies, and those ladies in that bar didn't wear anything—I mean, very little or nothing—and the chef told them it was my birthday. It was not my birthday. But he told them it was my birthday, and I didn't speak a word of English, and suddenly all those ladies are on top of me, and so how do you want me to go back to France after that? I had all those naked bodies all over me. Welcome to America! I love America!

That was my introduction to America! So I'm thinking, wow, you know, I stay here! That was twenty-two years ago. Now I realize that we have to give money to those ladies. [*He smiles.*] But you know, I still love it, and that was my first experience, but all joking aside, I found out over the years that in America people have a certain courtesy that we don't have anymore in Europe, such as politeness. New York, for instance, has a reputation for being tough and tearing people apart and everything. My brother was here last month, and he told me that the people are so nice, so polite, so helpful. . . . Try it today: go out with a map, a subway map, and stand on the sidewalk, and in less than a minute, someone will come up and say, "Can I help you?" It's amazing. I find people to be very nice in this country. In France, if you ask, "Where is the Arc de Triomphe?" and it's on the right, they're going to tell you it's on the left just because you're an American or whatever. So we've lost a certain courtesy, a certain politeness, in Europe, but especially in France and also Italy. So I think America has had bad PR. If the rest of the world knew real Americans, they would love this country. They would love America. I mean, it's a great country.

[*He pauses, serious tone.*] Listen. I came here with two suitcases twenty-two years ago. Today I have a multimillion-dollar company with sixty employees at seven locations where I do my business. I mean, I started from nothing. Nothing! I came here with not even $2,000 in my pocket. So it's amazing. If you have a dream, if you want to work, and if God gives you health—because without that you can do nothing—with a little bit of luck you can make it in this country. You have a chance.

Look at Mr. Mars. You know, the M&M Company. Mr. Mars Sr. [founder Frank C. Mars], the one who started the company, who invented M&Ms, the Snickers bar, the Mars bar—that guy to me is a hero because he started from nothing and today that company is worth, I don't know, maybe $25 billion, or more. [Annual sales in 2008 were $30 billion.] I mean, it is unbelievable, that company's power! I never met him. He passed away a long time ago. But from a distance I admired him. I learned about him. I read about him. His way of thinking. He is one of those people for me who was like, *wow*! Another person I admire, but who is not an American, is Leonardo da Vinci. This guy had a brain that's—I mean, he was an inventor, an artist, a visionary. That guy had a brain that was just sparkling, and when you think about those people, you just wish you had one-tenth of their brain, unbelievable people. . . .

I got my citizenship about ten years ago. I first got a J-1 visa. Then I applied for a five-year visa, then my green card. It's a long process. For my citizenship I learned the answers to all the questions. I knew more than my American girlfriend at that time. I passed my test. I succeeded, and then I took the oath with 280 other people. It was very emotional because suddenly there's the judge talking to you and telling you your duty to the country and you have to love this country to do it. And I love this country and I did it and I became an American and I'm very proud of it!

What I've learned about coming here to this country as an immigrant is you can't come here with an attitude. You have everything to learn before you're going to make it. You're not going to change people in this country; they're going to change you. You're going to bring a piece of your culture, but you're going to mix it together with the American culture. You're not going to impose it. You're not in whatever country you come from; you're in America, so be humble. Work hard. Have respect, and hopefully you will make it. If you have no humility, Americans will not forget. I mean, be humble and don't come off as Mr. Know-It-All; otherwise, you're not going to make it. I see that too often. Young chefs who come and say, "These Americans, they don't know what they're eating; I'm going to show them."

No, you're not going to show them! You're going to learn what they want and you're going to get as close as you can, and that's maybe what you're going to do: learn about the culture! You have to learn about a people's culture before you can offer something different, which means you have to respect the culture first.

I would go back to France to live maybe, but not to work. To live is fine because I love the lifestyle. I love France. But working there? No! I prefer the American way. I go back every year. My mom is there. I love to go to the beach. I love to enjoy France, but America is home now. I am more of an individualist, an entrepreneur, so that's basically why I like it here. It fits my personality. For some other personality, it doesn't fit. Everybody's different.

Chapter 11

1990s

By the 1990s, women accounted for more than half of all legal immigrants, shifting away from the male-dominated immigration of the past. Contemporary immigrants tended to be younger (ages fifteen to thirty-four) than the native population in the United States and more likely to be married than divorced. The 1990s also experienced a heavy influx of Hispanic and Asian immigrants, which hit a peak at the end of the decade. In 1990, for instance, more than 550,000 Vietnamese family members were settled in the United States. By 2000, that number was nearly nine hundred thousand. Mexican American family members were even more prevalent. According to the Pew Hispanic Center, legal Mexican Americans were 2.2 million in 1980, 4.3 million in 1990, and 7.9 million in 2000. Factor in another twelve million illegal immigrants, of which 80 percent are thought to be Mexican, and that brings the total Mexican population in the United States to roughly seventeen million people, or nearly 20 percent of the country of Mexico.

KEY HISTORIC EVENTS

★1990: President George Bush signs the Immigration Act of 1990, which he calls the "most comprehensive reform of our immigration laws in sixty-six years" because it increases legal immigration ceilings and employment-based immigration, emphasizing skills. On September 10, the main building at Ellis Island reopens to the public after a $165 million restoration, the largest restoration project of its kind in American history; its twenty-three interconnected medical buildings on the south side of the island continue to crumble and remain in a state of arrested decay.

★1993: A New York Times/CBS News poll finds that 69 percent of Americans surveyed favor a decrease in immigration, reflecting a continuing trend of opinion less favorable to immigration.

★1996: President Clinton signs into law the Illegal Immigration Reform and Immigrant Responsibility Act, which imposes new measures against illegal immigration and adds agents to the Border Patrol and to the INS.

★1997: Congress passes measures allowing hundreds of thousands of refugees from Central America and other regions to remain legally in the United States, while the US Commission on Immigration Reform, in its final report to Congress, endorses reductions in legal immigration.

★1998: As a result of the Illegal Immigration Reform and Immigrant Responsibility Act of 1996, more than three hundred thousand legal immigrants are deported by federal authorities because the act increases the types of crimes that would put legal immigrants in a "criminal alien" category.

★1999: US Supreme Court rules that foreigners are ineligible for refugee status if they committed a "serious nonpolitical crime" in their own country.

MIGRATION FLOWS

Total legal US immigration in 1990s: 9.8 million

Top ten emigration countries in this decade: Mexico (2,757,418), Philippines (534,338), Russia (433,427), Dominican Republic

(359,818), India (352,528), China (342,058), Vietnam (275,379), El Salvador (273,017), Canada and Newfoundland (194,788), Korea (179,770)

(See appendix for the complete list of countries.)

FAMOUS IMMIGRANTS

Immigrants who came to America in this decade, and who would later become famous, include:

Cesar Millan, Mexico, 1990, dog trainer
Pamela Anderson, Canada, 1990, model/actress
Sergei Fedorov, Soviet Union, 1990, hockey player (defected)
Milena "Mila" Kunis, Ukraine, 1991, actress
Glen Hansard, Ireland, 1991, singer/songwriter (movie *Once*)
Anna Kournikova, Soviet Union, 1991, tennis player
Maria Sharapova, Russia, 1994, tennis champion
Ryan Gosling, Canada, 1996, actor
Xavier Malisse, Belgium, 1998, tennis player
Byung-Hyun Kim, South Korea, 1999, baseball pitcher

CESAR MILLAN
BORN AUGUST 27, 1969
EMIGRATED ILLEGALLY FROM MEXICO, 1990, AGE 21

His story is remarkable. It personifies the American Dream and the immigrant quest for freedom. He grew up on his grandfather's farm in Culiacán, Sinaloa, Mexico. When he was twenty-one, with images of Disneyland and Rin Tin Tin dancing in his head, he said goodbye to his family and headed north to America alone in his goal to become the "best dog trainer in the world." Though he spoke no English and had only $100 in his pocket—the family savings, given to him by his father—he crossed the border illegally at Tijuana with the help of a smuggler called a "coyote." He went on to found the Dog Psychology Center in Los Angeles and became known for rehabilitating aggressive dogs. Today he is internationally known as "The Dog Whisperer" from his hit television show, which first aired in 2004 and is now broadcast in more than eighty countries worldwide. "Mexico is my mother nation, but America is my father nation because America gave me the direction that I should take," he said, having received his citizenship in 2009. "So how do I feel about finally being part of a country that I'm in love with? I have a great amount of appreciation because my children were born here, and I met my wife here, and the world got to know me here. It was hard to touch my dreams, but this is the place in the world where dreams come true."

Growing up on my grandfather's farm in Mexico was a traditional, physical way of growing up for any child. We didn't spend a lot of time in the city, and being around trees and going to the river and surrounded by chickens and cows was the norm. My grandfather never panicked. He never got angry. He was the epitome of calmness—calm assertiveness.

My mom was born on a different ranch, and my dad was born in Espadino. And normally the woman follows the man in my country, and Mom is just the sweetest, most supportive woman on the planet, and my dad is a very driven individual with big goals to make it outside the ranch. And he did. He did it for himself as much as he wanted to do, and so I grew up with a combination of assertive people [who had much] love.

Fig. 48. Cesar Millan with Preston. Photograph used by permission of Robin Layton.

Growing up on the farm, I learned that the best school in the world is Mother Nature and to work with what you have: honor the earth, honor animals. My grandfather always said, "Never work against Mother Nature," and then I came to America and found out about a guy named Gandhi who said pretty much the same thing in different words. You know, I have my own Gandhi. My grandfather was my hero.

I was "El Perrero" ["The Dog Boy"]. That's a negative label that they give to people who are around certain animals, and in this case, dogs. When I was growing up, dogs for us were like family members—friends and helpers and everything. . . . We moved to Mazatlan about the time I needed to go to kindergarten. We started going five days to the city and then came back on the weekend. We had to go to Mazatlan because there were no schools near the ranch.

Then at age thirteen, I was going to a judo competition and I told my mom I wanted to be the best dog trainer in the world, and she said "Of course you can. You can do whatever you want." So from that point on I declared that this is what I wanted to be in life. I wanted to be the best because there were trainers who started coming to Mazatlan, and I asked why those dogs do what they do, and that's when they explained to me about people who train dogs. Being a veterinarian was another choice . . . and then the reruns of *Lassie* and *Rin Tin Tin* started happening in Mexico. So I had adoration for America because Disneyland and Hollywood were here, and that's where Lassie and Rin Tin Tin were. [*He laughs.*] So I was already in love with this country. . . .

The day I left for America was December 23, 1990. Something in me said, "I want to go to America." I told my mom, and she said, "Where are you going?"

I said, "I'm going to America."

"But the day after tomorrow is Christmas."

"I know, but I have to go."

So she called my dad, and my dad came and gave me the family savings, which was one hundred dollars. And with that money and my savings I paid for my bus ticket, and then I tried to save the hundred dollars so I could eat once I crossed the border. But I finished using that money to pay the coyote guy, so when I finally was able to jump [the border] I didn't have any money. I was trying to cross from Tijuana. The coyote charged me one hundred dollars. For me, that was God sending me somebody to tell me to cross because I was already trying for two weeks and no luck. I was trying to cross on my own because I was trying to save the money. I was trying to imitate how they do it, but since I didn't know the roads, I didn't know when the immigration officers changed. I didn't know anything about the whole system, and those people master it.

I spent Christmas and New Year's on the border because I crossed two weeks later. I didn't know anybody. Some people were having a good time, but when you're on the border, that's a whole different world. It's like if you go to Tijuana and you go to the places where people celebrate, where the Americans go and drink, they don't know we're crossing. They have no idea, and they don't care! They're just buying dollar stuff, beers for a dollar, and it doesn't matter what day it is, or that it's New Year's, but for the immigrant that's not on your calendar, it has nothing to do with your life. Your life is to find a way to cross the border.

The border fence goes into the ocean at Tijuana, and I tried that, but it's just so hard. I didn't see a realistic way because you're sinking in the sand! And also where am I going to put my boots? You know you've got to carry the boots and it's not like we're crossing the Rio Bravo where you put your clothes over your head. I think the ocean is a little more risky, and normally people do the ocean at nighttime because daytime it's open! It's like, "Here I am!"

No, you look for the bushes; you look for areas where you can hide. It's the hunters and the rabbit. Also, at the ocean if they catch you, it takes longer for them to release you. But if they catch you close to the border [inland], they throw you out right away. I mean, I tried everything.

During the two weeks, I walked the entire border there. I saw people being dragged by the current because at that time it was raining a lot in Tijuana, so you could see people being taken away by the current of the water, especially the elderly people, pregnant people, children. It's really sad. It's just a sad story. It's a journey. It's like climbing Mount Everest. It was not a river—there were just areas because it was raining so much that it created canals. And then the coyotes—I guess this was their path in the past, and it was muddy and rainy, and this current just took these people. I don't know where it took them. And I walked the border fence; you can absolutely do it in two weeks, because you're not thinking, you're in survival mode, and your adrenaline is so high you're not thinking. What you're really thinking is worthless.

To survive you sweep floors, you ask for food, they see you're dirty. Some people give you tacos, some people say no, but you can survive because your adrenaline is feeding you, and somehow your body conserves whatever you eat. I ate tortillas. I ate whatever people gave me because I wanted to save my hundred dollars. I slept in the street. The street was my house. [*He pauses.*] You don't know how America looks. You can't even visualize it—all you know is "I have to cross." It's a very simple concept. In my case I didn't know the territory, so once I go through this hole at the bottom of the fence, where do I go? Do I run in a straight line? Where do you go? I just had no clue.

I wasn't scared. Everybody asks me, "Did you ever have fear?" But I never had fear. It's just something that was instilled in me since I was little. I'm not afraid of dying. I'm not afraid of anything—what's the point? I have natural fear of fire or tsunamis or things like that. That's natural fear, but psychological fear? When you're little and they send you in the middle of the night to go and find the donkey, you face a lot of fear! [*He laughs.*] And so I was blessed to be with two people who were not afraid of anything—and they're good people, great people actually, my father and my grandfather. . . .

The coyote found me. I was at the border because that was my job: to jump the border. I tried early in the morning; I tried in the afternoons, midnight. Then one day this guy came and said, "Do you want to cross the border?" And I said, "Yeah." And that's when he asked for one hundred dollars, and I thought, OK, that's kind of weird. It was just him and I. That's why I felt like this was divine, his [God's] intervention, because this guy came from nowhere and he was filthy dirty. I mean, I grew up to learn not to trust people like this, but inside of me, I felt like I could trust him. It was an internal feeling that happened, you know?

We started crossing at seven p.m. I went to a place where this lady had a little coffee shop, a very humble coffee shop, and she sold gum, which is pretty much what keeps you awake: coffee and gum. There was a hole right behind her, and it was like she was guarding this hole. But this coyote knew the way. . . . He knew how to go through the tunnel under the freeway, which was a very scary moment for me: . . . we run, we run against traffic. You can see the cars, they're beeping at you—beep, beep—and then you've got to cross four lines [of traffic] and it feels like somebody's going to hit you—and I'm in boots, I'm wet, I'm full of mud, I'm a wetback. I am really wet!

After we crossed, the coyote brought me to a gas station and across the street from the gas station was the Border Patrol [headquarters] and I thought, "Oh my God, he brought me to the Border Patrol! He lied to me!"

Fig. 49. The Tijuana border, a region where many immigrants like Cesar Millan have crossed in search of the American Dream. Photograph used by permission of Sara N. Coan.

No, what he did was he got me a taxi, which he paid for, so that it could take me away from there to San Diego downtown. I mean, this guy was an angel! He charged me one hundred dollars, maybe he made eighty dollars, and it took us hours to cross the border. Coyotes are not exactly known as humanitarians. They're just paying attention to how much money they're going to make.

When I got across, I celebrated like never before. I was alone. I celebrated the Mexican way—you know, we do the whole scream! I had no money because I gave it to the coyote, so I couldn't even buy a drink or anything. So what happened was I found a place under the freeway where I could go to sleep, and I slept for a whole day. But you don't sleep because you feel like you have to be on alert. So you sleep for two or three hours at a time because you're afraid people will take things from you while you sleep. They can kidnap you; so many bad things can happen.

I mean, I know I didn't do this on my own. [*He chuckles.*] My mom and God and my father praying were part of it. I am a very faithful human being. I am a man of instinct and a man of faith; that's what I came to America with. But that was my lowest, you know? I didn't bring any clothes, but I took that instinct and faith. And I prayed every day. I never stopped, and I never will! You know, when you grow up in a third world country, your instinct and your faith keep you alive. It's not your intelligence, and it's not your emotions because for the most part men can't cry so you learn to numb your emotions. You learn not to speak about emotions or to not show emotions, but instead rely on your instinct for survival and faith and hope that one day things will change. . . .

I don't see life as hard. I lived the hard part of life already growing up in a third world country where you have to walk for water, you know? I am so constant to challenge. I'm so constant to believe that things will get better and so you can go through challenge, suffering, and at the end you're going to achieve what you're looking for. There's just no other way around. The storm doesn't last forever. So that mentality keeps you alive; it keeps you hopeful and allows you to not lose your patience because one of the things that happens is that people lose their patience and then they go back or they give up or they start drinking, and I can't give up. I never did.

After I woke up [under the freeway], I started looking around. I was in San Diego, so I didn't know anything about San Diego. I didn't have any need to stay in San Diego. My goal was to get to Disneyland or Hollywood because that's where Rin Tin Tin was, where Lassie was. I have to find the castle, the Disneyland castle, because every time I saw a Disney® show I saw the castle, and that's where Disneyland is. [*He pauses.*] I didn't know anybody here. [*He laughs.*] I was so naïve to think that Rin Tin Tin was going to be there, but that's what Hollywood and Disneyland sell you. As a kid in Mexico, I would watch *Rin Tin Tin* and *Lassie* on TV, and I thought, "I've got to meet their trainer. Those people are going to teach me how to train dogs. . . ."

In San Diego, I started walking around and learning the culture of America. I learned the sentence, "Do you have application for work?" That was my first sentence. And then eventually I walked by this grooming place, and I said this sentence to these ladies, who gave me the opportunity to work for them, and that's when I started showing that I can work with aggressive [dog] cases, and that day I made sixty dollars! In Mexico it was a dollar a day. I went to 7-Eleven, and with ninety-nine cents I bought two hot dogs, and then I saved $1.69 to buy a Big Gulp™ so I could get the free refill—so you can live in America back then on a dollar a day.

I worked at a grooming place in Chula Vista [a suburb southeast of San Diego]. Two very nice Caucasian ladies gave me the opportunity to work for them, since I didn't speak English. They were elderly ladies when I met them, and they were hippie-like. They found out I was living in the streets, so they gave me the keys. So I slept in the grooming salon in the back, and then when I saved $1,000, I said, "I have to go." It was not my goal to stay in San Diego. My goal was to get to LA. I never saw them again. You just move forward. When you're an immigrant, you're just moving forward. I wanted to be the best dog trainer in the world; that was very clear in my mind. But I had saved $1,000, so the first thing I did was I went out and bought my first pair of Original Levi's®! [*He laughs.*]

I took a Greyhound® bus to LA, and I left in the middle of the night because there's another border you have to go through near San Diego and then you learn that on a certain day, immigration people are not checking, they're not stopping buses. I arrived into downtown LA, and Skid Row was right there and I got to experience the first homeless people I'd ever seen. They were on drugs, and I was not around people who were doing drugs or homeless, so that was a shocking experience for me. I was not afraid of anybody. I just walked toward downtown LA, and

I saw the buildings, and I said, "Well, you know, that's what downtown is; that's where the big buildings are," so I walk toward there, and I found a place where I could sleep, and the next day I looked through the Yellow Pages: "Dog Training Facilities."

I was hired by one in Gardena [a suburb southwest of Los Angeles]. I became the kennel boy. I learned how to take care of dogs and fed them. After I went to work at the dog training facility, I stopped looking for Lassie and Rin Tin Tin. [*He pauses.*] After my kids were born, I took them to Disneyland, but by then I wasn't looking for that. By that time, I became knowledgeable, and by then my wife, Ilusión, told me Disneyland is not where they train dogs. So that was a big disappointment.

I created a reputation of being a guy who can work with aggressive dog cases, and then I met a guy named Jay Reel, and he offered me a job as a carwash guy. I worked with his golden retrievers. I was not very happy working in the kennel. I worked sixteen hours a day, seven days a week. I worked there for almost a year. But I met good people; I met Jay, and he said, "You don't look too happy. I'll give you a job; it's not about dogs, but I can bring you the dogs of my friend and you can train them for him. You're good."

So I start washing cars. At the same time, I was training dogs: teaching them to carry the bucket, carry the towel, bring me the water hose. They were my helpers, you know? And then he taught me about discipline in the American culture and about time. Because when you live in Mexico and you say you're coming, you come thirty or forty minutes later. So he taught me about being more disciplined with time. He not only let me work for him, he also took me to get my driver's license. He gave me a car to drive for free. We're still very good friends. By this time, I had gotten married and had a child. And then one day, he went to Lake Havasu, and before he left, he said, "By the way, you're fired!"

I said, "Why?" [*He laughs incredulously.*] "Why are you firing me?"

"Because you're ready to do it on your own—I'm certain."

It's like: "What are you talking about? I have a child. I'm married. . . ."

"No, no, you're ready."

And it was "Bye-bye." [*He laughs incredulously again.*] Just like that.

I was a good car washer, but at the same time, he knew that my future was with the dogs, and he saw something in me, and he said, "No, you're ready to go out on your own. You just have to go for it!" One thing, though: he still let me drive the car, and without the car I couldn't go and pick up dogs. So he said, "Keep the car. Just make sure to take care of it, and, you know, call me."

I was thinking, "Oh my God, what am I going to tell Ilusión?" I just got fired. I can live on one dollar a day, but when you have a child and a wife, one dollar a day is not gonna make it. And then the rent. After I stopped being so chaotic about it, I just went back to my normal state and calmly, confidently figured, "I'll just go out there and tell people I need a job." But what happened is I started walking more dogs. I became the Mexican guy who can walk a pack of dogs. And so I was walking thirty, forty dogs at ten dollars per dog—that's $300–400 a day, and so that was great.

That's when I found out that in America it's illegal to walk dogs off a leash. I mean, I had no clue. In Mexico, everybody walks dogs off the leash. Actually, it's more difficult to walk a dog on the leash. If my clients can't control the dog, I would say, "Take the leash off!" and the dog follows them. That's the nature of the dog. That's the nature of an animal, not to have a foreign object on his body. I mean, when I grew up I never saw a leash on a dog! So that was shocking to me, and that's when the whole thing about dog psychology versus dog training came to my awareness. "The Energetic Mind: The Revolutionary Style of Dog Training" I was calling it back then. I created business cards, passed them around, went to dog parks where people were training dogs. That's how I got to meet many African American dog trainers, and then we started networking, and they passed me clients who were not able to control or train their dogs. . . .

The businessman in me came out later. I have a mind to work with people, and I have a mind to follow sometimes, but when the fundamentals don't match my core, I can't be part of that group, you know? It's just very difficult, and that's when I thought maybe I should open up my own business. I didn't know how. I didn't know what it entailed. I was totally clueless about business. What am I going to call myself? That's when I came up with "The Dog Psychology Center of Los Angeles." America will not buy a title that says, "Common Sense for Dogs," you know? And that's when I realized that a lot of people go to psychologists. And so, OK, Americans will buy a title if it has "psychology" in it. So then, I thought, how much is it going to cost? Many people around me said, "You're not a psychologist; you can't get that title." So it was a little discouraging, but at the same time, I thought, it doesn't hurt to try! Everybody told me, "You can't jump the border," right? So it's like the same metaphor.

I actually saved $300 because I thought it was going to be that expensive. Back then I had no money. I went to City Hall and applied for the name so I can have a license: the Dog Psychology Center. And it ended up costing me fifteen dollars. Just like that. Nobody owned the name, and you didn't have to be a psychologist to own a title like that. You can't call yourself a psychologist, but you can call places [psychology centers], so that was very empowering. I ended up with $285 back, which allowed me to buy Pampers® for Andre [his son] and formula and all that stuff. [He laughs.] That was a very proud day for me to have a title for my place, even though it was in South Central Los Angeles, a really beat-up place, a place where people said, "Nobody's going to come to South Central because people get killed in South Central."

But months later, dogs from Beverly Hills started arriving in limousines to my place! [He laughs.] Having Nicolas Cage as a client, who lives in Bel Air, helps! One day his butler called me and said, "Mr. Cage would like to meet you." And I didn't know who Mr. Cage was until he said, "Nicolas Cage."

"OK, very good, I am available tomorrow. I would like to come and evaluate the situation. . . ." So I did, and he had a pack of dogs. Most of the people, let's say 85 percent of my cases, are about aggression, especially when you have a powerful breed like a Doberman, Rottweiler, German Shepherd, or pit bull. He [Cage] had already called the other professionals, and there was one guy left and he's in South Central, so you might give him a try. [He laughs, then playfully:] "He's in South Central;

he knows how to handle aggression. Don't you worry about it!" More than anything, you train the people. For the most part, their time is invested in other areas and dogs are more for affection purposes, so normally when I finish training the people, it helps.

Some early clients were Redman, who was really a hot commodity. He was a rapper and he helped me in the rap community, and Jade, in the hip-hop community. In the actor community, producers like Barry Josephson helped me, and Roman Phifer helped me in the NFL community, and someone in the NBA circle, and the billionaire circle—and so you've got all these amazing people who are successful, but they have trouble with their dogs or a lot of trouble with their dogs, and everybody has a circle, and once somebody lets you in, the networking begins. And to me, it's always about being truthful, having integrity, and that's how you create the loyalty of your clients. . . .

I saw my mom again after I got my green card. I got the green card five years after I married Ilusión [1997], and I got my citizenship last year [2009]. My mom came here because she wanted to meet my son. You know, my mom never had a passport in her life, never flew on a plane, but she got a passport and a visa and she came. She came alone. And I remember we had like thirty minutes of letting it go. She's just pure love, and I understand sacrifice because of her. At that point, I hadn't seen her in eight years! I mean, she definitely raised a very strong human being. And she was proud of me. . . .

Soon after that, I went back to Mexico for the first time since I came here. I went back and I ate everything. [*He laughs.*] No apprehension—I was going back home. I wanted to see my family; I wanted to see the ranch. We flew. We didn't go through Tijuana. To go through this border [at the airport] [*sighs in relief*] and have it [my passport] stamped was like [*laughs heartily*], "Wow! So you're saying I don't have to run?" [*He laughs.*] But I still see them [Border Patrol agents] in uniform and will get nervous even though I have papers in my hand, you know? It took a while, a few trips for me to get over that: that I don't have to run, I don't have to hide, I don't have to feel uncertain about the uniform. It's sort of a Pavlovian response; they trained me well! [*He laughs heartily.*] Now when I'm at the airport and security people see me, they bring me all the way to the front. I cut the line, and they say, "Will you help me with my dog?"

The TV show happened as the result of an interview I did in 2002 with the *Los Angeles Times*, and they followed me for three days. At the end, the reporter asked me, "What would you like to do next?" And I said, "I would love to have a TV show." The newspaper story came out on a Saturday, and by Monday a whole bunch of producers were outside the warehouse in South Central Los Angeles—the very place where people said nobody's gonna come! [*He laughs.*] That's where the TV show was born: South Central Los Angeles.

So I said to the producers, "One of the things I want you to do is walk through the pack. And the pack is going to evaluate if I can work with you or not." [*He laughs.*] "The pack will growl. The pack will walk away from some people. The pack will give them their back, and that means you can't work with me." Well, one of the producers walked through, and the pack came to them, and we've been together ever since.

You can always count on the dogs. As I said, I'm a man of instincts and a man of faith. That's how I jumped the border: all those angels given to me by God—the divine intervention, the divine help. So gratitude is always how I begin each day. I begin with prayer, and I always pray around dogs because they always believe what you believe. Sometimes you can pray around people, but they don't believe what you believe, so they're blocking your prayer! But you can always count on the dogs because when the dogs are around me they're my anchor, so you just go into an automatic state of mind and you're not in conflict; you're just clear. And that's what I want to bring to people's lives: that when you are with a dog, conflict should not be in your being, and a life without conflict has joy, has happiness. . . .

My number one hero is my grandfather, who taught me never to work against Mother Nature. But also Oprah because she is a true American Dream. She comes from a poor background, abused background. She knows how to deal with uncertainty and has the respect and loyalty of the American people. Even though she's a black woman in America, she pretty much rules the world. You're talking about somebody who has a really bad background and made the best out of it. She won against all the odds. That just shows you that the willpower of a human being has more importance than the lack of knowledge of a person.

The proudest moment for my dad—that "My son made it!"— was when I was invited to the White House in 2006 because he's a politician at heart. My dad works for the oldest political party in Mexico, so when I was invited to the White House, Mr. Bush was there, and I was right next to the king of Spain, and all these amazing people were in the front row a few feet away from Mr. Bush. But when I first arrived at the White House, everybody formed a line. But everybody has to be checked, so I went in front of the line passing all these important people and everybody's like, "Who's this guy?" And I heard a Secret [Service] agent say, "That's the Dog Whisperer. Don't you see the show?" That was an amazing experience. I gave Mr. Bush a "Pack Leader" hat and a "Pack Leader shirt," and he sent me a letter thanking me.

I love that quote from Mr. Kennedy, "Ask not what your country can do for you, ask what you can do for your country." That is a true pack leader, you know? Because in the dog world, the pack leader is not there for himself. He's there for the pack, and so that quote of Mr. Kennedy is so animal-like, so instinctual-like because it's all about service. That's the state of the divine, and that's to be enlightened: that you want to help the world to get better in some shape or form, and that whatever your situation in life, the situation with everything is just your growth. The point is that you understand that things happen for a reason, and you find what the reason is, you act on it, and move on. You live in the moment, and you live calm-assertive, like my grandfather. He's no longer with us, but he would have given me the simplest solution for anything—and it would be like: "What? It's that simple?" Yeah! Life is simple. We make it complicated. It goes back to that. The human loves to complicate things. The intellectual loves to complicate things, and emotions sometimes get in the way of you seeing logical simplicity and really taking advice from anybody.

I'll tell you a story. One day I was in New York, and I was walking with my brother. We had finished a nice Italian dinner, and then I see this homeless person with dreadlocks, and he said, "Hey, you! You're the Dog Whisperer!" [*He laughs.*]

"How do you know?"

"I watch TV! You're really good!" [*He laughs.*]

And the first thing that came out of my mouth because he seemed so happy was, "So how do you stay so happy?"

And he said, "I go with the flow."

The next day I get to meet a billionaire, and this guy owns cruise ships and casinos, and I said, "Sir, you seem very happy. How do you stay in that state?"

And he said, "I just go with the flow." [*He laughs heartily.*] But going with the flow doesn't mean you let people push you around. That's not what they're saying. It's just that you don't fight things that are happening. You go with the energy. Like my grandfather always said, never go against Mother Nature.

CARLOS ESCOBAR
BORN FEBUARY 5, 1970
EMIGRATED ILLEGALLY FROM MEXICO, 1996, AGE 26

He came to America alone. He came to embrace the American Dream that so many people talked about back home in his village in Mexico. Carlos was twenty-six years old when he left his wife, mother, and young son. He crossed the border illegally with the help of a coyote. Once across, he journeyed north to a small town outside Sonoma, where he got a job at a vineyard as a migrant worker earning eight dollars for a twelve-hour workday. He eventually learned English and got a better-paying job in a lumber mill, earning more in a month than he did in Mexico in a year. It took more than seven years before he was able to get his green card and bring his wife and son to America. Today, Carlos, at age forty, a devout Catholic, lives happily in northern California with his family. He recently became a US citizen, but his greatest pride is his son: "my papi, my Pedro," he said. "Pedro is going to college now and working hard to make his dreams come true. He wants to be a lawyer and one day help other Mexicans who immigrate here." He paused. "We miss Mexico sometimes," he said, "but we are happy here, thank God. Will we return one day? Maybe. Just not today."

My young son, Pedro, was five years old and he just kept crying. It was the day I left Mexico. I was about to begin my journey to America to find a new job and a better life. I had been a laborer, a construction worker, but the company I worked for closed and I couldn't find work. I desperately needed money to support my family. My mother ran a small bodega {store}, but it didn't bring in much money. All four of us lived out back in an apartment. I wanted my son to have a good education and maybe one day go to college, which was never a possibility for me. I wanted to give him a good life. I did not want my boy to go through what I did; which is why I decided to come to the United States. When I was little, I sold food on the street so my family could eat. My father left us when I was little. I was an only child. . . .

One afternoon my wife, Rosalinda, and Pedro were at the bodega with my mother. Nobody said anything. They knew. I bent down to my boy, my papi: "I am going to America, but I'll be back soon, don't worry." Pedro had tears in his eyes. "But why?" he asked and gave me a big hug.

I felt like my heart was going to break. A short time later, a friend of mine came by with an old pickup truck and drove me about 250 miles to the north. I had cash with me and the name of a person, this coyote I was to meet there. . . .

Fig. 50. The California–Mexico border Carlos Escobar crossed in his quest to find freedom. The fence literally extends into the Pacific Ocean, north of Tijuana and south of San Diego. Every few minutes, Border Patrol helicopters do regular reconnaissance flights along the fence, out to the ocean and back, in search of illegal immigrants trying to sneak across the border or swim through the polluted waters of the "Tijuana Slough." Photograph used by permission of Sara N. Coan.

We met at a small run-down motel a few miles from the California border. The coyote had many people living in this horrible, dirty, tiny room waiting to cross. Many of them were there for weeks; some, months. He told us not to go outside until it was time to leave. He said it was for our safety, and he warned us. He said there were a lot of dealers, a lot of drugs, gangs, and people had been murdered, robbed, disappeared, and if we went outside there was nothing he could do to protect us; we were on our own. But some people didn't care, and they took a chance, even if it meant smoking a cigarette. . . . I stayed in that room for eight straight days, imagine! We slept on the floor. There were cockroaches everywhere. The toilet didn't work. I will never forget the smell. It was not something I can describe. There are no words for what it was like. As if that weren't enough, everyone was going crazy, so some people would sneak out at night.

I remember one young girl—she was so sweet, so pretty, dark hair. Maybe sixteen, seventeen—practically a child. Her name was Carlita. Me and some of the older ones in the group sort of looked after her like a parent. Well, one night Carlita went out for a cigarette. She had been gone quite a while, maybe a couple of hours, and we started getting worried. Then, later that night, we could hear screams, the voices of men. I moved to the door to go after her, to save her, but some of the others held me back. [*He pauses, emotional.*] I never saw her again. . . .

We walked across the desert into Arizona. We traveled at night. It took three days to cross. We were sore, hungry, thirsty. At one point we didn't have a drink for nearly two days, but we just kept going, kept walking. We ran out of water because the coyote said not to carry too much with us because he said it would slow us down. Of course, he made sure there was enough water for him. He wouldn't share it either, the bastard! And a rich one, too! It cost me more than $3,000 to cross. . . .

There were fourteen of us. There were lots of rattlesnakes, scorpions, heat, dust. And when it rained, lots of mud, so it was slow going. You had to be careful where you stepped. One bite from a snake or scorpion and you're gone like that [*snaps fingers*]. I could see the lights of the American Border Patrol off in the distance. The coyote told us that many like us did not make it, and there was no reason to doubt him. In fact, at one point, just off the trail in a ditch, I saw what looked like the entrails of something covered with black flies. Thousands of black flies. It could have been a cow or a dog,—I wasn't sure—until I saw what looked like a human skull and bones in the dirt. So apparently we were not the first to come this way and I remember thinking, "This loco. This is crazy. I wish I had never come."

Once we made it across, we had to lie down in a van. The coyote's brother drove, and we finally got some water. It was a long drive, many hours to the north of San Francisco to work in the vineyards. We were known as the *mojado*, or the illegal ones. . . .

When I arrived, my English was very poor but enough to get by. I wanted to go to school to learn, but I had to work all day, and they were long days. I did this so I could send money back home to Rosalinda and my mother. I would study English in the nighttime after work, and there were several others. It was a group of us: the workers, the mojado. We used to meet in the basement of a small mission church. It was sort of a like a Bible study group except we also learned English. A local woman who once lived in Mexico translated back and forth into Spanish. She taught us. She was a good woman. In her fifties. Her name was Zulma. She gave us books to read, but more importantly, she gave us hope. And then the years passed—and I learned and I worked, I prayed, I wrote letters. I sent money back home. This was my life for a very long time.

Many of the mojado—the ones in our church group, anyway— returned to Mexico. They were not happy because the life was too hard. We lived in shacks on the outer fringes of the vineyard fields. There was some electricity but no plumbing. No running water for showers. We had to go to a communal building for that. And the bedsprings were rusted and the mattresses filled with mold. One friend of mine got sick. He had no money for a doctor, much less medical insurance, and he said, "I do not want to die in California. I want to die in my country. I want to die in Mexico," and he went home. For others, they never intended to stay anyway. Their plan was simple: come here, work, make the money, take it home, and hopefully take enough where you can set yourself up somehow. For the ones that stayed, like me, Zulma helped us get green cards. . . .

It took me over seven years to raise the money to bring my Rosalinda and Pedro to America. By that time, my mother had passed. The last time I saw her was the day I left Mexico to come here. But the day I saw my wife and boy again, that was a day! My family was together again. Pedro had become a big boy now, almost thirteen years old, and Rosalinda looked like an angel. Beautiful. This was the greatest day of my life. [*He pauses.*] My next one will be when Pedro graduates college. He wants to go to law school. He said he wants to help others come here, the way he wishes someone had been there to help his padre.

GOLLY RAMNATH
BORN OCTOBER 15, 1957
EMIGRATED FROM TRINIDAD, 1998, AGE 41

She came to America to escape a bad marriage and start a new life. Her dream was to get an education, but her background went only as far as primary school. Relying on domestic jobs to support her, she passed her high school equivalency exam and finally, at age fifty, earned an associate's degree. That same year, 2007, she married her second husband, with whom now she lives happily in Bay Ridge, Brooklyn. In 2009, she earned her bachelor's degree in English education and is working toward her master's to become a teacher. "I am very happy that I came to America," she said. "I can honestly say that my life began at fifty when I graduated college."

I left Trinidad because I was in a very bad marriage and I wanted out. The children were old enough where they could take care of themselves, and I thought it was time. I am from India; my grandparents are from India. My great-grandparents went to Trinidad as indentured laborers, and then my grandparents followed. My grandmother was born in India, but my mother was born in Trinidad. So we've had two or three generations of our family in Trinidad. So Trinidad is my home, not India.

I was married for twenty-five years. Yes, it was survival of the fittest. I have three children, three girls, but when I got married, he had two children that came to live with us, and they were the cause of the bad marriage. It was like I had no say and they had all the say in the marriage. They became the bosses. I felt like the slave. Indians are very obedient and humble, and they take care of their home and their family. I got married to someone who is not Indian. He was African: a black man from Trinidad, which was a no-no in my culture. So as far as my family was concerned, I was dead. I thought they would have softened up after a while, but they never did until I left for good.

So for twenty-five years, the relations with my family were bad. I mean, my mother, my sister, and I spoke to each other, but there was always a distance. It's only after they realized I had left him for good and filed for divorce that I felt welcomed back into the family. This happened when my mother was dying. I was already here [America] in 2002 when my mother got really sick, and I went home to see her. She was at home with my sister in Trinidad, and I think she died peacefully, knowing that I would not be going back to him.

Fig. 51. Golly Ramnath. Photograph used by permission of Nur Coan.

What many people don't understand about a third world country: Once you get married, that's it. You have no other choice. So in my situation, I got married to someone who my family did not approve of. I had no education to find a job on my own. I had nobody to take care of my children in case I did get a job. I couldn't just leave them with anybody because I couldn't afford to pay a babysitter, and to get a good job, you have to have a good education. At that time I only had a primary school education.

I knew when I filed for divorce I would have to leave Trinidad. I filed over here [United States]. . . . His eldest daughter was like the main person in his life. She's a grown woman now. But I came here in 1998 to escape him. That's what I did.

A friend of mine had come to Trinidad for Carnival in February of '98, and I told her what was happening with me and that I wanted to get out, and she said, "OK, I'll help you." She provided a place for me to stay in her apartment in Brooklyn. I came in April 1998 on a tourist visa. My eldest daughter was already over here in America, in Brooklyn. She came here before me in 1998 when she was nineteen on a holiday [tourist] visa, but later on she got a student visa. I found a job in Greenwich [Connecticut] as a live-in. I took care of two girls; taking them to school, getting up in the morning, packing their lunch, helping fix their dinner [and so on].

I worked there for five and a half months because I didn't want to overstay my visa. But I went back home, and within two weeks I was ready to leave. I couldn't stand him! I didn't want to leave because of the children, but I couldn't be around my husband at all. It was just too much! I didn't know what to do because I had left the two children in Trinidad. One was thirteen and one was eighteen. It was very difficult for me to leave them, especially the younger one. One was getting ready to go to university, and the other one was just into high school. When I told my husband I got a job [in America], he didn't say anything because I needed to pay the university fees. So that was my excuse, right?

And over the course of the next five years, that's what I did. I went back and forth. I had a ten-year tourist visa, but you have to go back every six months. So I would go to Trinidad and then come back to Connecticut to continue the job. I did that every two or three months because of the visa and because my mother was very sick and I didn't want to overstay my time here [in the United States]; then if something happened to her, I wouldn't be able to travel back. When I came back, although my husband and I lived in the same house, we didn't have much to say to each other. We slept in separate beds. I slept with the children. So it was under the same roof, but it was very far apart, and he was dating other people, also Indian women. . . .

By 2002, my mother had died, I had filed for divorce, my children had grown, and my eldest daughter was here in Brooklyn. I always wanted to have an education, so I started my GED classes on Saturdays while I worked in Connecticut from Monday to Friday. In my culture, the girls are not pushed for an education. You're pushed, really, to take care of the house and your family, and that's it. You get a primary education, and that's it. You know how to read and write, but you have to cook, clean the house, learn to sew, and take care of the husband and your children. That's it.

I got my GED in 2002, then my associate's degree in liberal arts at Manhattan Community College. I went to Brooklyn College for another two years, and I got a bachelor's degree in 2009 in English education. Presently, I'm doing my master's at Brooklyn College to be a teacher. I would love to be a teacher, only there are no jobs for us right now. My eldest daughter is also at Brooklyn College with me, doing her bachelor's in business. My other daughters chose to stay in Trinidad. They didn't want to come here. One has a degree from a school of chartered accountants. The youngest one started her own business doing web design. My relationship with them is very good. They understand what I went through.

[*She pauses.*] I came to America to find a better life, but I realized that to have a good life here, you need to be educated or else you're stuck in a menial job. For me, an education is something I always wanted. It was like chasing an elusive dream. I graduated with my bachelor's degree when I was fifty-two years old! So you have to stay focused on your goals, and you cannot give in to the stumbling blocks that will come into your life. There are distractions, but you have to persevere. You have to. People say this country is the land flowing with milk and honey, but you don't see that milk and honey *until* you work for it. You cannot come to America and be lazy. If you come to someone's country, you have to be an asset to that country. That's what I believe. You have to have people respect you, and that is what I strive for. . . .

I am very happy that I came to America. I can honestly say that my life began at fifty when I graduated college. I'm hoping by the time I graduate with my master's the economy will be better. My husband, thank God, can provide in the meantime. I do part-time babysitting to earn extra money, and I meet babysitters in Brooklyn Heights and I tell them, "You need to go to school!" And they look at me so funny. And I'm like, "No, you have to get an education! That is the key to success in this country." And they look at me like, "What is wrong with this woman?" That's how I feel. I've always wanted to pursue an education, and my second husband is very supportive of this. I think that's what I love about him.

Chapter 12

2000s

Census Bureau data show that immigrants who arrived in this decade were better educated than those who arrived in the 1990s. Likewise, children of immigrants were more financially successful than their parents and had more professional skills. The survey also points out that out of an estimated US population of 310 million people, more than 35 million were born outside this country. The bulk of immigrants since 2000 have come from Mexico and Latin America, but also from Asia and India, which have experienced a "brain drain" of sorts—particularly in science and technology—as many of their most intelligent and best-educated citizens have migrated to the United States and other Western nations to pursue better opportunities.

KEY HISTORIC EVENTS

★ 2001: The September 11 terrorist attacks on the United States result in tighter screening procedures of refugees and the suspension of resettlement programs; the Patriot Act grants the government broad new powers to allow law enforcement and intelligence agencies to investigate and detain aliens suspected of terrorist activities.

★ 2002: The Department of Homeland Security is created through the merger of twenty-two US government agencies, among them the INS, to prevent and respond to terrorism.

★ 2003: With the INS dissolved, immigration administration services such as permanent residence, naturalization, and asylum become the responsibility of US Citizenship and Immigration Services (USCIS), while immigration law enforcement services such as investigations, deportation, and intelligence become the domain of US Immigration and Customs Enforcement (ICE); Border Patrol and Customs inspectors are combined to form the newly created US Customs and Border Protection (CBP).

★2005: The number of legal immigrants who have become naturalized US citizens reaches its highest level in twenty-five years.

★2006: The issue of immigration reform generates rallies and protests in cities across America, largely in support of granting illegal immigrants some type of legal status.

★2007: Economic recession commences, later to become a worldwide recession on par with the depressions of 1893 and 1929.

★2008: Poor economy leads, for the first time, to a "reverse immigration" phenomenon that has many Americans heading overseas for jobs in Asia and Canada, while a new trend of "reverse revenue" sees Mexican families sending money north to the United States to help immigrant kin—both legal and illegal—who can't find employment; as the recession deepens, more and more migrants return home, unable to find work.

★2009: After a major government crackdown on illegal immigrants, ICE reports a record 392,862 immigrants deported from the United States, about half of them convicted criminals; ICE also confirms there are more than 325,000 people in the country who have been ordered deported but can't be sent away because no country will accept them. Simultaneously, according to ICE, the United States sees a rise in children born to illegal immigrants: more than 4 million in 2009, up from 2.7 million in 2003, with that percentage likely to increase.

★2010:   Arizona governor Jan Brewer signs SB 1070 into law. The controversial measure requires Arizona police officers to question anyone they reasonably suspect of being illegal and to detain them if they cannot provide proof of status. Critics of the legislation say it encourages racial profiling, but supporters say the law simply enforces existing federal law. Several lawsuits are filed challenging SB 1070.

MIGRATION FLOWS

Total legal US immigration in 2000s: 10.3 million

Top ten emigration countries in this decade: Mexico (1,706,993), China (599,914), India (597,032), Philippines (549,024), Russia (488,115), Vietnam (292,143), Dominican Republic (291,603), Cuba (274,028), El Salvador (252,526), Colombia (235,698)

(See appendix for the complete list of countries.)

FAMOUS IMMIGRANTS

Immigrants who came to America in this decade, and who would later become famous, include:

Catherine Zeta-Jones, Wales, 2000, actress
Steffi Graf, Germany, 2001, tennis champion
Mats Wilander, Sweden, 2001, tennis champion
Hideki Matsui, Japan, 2002, baseball player
Yao Ming, China, 2002, basketball player
Rachel McAdams, Canada, 2002, actress
Somdev Devvarman, India, 2005, tennis player

Rachel Weisz, England, 2006, actress
Sacha Baron Cohen, England, 2007, actor/comedian
Markéta Irglová, Czechoslovakia, 2010, singer/songwriter
    (movie *Once*)
Zeituni Onyango ("Aunty Zeituni"), Kenya, 2010, President
    Obama's half-aunt (deportation waived)

Fig. 52. The highest point at the California–Mexico border, near Campo, California. Border Patrol agents use this perch for long-range surveillance of illegal immigrants trying to cross. There is a one-mile buffer zone from the fence to the legal beginning of the Mexico border (to the right). Photograph by the author.

KIRIL TARPOV
BORN MARCH 25, 1957
EMIGRATED FROM BULGARIA, 2000, AGE 43

He is a music teacher and conductor from Plovdiv, Bulgaria's second-largest city. He came to America as part of a cultural exchange program and to give his adopted son, Angel, a better life. Like the Ellis Island–era immigrants before him, he worked and sent money back to his mother in Bulgaria until he was able to bring Angel, a gifted cellist, to America so that he could pursue a music education. They eventually settled in the Midwest. He remembers being new in America and working on Wall Street, a few blocks from the World Trade Center, when the 9/11 attack occurred. "I called to Bulgaria and I hear the voice of Angel, my son." {His voice cracks.} "He doesn't know what happened, and I didn't tell him. He just wanted to hear my voice, and I wanted to hear his. And when I hear his voice, in this moment, I realized maybe our building is going to be the next one and I'm never going to see him again and I start crying and I closed the phone."

I came to America to visit in 1999 as part of a Bulgarian group for a cultural exchange program. I came here with a regular work visa because at that time I was involved with the cultural exchange between Bulgaria and the United States. I was working with a music foundation in Bulgaria in cooperation with another foundation in New York. We had started this cultural exchange program in 1998, and we organized different seminars and workshops in Bulgaria, and here we worked in the American educational system—in the high schools and universities—with the idea of creating a Bulgarian-American Arts Festival. We would have concerts at the Bulgarian Embassy in New York. . . .

When my visa expired, I had to return to Bulgaria. Then I received an invitation from the Bulgarian Eastern Orthodox Church based in New York to become their music conductor, and they offered me a work visa, which enabled me to continue my work in the cultural exchange program here, and on April 1, 2000, I was in the United States and have been here ever since.

I came here to continue my work in this cultural exchange program, but the other reasons were to have a future as a musician, and second, to give a chance to my adopted son because he has dark skin—his parents were Egyptian, and back in Bulgaria we have a lot of problems with people

Fig. 53. Kiril Tarpov. Photograph used by permission of the Tarpov family.

with dark skin color, and I soon realized it's going to cause a lot of problems for him—and for me to give him a chance at a better life. That's why when I had this opportunity from the church to come to the United States, I started thinking, why not become an immigrant? With a work visa, I could get a green card, maybe, and become a normal American. . . .

I adopted my son in 1996 after I came back to Bulgaria because I wanted to have a child. With my ex-wife, we didn't have a child. . . . I asked all my friends to help me find a way to adopt a child, but because I was single; the advice was to have one child and see if it works. At the time, I was a music conductor with a new Bulgarian opera, and we had a big tour in Europe and then two weeks in the United States. It was my first time here. My first stop was in New York. I remember when I stepped down from the bus in the city after arriving at the airport, I thought, "This is my city; this is where I want to live."

Then, one day, a friend of mine called me to go to an orphanage because they're going to move the kids from one facility to another and it's a good time to see the kids. They were around three to three and a half years old. This was in Plovdiv, my home city, which was the second-biggest city in Bulgaria after Sofia, the capital. So I went to this orphanage around lunchtime. They had just woken the kids from their afternoon nap for lunch, and I looked at them, and I saw one boy's big smile, and I just said, "This will be my son." I called him Angel.

Later they introduced me to him. After that, I started to prepare the necessary documents, and there was the hearing for the adoption. But I wasn't able to be there in court because I had a performance in France between Bordeaux and Marseilles, and that's when I got a call from Bulgaria: "You're a father now!" We had a big party, and then I brought him home, and after that, we started our life together.

Life in Bulgaria in 1996 was hard because the Communists were in the government, and this was one of the terrible years. I had found a job as a music teacher from the teacher's union in one of the schools so I could raise my son. It was very difficult because at nighttime I went to support the people who were against the Communists, and during the day I had to teach the kids and I had to raise my son, and it was an unpleasant time. The pay was not good. To give you an idea, for my two-week tour in United States, I was paid thirty-six dollars per day as a conductor. This was like a whole year's salary for a teacher in Bulgaria—can you imagine? And I wasn't a regular teacher; I was a well-known music teacher. So money was one real motivation to come to United States.

After the adoption, I also realized Angel was very talented musically, and it was impossible to give him a future in Bulgaria. He started to play the cello when he was four and a half years old. I got him to a teacher for lessons, and I saw he had natural talent with a good ear.

When I came here in 2000, I left Angel with my mom. The Bulgarian church had given me a work visa, but they didn't give me any salary, so I had to find work to pay my expenses and to send back money to Bulgaria for Angel. So I started to work at a coffee shop on Wall Street in New York, and at this time I didn't speak any English. But I was working with the customers, and it's amazing how kind they were. They took their time to explain things to me, what things meant, like "bagel with cream cheese," because I didn't know. Or what does it mean when they order "coffee with cream" or "[coffee with] skim milk," for instance? When the customers had a break, they'd come down from their offices to the coffee shop. Some of them came just to help me and teach me, and that's how I started to learn English. That's why I respect and I love New Yorkers.

I was here when the 9/11 tragedy happened. We helped a lot of people with water and everything. There were people who lost consciousness. From the outside they came in or were brought in not breathing, and we helped them. That day, in the beginning, somebody said a plane crashed into one of the Twin Towers. At first I thought it was some spoiled kid without any license to fly who crashed into the tower, and then when the second plane crashed, everything started going so fast, and we realized what happened.

After the collapse of the first building, everybody started knocking on the windows of the building to let them in, but security had locked the doors. It was a huge lobby of an atrium building at 60 Wall Street. Upstairs were several big financial companies like J. P. Morgan. Everybody started knocking on the windows to come in, but the people on the inside started screaming, "Don't let them! Don't let them in!" I thought, "You can't keep these people outside! Let them in!" They were covered in dust and debris. We let them in, and we helped them wash their faces because they couldn't see anything, and we helped some to start breathing because they were choking, coughing from the dust. We gave them water to drink to clear their throats. A few minutes after that, I find the phone, and I called to Bulgaria because the coffee shop had international connections because the owner was Turkish. I called to Bulgaria, and I hear the voice of Angel, my son. [*His voice cracks.*] He doesn't know what happened, and I didn't tell him. He just wanted to hear my voice, and I wanted to hear his. And when I hear his voice, in this moment, I realized maybe our building is going to be the next one and I'm never going to see him again, and I start crying, and I closed the phone.

Then the second building collapsed, and they sent us to the basement, and everything down there was dark; we were below street level. Up until then, we didn't have a chance to think about what happened outside, and then I realized what kind of tragedy it was. Then security said, "Go out! Everybody out! Everybody out!" and around one p.m., security had us leave the building, and we walked. Everybody walked home.

SISTER CHRISTINE FEAGAN
MARSHALLTOWN, IOWA
AMERICAN BORN

Far removed from any border, the heartland of America is not necessarily thought of as a place filled with immigrants, but its face is changing. The push-pulls of immigration on a national level can be seen and felt in places like Marshalltown, Iowa. Originally from Illinois, Sister Christine is an immigrant of sorts, having spent fifteen years in Bolivia before returning to the United States. She came to Marshalltown in 1999 to become the director of the Hispanic Ministry Office. Since that time, she has watched the town transform from a sleepy Corn Belt community right out of the movie Field of Dreams *to an immigrant hotbed where nearly a third of the population (and rising) are immigrants, primarily Hispanic. The American Dream may still be alive, but the voices being heard are increasingly Hispanic ones. Marshalltown's population of approximately twenty-six thousand has remained virtually unchanged since 1999; as the immigrants have come, many of them illegal, the locals have left. There is a huge black market for Social Security cards, driver's licenses, and the like.*

Sixty-two years old and fluent in Spanish, Sister Christine is a trusted figure and advisor to the Hispanic community here, who have relied on her for everything from immigration help and advice to language interpreting to friendship and moral support. While poor English, illegal status, and fear of deportation keep some in the shadows, people like Feagan provide hope, as most immigrants here live in fear of ICE. Stealth undercover raids in 1996 and 2006 at the Swift meatpacking plant, a major employer, still resonate with residents, both legal and not. "I think it would be great if everybody wore sunglasses and the colors looked the same," Feagan said. "I think a lot of it is not just an immigration issue—it's a race issue. I really do. Because when people talk about immigration, they talk about Mexicans."

I've been in Marshalltown since September 1999. Since then I've seen a lot of changes: demographic changes, growth in the community and in our parish. When I first came, for example, there was one Spanish mass on Sunday in early afternoon. We now have a Saturday night mass and a Sunday morning mass, and the church is overflowing on Sunday. The parish has changed from being about 20 percent Hispanic when I came to about 65 percent Hispanic now. Most of the people come from Mexico. We have a few from Guatemala, some Salvadorans. Some people originally settled in California and then moved here. Some settled in Washington State and then came here. Some came from Nebraska. It's hard to tell among the Hispanics who's illegal or legal. They all look the same. [*She laughs.*]

Originally, the Hispanics who came here were mostly single men, and now a lot of them have brought their families up and applied for legal permanent residency. A lot of those legal permanent residents recently became citizens to speed up the process of bringing up family members because otherwise the wait time is years to bring family members from Mexico.

I'm the director of the Hispanic Ministry Office, and that's another thing that's changed. When I first came, a lot of people would ask us for help to get their telephone set up, or help them about paying a bill at a hospital, and so we would do a lot of interpreting and accompanying them on appointments. Now, if you go to the bank in town, there are Hispanic tellers, and if you go to the hospital, there are interpreters; just about any place you go now, you will find Spanish-speaking people. What I'm saying is there is an awareness that they [Hispanics] are here and so we need to serve them. Today the total population is about the same compared to '99, but it's changed demographically. As Hispanics have moved in, the Anglos have moved out.

I am the Hispanic minister at the church. People come here, to me, if they don't understand their rent bill, and we have a counselor that comes two days a week, so it's like an outreach office, and a lot of people come and say, "I need work. Do you know of anybody looking to hire for housecleaning, taking care of kids?" or whatever. In the office here we do a lot of work with immigration papers for when people are applying to bring up a relative, or they need to renew their green card, or they're applying for citizenship, or they need a permission letter that says one parent is going to go with the kids down to Mexico and they need the other parent to have a notarized letter giving permission. People will come in and they'll need a recommendation letter for immigration purposes that says this person or family are registered members of the parish. There's a lot of that kind of thing. And then there's a lot of people who just come in because they need somebody to talk to—just personal issues, things that are going on in their life.

I lived in Bolivia for fifteen years. I studied Spanish and French for ten years before I went down to Bolivia. I grew up in northwest Illinois. I came from a Catholic home, but I would say we weren't overly religious. When I came back, I was in Chicago on the South Side, working in a parish that was basically Mexican, and then a friend told me about an opening here for a Hispanic minister, and so I came. I did missionary work in Bolivia and was an immigrant there [*laughs*], so I have compassion.

Fig. 54. The greeting upon arriving at a Border Patrol checkpoint in Jamul, California, approximately twenty miles north of the Mexican border. Photograph used by permission of Sara N. Coan.

In Marshalltown, there are problems for the undocumented people in that they're afraid all the time that they're going to be arrested by ICE, which stands for Immigration and Customs Enforcement. There are two arms of immigration. There is USCIS, which is United States Citizenship and Immigration Services, which would be like when you apply for something or you become a naturalized citizen. Then you have ICE. . . . That's your Border Patrol and what used to be INS. ICE has no office in Marshalltown. They come from Des Moines, which is about fifty miles away, and then wherever else, because I'm sure the agents who came in December of 2006 were from a lot of different places.

They're afraid of what's happening in other places in the country and that it's going to happen here. They're afraid that if they lose their job, how will they survive? Where will they go if the [social] climate is the same in other places? They're concerned for their kids' well-being. People here are happy to be here. They like Iowa. They like Marshalltown. We have a good school system. There's plenty of work. There's plenty of space, and I think that's what's attracted them. And it's peaceful. It's not crowded.

The major employer is the Swift meatpacking plant—hogs, pork. And then there's Lennox Industries, which makes heating and air conditioning units. But not too long ago Lennox laid off three hundred people because they sent part of their air conditioning production to Mexico. And then we have Fisher Controls, which is now part of Emerson, although very few Hispanics work there because it's a lot more specialized, so they don't have the training or educational background to be able to fit in. Fisher makes parts for boilers and heaters. Then we have the Iowa Veterans Home, and a lot of people work there in light housekeeping. We have the Meskwaki [Bingo] Casino [Hotel] twenty miles away. . . . If they don't have good papers they can't work there. The same with the Iowa Veterans Home. And the Swift plant uses E-Verify® [an online system for checking employees' eligibility], so that's why during the 2006 raid Swift was not legally at fault for employing [those] who turned out to be illegal immigrants: because they had done "everything" they were "supposed" to do to make sure that people were documented.

By "good papers" I mean they [Hispanics] have their own Social Security number and are using their own name—that they are here legally. People [illegals, mainly] will see a roofing job going on, and they'll say, "Do you need work for the day?" and they work. Last year, there was a really bad hailstorm that happened in Eldora, which is about thirty-five miles from here, and so there was a lot of repair work, houses that needed to be re-sided and roofs that needed to be redone, so that gave work to a lot of people, plus cutting grass or landscaping or whatever they can do. In my experience, people are willing to do *whatever*.

Typically, an illegal immigrant will try to get a Social Security number that's not being used by anybody else. It might be a three-year-old child, a retired person, or maybe it's somebody who is not working who sold their Social Security number for a year. That can be done, too. So Social Security numbers are used to get a job. Have you ever seen an I-9 form? Because now everybody has to fill one out when they seek employment. You have to show proof of being in this country legally. And you can either show from List A your passport or from List B your Social Security card and driver's license or something else that has your picture on it.

If you're an illegal, it would be really hard to get a job at Swift, but many do, of course. First of all, it would be really hard if you're Hispanic because now we have another group who've moved into Marshalltown: the Burmese. They are here as refugees. And so a lot of those people are now working at the plant. They came within this past year. I don't know how many of them there are, but their English skills are very low, and it's hard to find interpreters. Obviously, it's not anywhere near the number of Hispanics, but because they're here as refugees, that means they're under "protected status," so Swift prefers them.

A lot of people have come to Marshalltown because they knew somebody here. So now it's like the husband has brought up the wife and the kids [and] the brother has told his brother, "Hey, come on up. This is a really good place to be." The interstate highways have made it easier. They have become a pipeline. We have Interstate 35, a pipeline from Texas. We have Interstate 80, which takes you over to Arizona; there's a lot of people that enter from Texas and Arizona. So the interstates have

Fig. 55. A typical checkpoint like this one made more than forty thousand arrests in 2009 alone. Photograph used by permission of Sara N. Coan.

connected the dots and made places like Marshalltown more accessible. A lot of the Hispanics who were in California came here because work was getting scarce, the cost of living was too high, there's a lot of violence— so they're coming in many cases from California to Iowa. We've got a little group of people who were working in Washington State in the apple orchards and some from Nebraska and many directly up from Mexico, and a lot of them have come up legally. People hear the number twelve million and they think, "Oh my gosh, America is just crawling with these undocumented people," but there are three hundred million who live in the country. So twelve million is a drop in the bucket, you know?

I see immigrants in Marshalltown from Bosnia, Croatia, both legal and illegal. A lot of them come in through Canada. Some of the Bosnians have refugee status, which makes them legal. Other immigrants here are Sudanese and Somalis who have refugee status. Then there are those from El Salvador who have TPS or Temporary Protected Status, which means they can get a work permit. There was a man who had a kidney transplant twelve years ago. He's a legal permanent resident from El Salvador. He was working at the Swift plant for a long time and then he had serious breathing problems and a heart problem, so the doctor sent a letter to the plant that said he can go back to work but he can't work in the "cold" area, the meatpacking part where they freeze the meat. Well, they kept him there in the cold areas, and he ended up in the hospital two more times, and the doctors finally said he can't go back to work. Period. His health was too fragile. So I went with him to Social Security to apply for disability, and they never give it to you the first time, but they gave it to him—that's how bad he was!

The pecking order in terms of demographics in Marshalltown is the Anglo or white US citizens, which is still the majority; next is the Hispanic population. We don't have many Bosnians around here. We used to have more Sudanese than we have now, but a lot of them have gone to Des Moines. . . . Before I came here in 1999, there was an influx of Laotians, and they were here for a while and then they left. After the 2006 raid, we had a huge influx of African Americans from Chicago and Minnesota. Some of them, I'm told, just came here to apply for government benefits because being a small state, it goes through a lot faster. They were here for a while and then left.

Then there's Juan and Elizabeth. They were badly affected by the raid. Juan worked at the Swift plant for several years. Then in December 2006, there was the big raid, and he was arrested and eventually deported. It happened December 12, which is the Feast of Guadalupe, which is extremely important to the Mexican people. And so at eight o'clock in the morning, I got a phone call at home from one of the people here at the office, who said that immigration had landed at Swift. People had gone into work for their normal shift at 6:30 a.m., and everything was in operation, and then at 8 a.m. everything shut down, and people were all herded into the cafeteria. Now, Swift employs about 2,200 people, so for the first shift, figure 1,100. So they herded everybody into the cafeteria, but people ran and they hid. And some people got chemical burns because they hid where they shouldn't have hidden; some people hid in freezers; some hid up on the roof.

I went over there. It was a cold, damp, nasty day, and there were people all lined up from the outside of the fences looking in, and, of course, there were ICE agents everywhere. Not even the city police, because supposedly the city police had not been informed this was going to happen. The day of the raid, ninety-five people were arrested from Marshalltown. They were illegal, and it was several days before anybody knew where they were because they were just taken and put in different places.

So Juan was arrested and deported. But he couldn't stay away from his family that was up here. He had a three-year-old daughter and a five-year-old son, so he came back and got a job working in Pella, Iowa, which is forty minutes from here. One morning, ICE came to their house, and he had already gone to work, and so they asked the wife, "Where is your husband?" and she said, "I don't know," and they said, "You do know, and we want to talk to him." But she insisted she didn't know, and they said, "Where are your papers?" and she doesn't have any papers, but she said, "I don't have to show you my papers because you didn't come looking for me," which is correct. And they said, "We'll be back!"

So she was very afraid and hid for a few days with relatives, and then she got word that if her husband would turn himself in, ICE would not bring any charges against her because she, at one point in time, had used another Social Security number to work. And she had only worked for like three months, and that had been a long time ago.

Her husband eventually did turn himself in. He was brought to trial. He was sentenced to six months in prison in California, but he ended up being there almost two years! Then he was deported to Mexico, and he was given a "permanent bar," which means he cannot come back to the United States legally, *ever*! And then, with his wife, ICE did not keep its promise, and they brought charges against her for using a fraudulent Social Security number. There were actually four charges brought against her, and they brought it down to two, but she was sentenced to six months in prison, and her first concern was her children: "If I run from ICE, if I hide, and they don't find me, I'll be safe, but I'll never be able to be free with my kids."

Fig. 56. A Border Patrol agent and his German shepherd check vehicles for immigrants, drugs, and firearms in June 2010. Photograph used by permission of Sara N. Coan.

So Elizabeth bit the bullet and did the six months in Danbury, Connecticut, and this is after paying a lot of money to a lawyer. I think the lawyer really let her down. Just let her down. It's a really sad story. So she was sentenced to six months in prison in Danbury, Connecticut. This is a woman who had never been on a plane before, and I helped set it up so that somebody would meet her in Chicago. She took the plane from here to Chicago, and we had to pay her airfare. ICE did not even pay for her to go to prison!

Supposedly Danbury was a good women's prison. I mean, we have immigrant prisoners in federal prisons in Iowa, Illinois, and Nebraska, but she was sent there, and she doesn't speak English. She had never been away from her kids. So I had somebody meet her in Chicago who got her on a plane to New York. Then I had some people meet her in New York who drove her to Danbury.

She did her six months' time, and everybody was hoping that afterward they would let her return to Iowa and work on a process to be able to stay because she had been here for many years. In the last month of her being there [Danbury] they told her that she would have to make a declaration in court, but she didn't have legal counsel, so she agreed to take "voluntary departure." She thought she would have time to come back to Iowa to say goodbye and then get on a plane to Mexico, but she never came back to Iowa. Elizabeth was taken from Danbury to someplace out east and from there, sent to Mexico.

Now this is the thing. Her parents, who are elderly and they are legal residents, stayed in Marshalltown and took care of the little kids, who are now five and seven. And the parents had sold all of their property. I had gone several years ago to Mexico, and I visited these people, and they had a beautiful home because all the kids had helped to send money back, and they were very happy there, but they wanted to be here with their kids. So they moved everything up here. So when Elizabeth went back to Mexico, there's the house, but there's nothing in it! Not a thing.

So she goes back, and there's her husband and herself. There's no work. There's nobody up here to send money back to them, and their kids are here in Marshalltown. And then the concern was how to get the kids back to Mexico so they could be with them. Well, the little boy was in second grade. He didn't want to go back to Mexico. And the little girl said she really didn't remember her dad. I mean, these are little kids! Two years is a lifetime to them. So they were living with the grandparents.

A couple of months ago, when school got out, Elizabeth's sister and brother-in-law drove the two kids—and put as much as they could fit that belonged to Elizabeth and the kids into their vehicle—down to Mexico and left the kids there with the parents. Elizabeth's parents are still living in Marshalltown, but those kids have never lived in Mexico, so it's really weird and sad, and it shows how the system does not work. In this case, we're deporting de facto American kids! These children were born in this country; they are American citizens. They were not legally deported, but given the situation, they were.

Then there's Felix and Cynthia from Mexico City. They had worked with a lawyer, a so-called lawyer, on their immigration papers [and] work permits, and everything was in process. But they were caught in a trap because this so-called lawyer had applied for them to be here legally as asylees, and Mexico does not get asylum. And Cynthia also had a deportation order against her. A lot of people who've been here for many years have a deportation order from a long time ago, and ICE likes to call in its chips: "OK, you've got this against you. We're gonna get you now."

So she and her husband hired a real lawyer, who charged $10,000 to work on a case. So the lawyer decided to work on Felix's papers first as the main breadwinner. Felix worked in construction. He had a very good job. He's also an ordained deacon. He had his permanent residency and all that. They started to work on her papers, and one day—I think she was using another Social Security number with her own name, but ICE went to where she worked and arrested her. They took her away, and she did not come back home. She was taken to Des Moines. She wasn't there very long, and she was deported to Mexico. She was either given a ten-year bar or a twenty-year bar, which means she cannot come back legally within that amount of time. If she does come back and she gets caught, she will spend the remainder of that time in prison.

Now, they have four children: fourteen, twelve, seven, and five. So those kids are up here without Mom. Cynthia's mom came here and stayed for like six months. Shortly after Cynthia went back to Mexico, she [the mother] came and stayed here to help Felix get his feet on the ground in terms of how to handle these four kids without her. Cynthia's mom came on a visitor's visa. The kids were up here almost a year without seeing Cynthia. I mean, there's phone calls, and I don't know if they used Skype to talk—and Felix had gone back a couple of times to see her, but it's very expensive, so the deacon community helped him financially. He took the four kids down to Mexico two weeks ago to spend time with Cynthia, and then just before school starts, he'll go down and pick them up and bring them back. What Felix is hoping is that after being a legal resident for five years, he can apply to become a citizen, and then he can apply to bring Cynthia up as his spouse, so you're talking a long time.

So there's a family that's totally disrupted. She'll never get that time back again, and those kids will never get that time back again. I don't know if you have kids, but when one of the parents is gone, it's all up for grabs. The chaos that's involved is substantial because Felix works full time. The oldest boy is fourteen and the girl is twelve, and to expect them to take on the role of the adults in the house is asking a lot.

Then there's Martha and Moises from Mexico. When they came, they were both undocumented. And they settled in California and eventually made their way to Iowa, and there were lots of hard times and lean times in between, but today both Martha and Moises are citizens. They are realtors in town. Moises also works as a manager at the casino here, and their oldest daughter is married to an Anglo who's an engineer. They have a daughter who's in law school, another daughter who's in medical school, and the youngest son just graduated from high school and he's going to study graphic arts. So they really are a success story and where the American Dream should let everybody go. But there are way too many stories that are not like them. They are the exception rather than the rule, and a lot of it is personality, too. Martha's the kind of person who doesn't let anyone step on her. And a lot of other people—their whole life they've been stepped on, and they just want to stay out of the way.

Do the Anglo locals resent the Hispanics? There's some of that. But the people have also come to know the Hispanic people because they work with them, their kids are friends with them, they've seen them in the community. I think the Swift raid in 2006 did a lot to solidify positive attitudes in the community, but yes, there are some people who resent them, don't like them. And some people grudgingly say, "I guess it's a good thing they're here," because all of our schools have expanded. They've put additions on, upgraded them, so the schools have grown. The hospital has a new OB wing. We have more than forty Latino businesses in town, and so, economically, it's been a boon.

Supposedly there aren't going to be any more mass factory raids like ICE did in 1996 and 2006. What they do now is go door to door looking for people, and they do it whenever they want. I think they're doing it all the time in different places. They get out these old arrest warrants—deportation orders—and find where these people are. I can't imagine how much money it costs to drag somebody down. People I know have

Fig. 57. Sign at the Border Patrol checkpoint at Jamul, California, June 2010. Photograph used by permission of Sara N. Coan.

said to me, "When we're in public, call me by this name because that's how people know me." [*She laughs at the irony.*] To me, that is like the ultimate in poverty, when you have to give up your own identification: "My fake ID at work says Maria, so when I'm out in public I have to be Maria, but when I'm home I'm Christina." That's really bad. And it's all out of fear that an ICE agent is going to come up and tap you on the shoulder.

There are also people who will turn other people in out of jealousy or just wanting to hold fear over somebody, like, "I know you're illegal, and if you do this or don't do that I'll call immigration." Another thing that's a side effect are parents who don't have authority in the home because in a lot of cases kids will threaten them with calling immigration.

What boils my blood is that nothing is being done, truly. A couple of nights ago I went to Des Moines and saw the movie *Papers*, about five undocumented youths whose life in America is affected daily by their lack of papers and how their lack of legal status makes it impossible for them to drive or work or go to college. And we have an extremely high dropout rate in our high school, and a lot of them are Hispanic kids. One of the people in the film said that kids do really well until junior year, when they wake up to the fact that "I'm undocumented, so why bother? I'm not going to be able to go to college; I'm not going to be able to get a job. . . ." But we've also got some great kids who are working on getting this DREAM Act passed. These are kids who don't have documentation. Kids who are 4.0 in high school and took college-level courses. One girl said to me, "I took college courses when I was in high school because I wanted to graduate a year earlier than my friends, but now I'm two years behind my friends and they're going to graduate next year." So it's really pathetic.

Is the American Dream still alive here? I don't know. To me, the American Dream is that everybody can have an opportunity to be happy. Is that happening in Marshalltown, Iowa? For some people it is. But then again, with the whole immigration thing, I think you'd be hard put to find anyone in the Hispanic community who does not know someone who is going through life's realities as an undocumented person. You know, it's sort of like the thing with cancer: everybody knows somebody who is struggling with this.

I sympathize with Arizona to the extent that I know it's got to be really bad there because I know what it's like here. I'm sure there's a lot of violent activity and drugs—if not there, then just across the border— and so it's fear motivated. The problem is that fear is contagious, so I don't know where it's going to end. I think Arizona stepped over the line. I think it would be great if everybody wore sunglasses and the colors looked the same. I think a lot of it is not just an immigration issue, it's a race issue. I really do. Because when people talk about immigration, they talk about Mexicans. They don't talk about the Canadians who are here illegally, who I've heard is a huge number. They don't talk about the other groups who are here illegally. There are Europeans who are here illegally. They came on a visa from another country, and then it ran out and they just stayed. But they look like us [white Anglo-Americans] and they look like they're supposed to be here, so it's OK. In Fremont, Nebraska, the city recently passed a law that to rent you have to prove you are here legally. I mean, to rent! Everybody rents. And that's Fremont, Nebraska!

DREAM ACT STUDENTS

The Development, Relief, and Education for Alien Minors (DREAM) Act is a piece of proposed federal legislation first introduced in 2001 by Senator Orrin Hatch (R-UT) that would establish a path to citizenship for undocumented immigrants who arrived in the United States as children, only to find out they had no legal status as adults. It would transition these youth out of the shadows and into being full members of society, allowing them to pursue college, serve in the military, or work legally without fear of being deported back to a birth country they have little or no memory of—and whose language they perhaps do not even speak. The bill would directly affect an estimated 2.5 million "Americanized" but undocumented immigrant students.

"These determined and dedicated young people need the chance to become productive members of our society," said Representative Zoe Lofgren (D-CA), a supporter of the bill. "They never had a choice in their situation. Yet our law blames them for it and makes them pay a heavy price. We should not penalize innocent children for the actions of their parents, but should instead reward them when they succeed."

The DREAM Act—or, as some call it, the American Dream Act—has been voted on several times before the House and Senate, but its passage has remained elusive. In 2007, it came eight votes shy of the sixty votes needed for passage, and while it has received overwhelming support from the general public in polls, the initiative appears to have become a political football, consistently discussed but never resolved.

In September 2010, the bill was reintroduced again, this time incorporated as part of the 2010 National Defense Authorization Act, but it failed to get a single Republican to support it, even among those who had favored the measure in the past, and fell four votes shy of passage.

In December 2010, the House of Representatives passed the bill in a vote of 216–198, only to have it rejected by the Senate, which voted 55–41 to block it from going to President Barack Obama—a proponent of the measure—for his signature. It was a painful setback for the DREAM Act movement, as only three Republicans voted for it, and its failure appeared to leave the immigration policy of the Obama administration in disarray, at least temporarily.

Fig. 58. From left to right: Martine Mwanj Kalaw; Subcommitee Chair Representative Zoe Lofgren (D-CA); Marie Nazareth Gonzalez; Congresswoman Lucille Roybal-Allard (D-CA), a coauthor of the DREAM Act (in the US House of Representatives); and Tam Tran.

What follows is the oral testimony of three DREAM Act students who appeared on May 18, 2007, in Washington, DC, before the House Judiciary Subcommittee on Immigration, Citizenship, Refugees, Border Security, and International Law regarding a hearing on "Comprehensive Immigration Reform: The Future of Undocumented Immigrant Students."

These are their stories, in their own words.

MARIE GONZALEZ
EMIGRATED FROM COSTA RICA, 1991, AGE 5
WESTMINSTER COLLEGE, CLASS OF 2009

Raised in Jefferson City, Missouri, she graduated with honors from Helias High School, one of Missouri's top secondary schools. She was a member of the National Honor Society, the foreign language club, the tennis team, and the track team. She also volunteered extensively for the Vitae Society and the youth group at her church. She was also once chosen by Latina *magazine as one of their Women of the Year. "I would like to become an attorney one day. I would like to work for advocacy, for people who are underrepresented, whether that be {in} immigration or other issues."*

Good morning. My name is Marie Nazareth Gonzalez. I am a twenty-one-year-old junior from Jefferson City, Missouri, currently attending Westminster College in Fulton, Missouri. I'm majoring in political science and international business with a focus on communication and leadership.

My family is originally from Costa Rica. I was born in Alajuela, Costa Rica, but have been living in the United States since the age of five. My parents, Marina and Marvin, brought me to the United States in November of 1991. Having come over legally, their plan was to become US citizens so we could one day all benefit from living in the land of the free. We sought to live the American Dream: the promise of a better education, a better life, and altogether a better future—what any parent would want for their child. Strong values and good morals have been instilled in me from a very young age. As long as I can remember, my parents have worked very hard for every dollar they've earned and in the process have taught me that life is not easy and that I must work hard and honorably for what I want in life.

That is exactly what they did. When they came to the United States, they had no intention of breaking the law or of making an exception of themselves. Unfortunately, the law is very difficult and complex. I am not making excuses for what happened, just trying to clear my family's name. Throughout all our years in the United States, we worked very hard for what we had, thinking that one day soon we would be citizens.

In April of 2002, our family's dream of becoming citizens was halted by a phone call. My father had been working for the state as a courier for the governor's office. The job was not prestigious in any way, but my father was very devoted to his job and was loved and respected by his coworkers. On one occasion, the governor even publicly stated his appreciation for my dad while he was making opening remarks at an event for Missouri high school sophomores that I attended. All of that ended after an anonymous person called the governor's office requesting that our immigration status be confirmed.

From that day forward, my life became a haze of meetings with attorneys, hearings, and rallies. When they heard that we were facing deportation, the community that knew us in Jefferson City rallied behind my family and me to an overwhelming degree. They knew we were hardworking, honorable, taxpaying people, and they fought to allow us to stay in the United States. Members of our Catholic parish, where my mom worked as a volunteer Spanish teacher and after-school care director joined with other community members to form the "Gonzalez Group" to rally support by collecting signatures for petitions and organizing phone calls. My classmates, teachers, and others also got involved because they considered me an important part of their community.

I was in high school at the time, with graduation quickly approaching. I was in my class's homecoming court. When it came out in the newspaper that I was being deported to a country I had not known since the age of five, people all across the country responded. They started a "We Are Marie" campaign, and tens of thousands called and wrote letters on my behalf. When I was a high school senior and our family's deportation date was looming very close, they brought me to Washington, DC. I got involved in advocacy for the DREAM Act. Unlike thousands of others like me who would benefit from the DREAM Act, I had little to fear from speaking out, since I was already facing deportation. When I gave the valedictorian speech at a mock graduation in front of the Capitol, I became a national symbol of the DREAM Act.

Eventually all of the work of so many people on my behalf began to pay off. My representative, Ike Skelton, and both of my senators, Jim Talent and

Kit Bond, responded to the support from the community and got involved in the effort to keep me here. Eventually, though, all of our appeals were exhausted, and a final date was set for our family to leave the United States for good: July 5, 2005.

I remember that the weeks before that date were surreal. I was overwhelmed by the support I received. I appeared on national television, once with Senator Richard Durbin at my side, and was contacted by the media so often that I got tired of it. I thought, "Even if it is too late for me, at least it might help the DREAM Act to pass so that others like me won't have to face this ordeal."

Then, on July 1, 2005, I got word that the Department of Homeland Security had relented and would allow me to defer my departure for one year. When I got that news, I cried—simultaneously with happiness and grief. Even though I would be able to stay, my parents would have to leave in just three days. The Gonzalez Group had made shirts and organized a float for the Fourth of July parade. So, the day before their departure, my parents and I rode in the parade with other members of the group that had been such a huge part of our family. Hundreds cheered us on and voiced their support and sorrow.

My life since April of 2002 can be easily compared to a rollercoaster. There have been times when I have felt like I was on top of the world, living out my and my parents' dream of being a successful young woman in her college career, only to be brought down by the realization that at any moment it can be taken away. The deferral of my deportation has been renewed twice, each time for a year. Last month, when they gave me until June of 2008, they told me it would be the last renewal. If the DREAM Act does not pass by then, I will have to leave. I recognize that I am lucky to have been allowed to stay as long as I have. Others in my same situation have not had nearly the support that I have. Even so, it is hard not knowing if I will be able to remain in school at Westminster long enough to graduate.

I am only one student and one story. In the course of fighting to remain here, I have been lucky to meet many other students who would benefit from the DREAM Act, and one of the reasons I wanted to come here and testify is to speak to you on their behalf. Unlike them, I can speak about this issue in public without risking deportation. I share with them in their pain, fear, and uncertainty. Their stories are heartbreaking and similar. In my experiences and my travels, I have come to the realization that they would only be an asset to the country if only given the chance to prove themselves. The DREAM Act has the potential to not only impact the thousands of students who would qualify but also benefit this great nation by allowing these students to pursue their education and their dreams of success.

I can personally attest to how life in limbo is no way to live. Having been torn apart from my parents for almost two years and struggling to make it on my own, I know what it is like to face difficulty and how hard it is to fight for your dreams. No matter what, I will always consider the United States of America my home. I love this country. Only in America would a person like me have the opportunity to tell my story to people like you. Many may argue that because I have a Costa Rican birth certificate, I am Costa Rican and should be sent back to that country. If I am sent back there, sure, I'd be with my mom and dad, but I'd be torn away from loved ones that are my family here, and from everything I have known since I was a child. I hope one day not only to be a US citizen but to go to law school at Mizzou [University of Missouri], to live in DC, and to continue advocating for others who can't speak for themselves. Whether that will happen, though, is up to you—our nation's leaders—and to God.

MARTINE KALAW
EMIGRATED FROM DEMOCRATIC REPUBLIC OF THE CONGO, 1985, AGE 4
HAMILTON COLLEGE, CLASS OF 2003, AND MAXWELL SCHOOL OF CITIZENSHIP AND PUBLIC AFFAIRS, SYRACUSE UNIVERSITY, CLASS OF 2004

She was born in Lusaka, Zambia. After relocating to the Democratic Republic of the Congo, she came to the United States with her mother. After the death of her mother when she was fifteen, she came to study at St. Anne's–Belfield School in Charlottesville, Virginia. She excelled at St. Anne's and earned a scholarship to Hamilton College in New York. "I would like to give a voice to other individuals in my situation in terms of getting involved in nonprofit organization work {and} speaking at other forums such as this . . . without fear of backlash."

Good morning. My name is Martine Mwanj Kalaw. I am a proud New Yorker employed as a financial analyst with the New York Public Library, and prior to that I was a budget analyst at the New York City mayor's Office of Management and Budget. Although I have lived in the United States for twenty-two years, I have an immigration nightmare I'd like to share with you. In August 2004, I was ordered deported.

My mother brought me to the United States on a tourist visa from the Democratic Republic of the Congo when I was four years old. She fell in love with and married my stepfather when I was seven years old. When I was twelve, my stepfather died, and three years later, when I was fifteen, my mother died. My mother had been granted a green card and was in the process of applying for permanent US citizenship at the time of her death. However, neither she nor my stepfather ever filed papers for me. Thus, when my mother and stepfather died, I was left not only without parents, but also without a path to citizenship.

Although I had no home, I was able to excel through my academic performance and through self-parenting. I attended prep school in Charlottesville, Virginia, with the assistance of a judge, who acted as my benefactor. After graduating from St. Anne's–Belfield School, I attended Hamilton College in upstate New York on a scholarship and graduated in 2003 with a concentration in political science.

All of this time, I knew that I had immigration problems, but it wasn't until I was in college that I came to fully understand the extent of those problems. I needed a new Social Security card in order to secure a part-time job on campus. But when I naïvely went to the Social Security Administration for the card, they referred me to INS. The next thing I knew, I was in deportation proceedings. I persevered while my case was pending, despite the looming prospect of removal to a country in Africa where I would not be fully accepted and do not know the language.

Soon after college graduation, I was a recipient of the Margaret Jane White full scholarship, which allowed me to graduate with a master's in public administration from the Maxwell School at Syracuse University in 2004. Academia became my security blanket that allowed me to be something other than that scarlet letter "I" for "illegal immigrant."

Despite my academic record, I cannot escape the stifling nature of my immigration status and have therefore been unable to fully explore my full potential. My experience foreshadows what happens to immigrant students if legislation is not adopted to squarely address our status: we will be left in limbo, with a lot to give back to America but without provisions that will allow us to effectively do so. While I have been uplifted by the US education system, I have also been marginalized by the US immigration system.

In 2006, I met other potential DREAM Act beneficiaries who, like me, were facing deportation. They included Daniel Padilla, who graduated second in his class from Princeton University last year, and another young man who finished law school last year at Fordham. A third boy, a sweet and bookish teenager and honors student, talked about how it felt when the ICE agents came to his home in a case of mistaken identity but ended up arresting him anyway. He said, "They made me feel like a criminal . . . and I am not a criminal."

I sensed the desire that many of these students share—to absorb all that there is to offer from the US academic system and then to give it back to their communities tenfold. Unfortunately, instead of support they face a constant struggle to fight for legal representation, for a work permit, and for a future.

My particular story has a happy ending, I think. In summer 2005, I began to work closely with Susan Douglas Taylor, my current counsel, beacon of hope, and constant support. In the spring of 2006, the Board of Immigration accepted my application for adjustment of status and remanded my case back to the immigration judge for a background check. Unfortunately, the immigration judge put me through a series of hearings and sent my case back to the Board of Immigration Appeals to reconsider their decision. This nearly broke my faith.

Just last week my lawyer, Susan Taylor, informed me that the Board of Immigration granted me an adjustment of status and my case is won. However, I am apprehensive, and I do not know how to process this information because I have been let down so many times with immigration law that my heart fears any more disappointment. Furthermore, the timing of the decision also means that I may not qualify for work authorization after May 24 and I may lose my job.

Although my immigration nightmare may almost be over, it is just beginning for countless others. I was very apprehensive about coming to speak with you today in this very public forum. I worry, perhaps irrationally, that it might in some way have a negative impact on my case. Lord knows that I have gone to the depths of human frailty in trying to deal with my immigration struggle. But it is my obligation to do what I can to prevent this anguish for other students. So I am here today on behalf of many talented and hardworking students who, like me, have grown up in the United States, but who cannot tell their own stories because if they did so they would risk deportation. I hope that hearing my testimony will help them by making it more likely that the DREAM Act will become law this year.

TAM TRAN
EMIGRATED FROM GERMANY, 1989, AGE 6
UNIVERSITY OF CALIFORNIA–LOS ANGELES,
CLASS OF 2006, AND BROWN UNIVERSITY

She was born in Germany after her parents fled Vietnam. Her family came to the United States to reunite with other family members here. In December 2006, she graduated from UCLA with a degree in American literature and culture with college, departmental, and Latin honors. She has worked as a full-time film editor and videographer. "I would like to get my PhD in American studies and start a production company that translates academic work into the film media," she said. "I would also like to get involved with a nonprofit organization and create an oral history for individuals of marginalized communities."

I hate filling out forms, especially the ones that limit me to checking off boxes for categories I don't even identify with. Place of birth? Germany. But I'm not German. Ethnicity? I'm Vietnamese, but I've never been to Vietnam. However, these forms never ask me where I was raised or educated. I was born in Germany, my parents are Vietnamese, but I have been American raised and educated for the past eighteen years.

My parents escaped the Vietnam War as boat people and were rescued by the German navy. In Vietnam, my mother had to drop out of middle school to help support her family as a street vendor. My father was a bit luckier—he was college educated—but the value of his education has diminished in this country due to his inability to speak English fluently. They lived in Germany as refugees, and during that time, I was born.

My family came to the United States when I was six to reunite with relatives who fled to California because, after all, this was America. It is extremely difficult to win a political asylum case, but my parents took that chance because they truly believed they were asylees of a country they no longer considered home and which also posed a threat to their livelihood. Despite this, they lost the case. The immigration court ordered us deported to Germany. However, when we spoke to the German consulate, they told us, "We don't want you. You're not German." Germany does not grant birthright citizenship, so on application forms, when I come across the question that asks for my citizenship, I rebelliously mark "other" and write in "the world." But the truth is, I am culturally an American, and more specifically, I consider myself a Southern Californian. I grew up watching *Speed Racer* and *Mighty Mouse* every Saturday morning. But as of right now, my national identity is not American, and even though I can't be removed from American soil, I cannot become an American unless legislation changes.

In December, I graduated with a bachelor's degree in American literature and culture with Latin, departmental, and college honors from UCLA. I thought, finally, all these years of working multiple jobs and applying to countless scholarships, all while taking more than fifteen units every quarter, were going to pay off.

And it did seem to be paying off. I found a job right away in my field as a full-time film editor and videographer with a documentary project at UCLA. I also applied to graduate school and was accepted to a PhD program in cultural studies. I was awarded a department fellowship and the minority fellowship, but the challenges I faced as an undocumented college student began to surface once again.

Except the difference this time is I am twenty-four years old. I suppose this means I'm an adult. I also have a college degree. I guess this also means I'm an educated adult. But for a fact, I know that this means I do have responsibilities to the society I live in. I have the desire and also the ability and skills to help my community by being an academic researcher and socially conscious video documentarian, but I'll have to wait before I can become an accountable member of society. I recently declined the offer to the PhD program because even with these two fellowships, I don't have the money to cover the $50,000 tuition and living expenses. I'll have to wait before I can really grow up. But that's OK because when you're in my situation you have to, or learn to, or are forced to make compromises.

With my adult job, I can save up for graduate school next year. Or at least that's what I thought. Three days ago, the day before I boarded my flight to DC, I was informed that it would be my last day at work. My work permit has expired, and I won't be able to continue working until I receive a new one. Every year, I must apply for a renewal, but never have I received it on time. This means every year around this month, I lose the job that I have. But that's OK. Because I've been used to this—to losing things I have worked hard for. Not just this job but also the value of my college degree and the American identity I once possessed as a child.

This is my first time in Washington, DC, and the privilege of being able to speak today truly exemplifies the subliminal state I always feel like I'm in. I am lucky because I do have a government ID that allowed me to board the plane here to share my story and give voice to thousands of other undocumented students who cannot. But I know that when I return home tonight, I'll become marginalized once again. At the moment, I can't work legally even though I do have some legal status. I also know that the job I'm going to look for when I get back isn't the one I'll want to have. The job I'll want because it makes use of my college degree will be out of my hands. Without the DREAM Act, I have no prospect of overcoming my state of immigration limbo; I'll forever be a perpetual foreigner in a country where I've always considered myself an American.

But for some of my friends who could only be here today through a blurred face in a video, they have other fears, too. They can't be here because they are afraid of being deported from the country they grew up in and call home. There is also the fear of the unknown after graduation that is uniquely different from other students. Graduation for many of my friends isn't a rite of passage to becoming a responsible adult. Rather, it is the last phase in which they can feel a sense of belonging as an American. As an American university student, my friends feel a part of an American community, that they are living out the American dream among their peers. But after graduation, they will be left behind by their American friends, as my friends are without the prospect of obtaining a job that will utilize the degree they've earned. My friends will become just another undocumented immigrant. Thank you.

Postscript

Three days after Tam Tran spoke out on her immigration plight, ICE—in a predawn raid—arrested her family, including her Vietnamese father, mother, and twenty-one-year-old brother, charging them with being fugitives from justice even though the family's attorneys said the Trans had been reporting regularly to immigration officials to obtain work permits. The family was released to house arrest after Representative Zoe Lofgren (D-CA) intervened, but the Tran family was forced to wear electronic ankle bracelets just the same. "Would her family have been arrested if she hadn't spoken out?" Lofgren said of Tam, who was not at home at the time of the raid. "I don't think so."

In May 2010, Tam Tran, who was attending Brown University as a graduate student, was killed in a car accident in Maine. She was twenty-seven years old.

AFTERWORD

As America moves forward into the twenty-first century, its recent immigration patterns suggest its future demographic makeup. The US Census Bureau conservatively projects that by 2050, nearly 25 percent of the US population of more than four hundred million people will be Hispanic, largely fueled by emigration from Latin America and Mexico. To put this in perspective, in 1900, when the US population was seventy-six million, there were fewer than five hundred thousand Hispanics, or less than 1 percent. But it was a different world then.

When you look back to the Ellis Island era, you see a period in history greatly influenced by totalitarian regimes that had a huge bearing on immigration to this country. Germany and Russia alone had an enormous impact on the outcome of events in the twentieth century. The human suffering caused at their hands was both profound and incalculable, from the pogroms of the 1890s and World War I, to World War II and Stalinist Russia, Hitler's Germany, and Mussolini's Italy. Is it any wonder that those who fled the dictators and fascism of Axis countries comprise the largest portion of America's genealogical profile? How different would the face of America look today if the regimes of those countries had not so totally dominated the human landscape?

You also realize what a special breed our European ancestors were. They had to be. Theirs was a true test of Darwinism, for only the fittest survived, and those who did went on to help build this nation into an industrial and economic superpower that became the envy of the world. Their genetic code—so concentrated and so pure—gave America its ambition and work ethic, its persistence and determination, and its genius that made it a leader in all fields of endeavor, from science and technology to groundbreaking inventions that changed how we live our lives.

Over time, though, this European heritage thinned with each passing decade and year, as subsequent generations became more "Americanized" and further removed from their ethnic roots. Simultaneously, the gene pool experienced a sharp rise in new immigrants from all corners of the globe, which contributed a broader multicultural perspective and enriched the variety of the American mosaic.

We now look to these new immigrants to take the lead. To make their mark. To move this country forward in new directions and elevate us with their unique gifts and contributions. You have heard from many of them in these pages. It is up to them, and others like them, to help America redefine itself and enhance its prominence in the eyes of the world. The American Dream demands nothing less.

APPENDIX

STATISTICS: IMMIGRATION BY COUNTRY AND BY DECADE

1890–2010

Region and Country of Last Residence[1]	1890 to 1899	1900 to 1909	1910 to 1919	1920 to 1929	1930 to 1939	1940 to 1949
Total	**3,694,294**	**8,202,388**	**6,347,380**	**4,295,510**	**699,375**	**856,608**
Europe	**3,576,411**	**7,572,569**	**4,985,411**	**2,560,340**	**444,399**	**472,524**
Austria-Hungary[2,3,4]	534,059	2,001,376	1,154,727	60,891	12,531	13,574
Austria[2,4]	268,218	532,416	589,174	31,392	5,307	8,393
Hungary[2]	203,350	685,567	565,553	29,499	7,224	5,181
Belgium	19,642	37,429	32,574	21,511	4,013	12,473
Bulgaria[5]	52	34,651	27,180	2,824	1,062	449
Czechoslovakia[6]	-	-	-	101,182	17,757	8,475
Denmark	56,671	61,227	45,830	34,406	3,470	4,549
Finland	-	-	-	16,922	2,438	2,230
France[7]	35,616	67,735	60,335	54,842	13,761	36,954
Germany[3,4]	579,072	328,722	174,227	386,634	119,107	119,506
Greece	12,732	145,402	198,108	60,774	10,599	8,605
Ireland[8]	405,710	344,940	166,445	202,854	28,195	15,701
Italy	603,761	1,930,475	1,229,916	528,133	85,053	50,509
Netherlands	29,349	42,463	46,065	29,397	7,791	13,877
Norway-Sweden[9]	334,058	426,981	192,445	170,329	13,452	17,326
Norway[9]	96,810	182,542	79,488	70,327	6,901	8,326
Sweden[9]	237,248	244,439	112,957	100,002	6,551	9,000
Poland[3]	107,793	-	-	223,316	25,555	7,577
Portugal[10]	25,874	65,154	82,489	44,829	3,518	6,765
Romania	6,808	57,322	13,566	67,810	5,264	1,254
Russia[3,11]	450,101	1,501,301	1,106,998	61,604	2,463	605
Spain[12]	9,189	24,818	53,262	47,109	3,669	2,774
Switzerland	37,020	32,541	22,839	31,772	5,990	9,904
United Kingdom[8,13]	328,759	469,518	371,878	341,552	61,813	131,794
Yugoslavia[14]	-	-	-	49,215	6,920	2,039
Other Europe	145	514	6,527	22,434	9,978	5,584
Asia	**61,285**	**299,836**	**269,736**	**126,740**	**19,231**	**34,532**
China	15,268	19,884	20,916	30,648	5,874	16,072
Hong Kong	-	-	-	-	-	-
India	102	3,026	3,478	2,076	554	1,692
Iran	-	-	-	208	198	1,144
Israel	-	-	-	-	-	98
Japan	13,998	139,712	77,125	42,057	2,683	1,557

1950 to 1959	1960 to 1969	1970 to 1979	1980 to 1989	1990 to 1999	2000 to 2009
2,499,268	**3,213,749**	**4,248,203**	**6,244,379**	**9,775,398**	**10,245,003**
1,404,973	**1,133,443**	**825,590**	**668,866**	**1,348,612**	**1,488,473**
113,015	27,590	20,387	20,437	27,529	29,746
81,354	17,571	14,239	15,374	18,234	16,732
31,661	10,019	6,148	5,063	9,295	13,014
18,885	9,647	5,413	7,028	7,077	8,204
97	598	1,011	1,124	16,948	42,727
1,624	2,758	5,654	5,678	8,970	19,240
10,918	9,797	4,405	4,847	6,189	6,114
4,923	4,310	2,829	2,569	3,970	4,076
50,113	46,975	26,281	32,066	35,945	43,504
576,905	209,616	77,142	85,752	92,207	131,631
45,153	74,173	102,370	37,729	25,403	18,526
47,189	37,788	11,461	22,210	65,384	15,543
184,576	200,111	150,031	55,562	75,992	28,060
46,703	37,918	10,373	11,234	13,345	17,791
44,224	36,150	10,298	13,941	17,825	20,123
22,806	17,371	3,927	3,835	5,211	4,730
21,418	18,779	6,371	10,106	12,614	15,393
6,465	55,742	33,696	63,483	172,249	127,051
13,928	70,568	104,754	42,685	25,497	12,164
914	2,339	10,774	24,753	48,136	53,792
453	2,329	28,132	33,311	433,427	488,115
6,880	40,793	41,718	22,783	18,443	17,007
17,577	19,193	8,536	8,316	11,768	12,776
195,709	220,213	133,218	153,644	156,182	168,469
6,966	17,990	31,862	16,267	57,039	150,033
11,756	6,845	5,245	3,447	29,087	73,781
135,844	**358,605**	**1,406,544**	**2,391,356**	**2,859,899**	**3,348,321**
8,836	14,060	17,627	170,897	342,058	599,914
13,781	67,047	117,350	112,132	116,894	62,255
1,850	18,638	147,997	231,649	352,528	597,032
3,195	9,059	33,763	98,141	76,899	90,400
21,376	30,911	36,306	43,669	41,340	51,487
40,651	40,956	49,392	44,150	66,582	86,030

Region and Country of Last Residence[1]	1890 to 1899	1900 to 1909	1910 to 1919	1920 to 1929	1930 to 1939	1940 to 1949
Jordan	-	-	-	-	-	-
Korea	-	-	-	-	-	83
Philippines	-	-	-	-	391	4,099
Syria	-	-	-	5,307	2,188	1,179
Taiwan	-	-	-	-	-	-
Turkey	27,510	127,999	160,717	40,450	1,327	754
Vietnam	-	-	-	-	-	-
Other Asia	4,407	9,215	7,500	5,994	6,016	7,854
America	**37,350**	**277,809**	**1,070,539**	**1,591,278**	**230,319**	**328,435**
Canada and Newfoundland[15,16]	3,098	123,067	708,715	949,286	162,703	160,911
Mexico[16,17]	734	31,188	185,334	498,945	32,709	56,158
Caribbean	31,480	100,960	120,860	83,482	18,052	46,194
Cuba	-	-	-	12,769	10,641	25,976
Dominican Republic	-	-	-	-	1,026	4,802
Haiti	-	-	-	-	156	823
Jamaica[18]	-	-	-	-	-	-
Other Caribbean[18]	31,480	100,960	120,860	70,713	6,229	14,593
Central America	**649**	**7,341**	**15,692**	**16,511**	**6,840**	**20,135**
Belize	-	77	40	285	193	433
Costa Rica	-	-	-	-	431	1,965
El Salvador	-	-	-	-	597	4,885
Guatemala	-	-	-	-	423	1,303
Honduras	-	-	-	-	679	1,874
Nicaragua	-	-	-	-	405	4,393
Panama[19]	-	-	-	-	1,452	5,282
Other Central America	649	7,264	15,652	16,226	2,660	-
South America	**1,389**	**15,253**	**39,938**	**43,025**	**9,990**	**19,662**
Argentina	-	-	-	-	1,067	3,108
Bolivia	-	-	-	-	50	893
Brazil	-	-	-	4,627	1,468	3,653
Chile	-	-	-	-	347	1,320
Colombia	-	-	-	-	1,027	3,454
Ecuador	-	-	-	-	244	2,207
Guyana	-	-	-	-	131	596

1950 to 1959	1960 to 1969	1970 to 1979	1980 to 1989	1990 to 1999	2000 to 2009
4,899	9,230	25,541	28,928	42,755	50,010
4,845	27,048	241,192	322,708	179,770	206,285
17,245	70,660	337,726	502,056	534,338	549,024
1,091	2,432	8,086	14,534	22,906	28,402
721	15,657	83,155	119,051	132,647	94,143
2,980	9,464	12,209	19,208	38,687	44,372
290	2,949	121,716	200,632	275,379	292,143
14,084	40,494	174,484	483,601	637,116	596,824
921,610	**1,674,172**	**1,904,355**	**2,695,329**	**5,137,743**	**4,431,594**
353,169	433,128	179,267	156,313	194,788	222,724
273,847	441,824	621,218	1,009,586	2,757,418	1,706,993
115,661	427,235	708,850	790,109	1,004,687	1,057,416
73,221	202,030	256,497	132,552	159,037	274,028
10,219	83,552	139,249	221,552	359,818	291,603
3,787	28,992	55,166	121,406	177,446	204,598
7,397	62,218	130,226	193,874	177,143	173,212
21,037	50,443	127,712	120,725	131,243	113,975
40,201	**98,560**	**120,374**	**339,376**	**610,189**	**604,296**
1,133	4,185	6,747	14,964	12,600	9,370
4,044	17,975	12,405	25,017	17,054	20,914
5,094	14,405	29,428	137,418	273,017	252,526
4,197	14,357	23,837	58,847	126,043	161,650
5,320	15,078	15,651	39,071	72,880	63,542
7,812	10,383	10,911	31,102	80,446	78,124
12,601	22,177	21,395	32,957	28,149	18,170
-	-	-	-	-	-
78,418	**250,754**	**273,608**	**399,862**	**570,624**	**840,142**
16,346	49,384	30,303	23,442	30,065	46,391
2,759	6,205	5,635	9,798	18,111	20,976
11,547	29,238	18,600	22,944	50,744	111,453
4,669	12,384	15,032	19,749	18,200	19,454
15,567	68,371	71,265	105,494	137,985	235,698
8,574	34,107	47,464	48,015	81,358	105,441
1,131	4,546	38,278	85,886	74,407	72,181

Region and Country of Last Residence[1]	1890 to 1899	1900 to 1909	1910 to 1919	1920 to 1929	1930 to 1939	1940 to 1949
Paraguay	-	-	-	-	33	85
Peru	-	-	-	-	321	1,273
Suriname	-	-	-	-	25	130
Uruguay	-	-	-	-	112	754
Venezuela	-	-	-	-	1,155	2,182
Other South America	1,389	15,253	39,938	38,398	4,010	7
Other America [20]	-	-	-	29	25	25,375
Africa	**432**	**6,326**	**8,867**	**6,362**	**2,120**	**6,720**
Egypt	51	-	-	1,063	781	1,613
Ethiopia	-	-	-	-	10	28
Liberia	9	-	-	-	35	37
Morocco	-	-	-	-	73	879
South Africa	9	-	-	-	312	1,022
Other Africa	363	6,326	8,867	5,299	909	3,141
Oceania	**4,704**	**12,355**	**12,339**	**9,860**	**3,306**	**14,262**
Australia	3,098	11,191	11,280	8,404	2,260	11,201
New Zealand	12	-	-	935	790	2,351
Other Oceania	1,594	1,164	1,059	521	256	710
Not Specified [20, 21]	**14,112**	**33,493**	**488**	**930**	**-**	**135**

- Represents zero or not available.

1 Data for years prior to 1906 refer to country of origin; data from 1906 to 2009 refer to country of last residence.

2 Data for Austria and Hungary not reported separately for all years during 1860 to 1869, 1890 to 1899, and 1900 to 1909.

3 From 1899 to 1919, data for Poland included in Austria-Hungary, Germany, and the Soviet Union.

4 From 1938 to 1945, data for Austria included in Germany.

5 From 1899 to 1910, included Serbia and Montenegro.

6 Currently includes Czech Republic and Slovak Republic.

7 From 1820 to 1910, included Corsica.

8 Prior to 1926, data for Northern Ireland included in Ireland.

9 Data for Norway and Sweden not reported separately until 1869.

10 From 1820 to 1910, included Cape Verde and Azores Islands.

11 From 1820 to 1920, data refer to the Russian Empire. Between 1920 and 1990, data refer to the Soviet Union. From 1991 to present, data refer to the Russian federa-

1950 to 1959	1960 to 1969	1970 to 1979	1980 to 1989	1990 to 1999	2000 to 2009
576	1,249	1,486	3,518	6,082	4,477
5,980	19,783	25,311	49,958	110,117	138,176
299	612	714	1,357	2,285	2,404
1,026	4,089	8,416	7,235	6,062	8,400
9,927	20,758	11,007	22,405	35,180	75,006
17	28	97	61	28	85
60,314	22,671	1,038	83	37	23
13,016	**23,780**	**71,408**	**141,990**	**346,416**	**683,238**
1,996	5,581	23,543	26,744	44,604	75,032
302	804	2,588	12,927	40,097	89,209
289	841	2,391	6,420	13,587	20,177
2,703	2,880	1,967	3,471	15,768	39,276
2,278	4,360	10,002	15,505	21,964	33,010
5,448	9,314	30,917	76,923	210,396	426,534
11,353	**23,630**	**39,980**	**41,432**	**56,800**	**67,153**
8,275	14,986	18,708	16,901	24,288	33,247
1,799	3,775	5,018	6,129	8,600	12,844
1,279	4,869	16,254	18,402	23,912	21,062
12,472	**119**	**326**	**305,406**	**25,928**	**226,224**

tion, Armenia, Azerbaijan, Belarus, Georgia, Kazakhstan, Kyrgyzstan, Moldova, Russia, Tajikistan, Ukraine, and Uzbekistan.

12 From 1820 to 1910, included the Canary Islands and Balearic Islands.

13 Since 1925, data for United Kingdom refer to England, Scotland, Wales, and Northern Ireland.

14 Currently includes Bosnia-Herzegovina, Croatia, Macedonia, Slovenia, and Serbia, and Montenegro.

15 Prior to 1911, data refer to British North America. From 1911, data includes Newfoundland.

16 Land arrivals not completely enumerated until 1908.

17 No data available for Mexico from 1886 to 1893.

18 Data for Jamaica not reported separately until 1953. Prior to 1953, Jamaica was included in British West Indies.

19 From 1932 to 1972, data for the Panama Canal Zone included in Panama.

20 Included in "Not Specified" until 1925.

21 Includes 32,897 persons returning in 1906 to their homes in the United States.

Note: From 1820 to 1867, figures represent alien passenger arrivals at seaports; from 1868 to 1891 and from 1895 to 1897, immigrant alien arrivals; from 1892 to 1894 and from 1898 to 2007, immigrant aliens admitted for permanent residence; from 1892 to 1903, aliens entering by cabin class were not counted as immigrants. Land arrivals were not completely enumerated until 1908. For this table, fiscal year 1843 covers nine months ending September 1843; fiscal years 1832 and 1850 cover fifteen months ending December 31 of the respective years; and fiscal year 1868 covers six months ending June 30, 1868.

Source: US Department of Homeland Security

INDEX OF DATES

Page numbers in **bold** indicate photos and figures.

INDEX OF NAMES AND SUBJECTS

Page numbers in **bold** indicate photos and figures.